The Canadian General Election of 1997

The Canadian General Election of 1997

Edited by
Alan Frizzell and Jon H. Pammett

DUNDURN PRESS
TORONTO · OXFORD

Designer: Scott Reid
Printer: Webcom Limited

Canadian Cataloguing in Publication Data

The Canadian general election of 1997

ISBN 1-55002-300-4

1. Canada. Parliament — Elections, 1997. I. Frizzell,
Alan, 1947–   .   II. Pammett, Jon H., 1944–   .

FC635.C366 1997   324.971'0648   C97-931775-4
F1034.2.C366 1997

1   2   3   4   5   01   00   99   98   97

THE CANADA COUNCIL | LE CONSEIL DES ARTS
FOR THE ARTS | DU CANADA
SINCE 1957 | DEPUIS 1957

We acknowledge the support of the **Canada Council for the Arts** for our publishing program. We also acknowledge the support of the **Ontario Arts Council** and the **Book Publishing Industry Development Program** of the **Department of Canadian Heritage.**

Printed and bound in Canada.

 Printed on recycled paper.

Dundurn Press
8 Market Street
Suite 200
Toronto, Ontario, Canada
M5E 1M6

Dundurn Press
73 Lime Walk
Headington, Oxford
England
OX3 7AD

Dundurn Press
250 Sonwil Drive
Buffalo, NY
U.S.A. 14225

Contents

Introduction

> *It was the best of times, it was the worst of times, it was the age of wisdom, it was the age of foolishness, it was the epoch of belief, it was the epoch of incredulity, it was the season of Light, it was the season of Darkness, it was the spring of hope, it was the winter of despair.*

The familiar lines from Charles Dickens appear to sum up the situation for all of the Canadian political parties in the general election of June 2, 1997. They won some, but they lost some. They accomplished some of their objectives, but fell short in others.

The Liberal Party of Canada had returned to power in 1993 after a decade on the opposition benches. They had won a solid majority of 29 seats in the House of Commons, and had been relatively unscathed by subsequent attacks from a divided and scattered opposition. The ineffectiveness of all the opposition parties led to the general expectation that the Liberals would win a 1997 election handily, almost by default. They had received substantial (if at times grudging) praise for their performance in government and their ability to cut spending and reduce the deficit. They were the only party with credible claims to be a national party, supported in all areas of the country. The only question remaining about an election triumph for them was "when?"

The Liberal Party's own answer to this question turned out to be "sooner" rather than "later." Whether because the party's strategists were apprehensive about the potential situation later in the year, or just anxious to get the inevitable over with, they opted for a June election, only three-and-one-half years after their 1993 victory. Despite their eagerness for the election, however, the Liberals appeared disorganized. They mounted a shaky campaign which was light on specific issues and weak in leadership, and almost parleyed their majority government status into a minority, something most observers at the outset of the campaign thought was almost impossible.

All of the other parties could point to successful aspects of their campaigns. The New Democratic Party was able to make gains by improving their appeal to women and to the disadvantaged Atlantic region of the country. They did this through establishing their campaign issues of the need for government job creation, and the imperative of saving social programs from further budget cutting. The Progressive Conservative Party established their leader, Jean Charest, as the most popular federal leader in the country, and staked out a moderate position on the national unity/Quebec issue by championing "distinct society" status for that province. The Reform Party consolidated their Western base of support by branching out from their usual emphasis on economic issues like deficit reduction and tax cuts, and established themselves as the hard-line voice of English Canada toward Quebec separatism. The Bloc Québécois reinforced their status as the voice of Quebec in Ottawa and held on to the bulk of their support.

But just as all parties could claim some successes, all had prominent failures in their campaigns. The New Democratic Party failed to make any headway in recovering a presence in Ontario, lost ground in the West to Reform, and generally had a difficult time persuading voters they were major players in the political game nationwide. The Conservatives, despite a brief surge as a result of the victory of Jean Charest in the leaders' debates, did not establish themselves as the national opposition they desperately wanted to become; their seats are concentrated in the Eastern part of the country. Likewise, Reform failed to become a national party, marginalizing itself in Ontario by its anti-Quebec message. The Bloc Québécois lost seats and votes, and fell out of Official Opposition status in the House of Commons.

In some ways, the 1997 election was a logical extension of the results of the 1993 election. That event had left the Liberals as the dominant national party, with representation from all parts of the country and a substantial majority in Parliament. The Bloc Québécois and the Reform Party formed regionally-based opposition groupings, which competed for the right to form the Official Opposition in Parliament. The other two parties, the New Democratic Party and the Progressive Conservatives, fared very badly in terms of legislative seats in 1993. The 1997 result, which saw those two parties compete to secure the representation rights to the Atlantic Region, seemed to fill in the main gap. Ontario, the large central region of the country, was the stronghold of the Liberal Party. Though the Liberals resisted attempts to brand them as a regional party as well, the numbers in 1997 began to look more and more like it.

As seems inevitable in any Canadian election in which regional appeals come heavily into play, the first-past-the-post electoral system came under scrutiny after the result was known. The Liberals won the 1997 election by getting only 38% of the vote nationwide, an all-time low for a majority government. In three previous elections, the Liberals had formed majority governments with 41% of the national vote. The first of these instances was in 1921, when the Progressives entered federal politics, capturing almost one-quarter of the vote. The second was in 1945, when the CCF emerged onto the national scene and cut into the vote totals for the two traditional parties. The third was in 1993.

The injustice of such a result, from the point of view of equality in the translation of votes into seats, did not escape the other parties. The opposition stressed the lack of a popular mandate with which the Liberals formed the new government. Even the Bloc Québécois, which itself has more seats than its overall vote total would justify, joined the chorus in contesting the government's legitimacy. Academic speculation about the desirability of changing the electoral system to a more proportional model aside, however, the mechanics of the election result soon lost the attention of both the public and the political elites. It was politics-as-usual when Parliament resumed in September.

One disturbing result of the 1997 Canadian general election was the continuation of the downward slide in the voting turnout rate. Whereas the postwar norm has been for 75% of the voters to go to the polls in the average federal election, there was a sharp drop in 1993 to a turnout of only 70% of eligible voters. This time, the turnout rate slipped further, to 67% of eligible voters. As evidence in this book shows, even those people who did vote were less likely to be able to identify important issues in this election than had been the case in the recent past. And the accounts of the campaigns in this book are replete with evidence that the negative tone of many of the campaign attacks and advertisements was off-putting to many Canadians. It is conventional wisdom among political operatives that negative advertising "works," even when people say they do not like it. However, this judgement appears to ignore the fact that it may produce an increasingly small pool of voters to "work on." Champions of popular participation in Canadian public life have reason to be concerned with the conduct of the campaign of 1997.

However, those concerned solely with the results of elections may notice little change after the 1997 version from the situation after the previous election. The Liberal Party is still in office, albeit with a drastically reduced majority which is vulnerable to the "three D's" — Death, Defection, and Defeat in by-elections. Across the floor of the House of Commons, they face a regionally splintered opposition once again, with a few differences. The lead questions will be coming from the West, rather than Quebec. And the criticism will be coming from expanded caucuses of four parties, all eager to jockey for position as "the real opposition" for the future. As Canadian politics enters the new millennium, the uncertainties multiply.

One

Setting the Stage
by Anthony Westell

The extraordinary election of 1993[1] not only restored the Liberal Party to power after nine years in opposition, but left it without an effective opposition in the House of Commons, and the electorate without a credible alternative government. The Progressive Conservatives were reduced to two seats and the New Democrats to nine, neither having official party status in the House. Two new regional parties took their places across the aisle from the government. The Bloc Québécois, a separatist party committed to taking Quebec out of Confederation, formed the Loyal Opposition with 54 seats, but obviously was not a government-in-waiting. The Reform Party, with support largely in the West, had 52 seats. Under Prime Minister Jean Chrétien, the Liberals could and did claim to be the only national party, and this gave the government an unusually free hand.

The devastating defeat of the Conservative government in 1993 was due in considerable measure to widespread dislike and distrust of Prime Minister Brian Mulroney, and to a succession of scandals that created the perception of an administration riddled with corruption which overshadowed its achievements. All this deepened the perennial public cynicism about politicians and their motives, a disturbing trend in many democracies in the 1990s. While still in opposition, Chrétien had expressed his concern about the loss of public confidence in Parliament and government, and promised in his election program — known as the Liberal Red Book — that in office he would govern in such a way as to restore the public trust. Indeed, the Red Book itself was presented as a contract with the voters — long before the US Republicans popularized the notion — setting out what the Liberals intended to do and for which they could be held accountable. Other measures, both symbolic and substantial, followed. Chrétien had for years crafted his own log-cabin image as an unpretentious "li'l" guy from a small town in Quebec — although in fact he had become a millionaire corporate lawyer — and he reinforced this when he and his wife Aline — his closest political partner and adviser — moved into the official home of the Prime Minister, 24 Sussex Drive, without the customary redecoration and with government-issue furnishings. Almost at once, he appointed as his adviser on ethical issues a reassuring pillar of the old Ottawa Establishment, Mitchell Sharp, who had been a senior civil servant when the Ottawa Mandarins were among the most respected people in the country, and who served as a Liberal Cabinet Minister when government was thought to do good things for all the people. Later, the position of Ethics Counsellor was created to help ministers avoid conflicts of interest, and a special Senate-Commons committee was asked to prepare a code of conduct for members of both Houses. Lobbyists who had seemed to run riot during the Mulroney years were reined in, and Chrétien eschewed the grand gestures and strategies favoured by Mulroney, offering instead pragmatic daily management. Action when necessary, but not necessarily action, could have been his watchword.

As the 1997 election approached, the Liberals claimed to have honoured some 80% of the promises in the Red Book, but the opposition parties and the media scorned the claim, pointing in particular to the government's failure to get rid of the hated Goods and Services Tax imposed by the Mulroney Tories. But the overriding fact was that there had been a few indiscretions but no serious personal scandals involving Cabinet ministers during the three-and-half years of Chrétien's first government. The Prime Minister himself was spotless and retained a high level of public approval. Whether this record made any real headway in restoring public trust in the democratic process remains to be seen, but public confidence in the Prime Minister — and the absence of a credible alternative — probably did assist his Cabinet to make radical changes in policies in the two dominant issues of Canadian politics, the economy and national unity, without suffering the level of angry cynicism that might have been expected.

The economy

The Liberals came to power acknowledging that the federal budget deficit was a serious problem, but were equally or even more concerned with unemployment and slow growth in the economy. Both Chrétien and his finance minister, Paul Martin, seemed inclined at first to believe that if they could stimulate the economy and create jobs, revenues would increase. This, combined with restraints on spending, would reduce the deficit to manageable proportions in three years. After all, the Liberals had promised during the election not austerity but a return to the good old days of full employment and social spending. For example, as soon as possible after taking office, they approved in partnership with the provinces and municipalities, a $6-billion public works program designed both to create jobs and, more importantly, to promote a feel-good atmosphere that would strengthen consumer confidence and spending. Deep spending cuts, they feared, would merely create a new recession and a fall in revenues. Fiscal reality began to take charge when Martin discovered that the 1993-4 deficit was going to be much higher than the previous government had forecast. Even so, he was cautious in his first budget, in February, 1944, making modest cuts in predictable areas such as defense and foreign aid, and closing tax loopholes. "The challenge today is not rush," he said. "The challenge is to get things right." The truth seems to be that he was still taking the measure of the problem and discovering that it was not in fact the deficit but the national debt that grew with every deficit, costing more in interest, leaving less for constructive spending, and threatening eventually if not national bankruptcy the humiliation of appealing to the International Monetary Fund for help.[2]

By October, when he updated his budget forecasts, Martin had become a committed crusader in the battle to eliminate the deficit, balance the budget, and then to begin to reduce the debt. His new view was that growing the economy would not create jobs and reduce the deficit; rather, reducing the deficit would grow the economy and create jobs. Cutting spending became for the next two years the dominant theme of the government, to the dismay of Liberals on the Left of the party and the relief of those on the Right. Ambitious plans for reform of the social security system were shelved, and fiscal transfers to the provinces for social programs were slashed — forcing the provincial governments to accept the unpopularity of actually cutting programs. As it happened, most of the provinces were themselves tackling deficits — some were ahead of Martin in the process — and the country itself was changing moods: what had been a Revolution of Rising Expectations in the 1970s, when there seemed no limit to growth and spending, had gradually gone into reverse and what might be called a Revolution in Falling Expectations was becoming the consensus. That is to say, Canadians were coming to accept that things would get worse before, if ever, they got better. And they were right. Freer trade was forcing many corporations to retrench and restructure; the Bank of Canada continued, in its view, to choke inflation, and in the view of critics to choke the whole economy. Unemployment, reducing which had once been the government's priority, stood at 10.4% in its first year in office, 1994, and was still at 9.5% in May, 1997, just before the election. The number of the employed had only inched up, from 13,292,000 to 13,896,000. The worrisome problem of jobless youth actually became worse; among those aged 15 to 24, the unemployment rate rose from 16.5% in 1994 to 17.2 % (18% of males) in 1997. The average family income was falling, the gap between rich and poor widening, the number of beggars on the city streets increasing.

But by February 18, 1997, when Martin presented his fourth and pre-election budget, he was ready to claim victory, give or take a few billions. Program spending had been cut by $16.5 billion, or almost 14%, during his watch on the Finance ministry, and the deficit for the year was forecast at $17 billion, down from $42 billion in 1993–4. It was expected to fall to $9 billion in 1998–9 at which point the government would need to do no new borrowing. In reality, Martin was being cautious and many financial observers were convinced that he would achieve his targets a year ahead of schedule. The combined deficit of all governments — federal, provincial and municipal — which had stood at 7.4% of Gross Domestic Product in 1992, twice the average of the other industrialized democracies in the G-7 group, was down to 1.3%, or half the average. While the proportion of debt to GDP remained high, it was declining for the first time since 1974, and was forecast to fall rapidly as the deficit disappeared. Writing a Report Card on the Liberals in the 1997 edition of the annual survey *How Ottawa Spends*, Editor Gene Swimmer, a professor in the School of Public Administration at Carleton University, gave them an A grade for their handing of the deficit which he found "impressive by international as well as Canadian standards."[3]

Even better for the government, the economy was at last showing some vital signs, driven by exports to the growing U.S. economy, and optimists predicted the creation of 300,000 new jobs during the year. While on the eve of the election the country at large was still not feeling good about the economy, the deficit had been removed as an issue — of which the Reform Party had made much in 1993 — and Martin had become one of the most respected leaders in Canada. It was his legacy that all of a sudden politicians were talking not about cuts, but about how best to spend the surpluses when they began to appear in a year or two. Reduce taxes, increase spending, or pay down the debt? The Liberals, naturally, suggested a bit of all three — and were in a position where they might actually be able to make real the gauzy visions of 1993.

National unity

As Justice Minister in 1981, Chrétien played a key role in patriating the constitution from British safe keeping, and inserting into it a Charter of Rights and Freedoms. But this was done over the objections of Quebec. As the provincial government at the time was formed by the Parti Québécois (PQ) which was intent on taking the province out of Confederation, it could be said, and was, that no constitutional settlement would have been acceptable. But the PQ was not alone in resisting the new constitution, and Quebec has not since signed on, although it is of course bound by it. One consequence was that Chrétien came to be seen by many of his fellow Quebeckers as some sort of traitor. When the Quebec Liberals returned to power in 1985 by defeating the PQ, they offered terms for a settlement. Prime Minister Mulroney jumped at the opportunity and succeeded in persuading all the provinces to agree to a deal, the Meech Lake Accord. Chrétien opposed the Accord which eventually failed to achieve ratification in provincial legislatures, and he was again seen in Quebec as opposing the interests of his own province. So when he became prime minister in 1993, he was widely popular in English-speaking Canada, but not in Quebec. In that province in fact, the big winner in the election was not Chrétien's Liberals but the separatist Bloc Québécois which, as noted above, became, bizarrely, the Official Opposition in Ottawa.

None of this seemed to disturb Chrétien. He insisted that he had not been elected to talk about the constitution: Canadians, including Quebeckers, were fed up with it and wanted to focus on the economy. But the situation changed again in 1994 when Parti Québécois, under a hardline separatist, Jacques Parizeau, returned to power in Quebec and began planning for a referendum on separation. Chrétien remained sanguine because he was deeply convinced that his compatriots would never actually vote to leave Canada. The separatists seemed to have agreed because they decided not to offer a clear choice between remaining in Canada and becoming sovereign. The PQ, the BQ, and the minor Action Democratique party agreed instead, in June, 1995, to propose a new economic and political partnership between Canada and a sovereign Quebec, an outline of which was then debated and approved in the Quebec legislature, the National Assembly. This eventually gave rise to the referendum question which was something less than crystal clear: "Do you agree that Quebec should become sovereign after having made a formal offer to Canada for a new economic and political partnership within the scope of the bill respecting the future of Quebec and of the agreement signed on June 12, 1995."

Still Chrétien and his advisers remained confident that Quebeckers would vote No on referendum day, October 30. As the campaign began most of the polls supported that confidence, and the separatist campaign failed to gain momentum. The talk in Ottawa was of a repeat of the result of the 1980 referendum when 60% voted against separation. The tide began to turn when PQ Premier Parizeau, an able but arrogant and pompous figure in effect ceded the leadership of the failing separatist camp. Bouchard had had a curious career, first as a Liberal, and then as a minister in Mulroney's Conservative government, from which he resigned in a dispute over the Meech Lake Accord to become a separatist and found the BQ. His strength was his oratory and his political style — a grandeur reminiscent of Charles de Gaulle. Bouchard infused the campaign with an emotional appeal to Quebec nationalism, and persuaded many Quebeckers that it was not really about separation and sovereignty, but about achieving a new status within Canada. No matter how often federalists said that there would be no new partnership, many, probably most, Quebeckers remained convinced that they could have both sovereignty and MPs in Ottawa, the Canadian dollar in their pockets, and a Canadian passport when they travelled abroad.

As support for the separatist proposition began to grow, and then took the lead in the polls, the Quebec Liberals leading the federalists increased their pressure on Ottawa for proposals they could offer Quebeckers as an alternative both to separation and to the status quo. Finally, Chrétien yielded, and in a speech in Verdun, Quebec, he promised constitutional recognition of Quebec as a "distinct society" within Canada, and that no changes in the constitution affecting Quebec would be made without its consent. These were significant concessions because they had been two of the key provisions in the Meech Lake Accord which Chrétien had helped to defeat.

Whether by coincidence or not, the polls then began to show a decline in support for the separatist option, and when the votes were counted Chrétien and the federalists scraped through with the barest of margins: 50.6% voted No to separation; 49.4% (including a majority of French-speaking Quebeckers) voted Yes.

Although Chrétien could claim to have won, he had shown himself to be out of touch with his own people, a prime minister without much honour in his own province. He was eager to redeem the promises he had made during the campaign, but even that proved difficult. There was strong opposition, particularly in the West, to recognizing Quebec as a distinct society — although in history, language, and culture it obviously was — because that would appear to give it a special status not enjoyed by other provinces, and if Quebec was to have a veto over constitutional change, the other provinces, or at least regions, would demand one also. It soon became apparent that Chrétien could not get the support of enough provinces to amend the constitution, and he was forced to act instead by way of a Parliamentary resolution which was no guarantee of change because it could of course be altered by a simple vote in any future Parliament.

This and other measures intended to conciliate Quebec became known as Plan A. Plan B was to make clear to Quebec that however the vote might go in a future referendum, separation would not be easy. The Throne Speech opening Parliament in February, 1996 declared that in the event of another referendum: "The government will exercise its responsibility to ensure the debate is conducted with all the facts on the table, that the rules of the process are fair, that the consequences are clear, and that Canadians will have their say in the future of the country." How all this was to be resolved by a referendum initiated by the National Assembly of Quebec was not clear. Ottawa next asked the Supreme Court for a ruling on whether a unilateral declaration of independence would be legal. Chrétien repeated that a simple majority of 51% would not be enough to justify breaking up the country. And aboriginals in Quebec and others argued that in event of separation, they would want to remain part of Canada, envisaging the partition of the province.

Thus the unity issue which Chrétien had declared in 1993 to be dead was back, and near the top of the political agenda as the 1997 election approached. One result was to revive the Conservative and Reform parties. The new, young PC leader Jean Charest, had been one of the most effective campaigners against separatism during the referendum in his home province, in alliance with the Quebec and federal Liberals. In Quebec, he emerged as a spokesman for federalism and in the rest of Canada he had a new credibility as the leader of the party which had founded Canada and had always recognized Quebec's special place in Confederation. On the other hand, Reform leader Preston Manning, Charest's rival on the Right, had a new issue to replace the fiscal clothes stolen by Martin. He spoke primarily for the West in rejecting any sort of special status for Quebec, insisting that all provinces must be equal, but offering to devolve many Ottawa powers and programs to Quebec and the other provinces. It was this difference on constitutional policy that made impossible the union of the parties on the Right, Reform and Conservative, that many ideologues saw as a prerequisite to defeating the Liberals.

Meanwhile, the Official Opposition party, the Bloc Québécois, meanwhile, fell into disarray when Parizeau, having lost the referendum, resigned as Quebec Premier and was replaced by the man who had nearly won it for him, Lucien Bouchard, the founder and leader of the BQ. Recognizing that Quebec would not be willing to face another referendum for a few years, Bouchard settled down to build confidence in the future by showing he could provide good government, and the BQ in Ottawa drifted more or less leaderless toward the 1997 election.

Other issues

The decline of fish stocks on the Atlantic coast became a major policy problem during the 1993–97 period, with consequences probably both plus and minus for the Liberals. To give cod stocks in particular a chance to recover, the government in 1994 introduced the Atlantic Groundfish Strategy, known as TAGS, the essence of which was to compensate the fishing industry for not fishing, with payments of $1.9 billion over five years. Far more people than expected applied for aid of one sort or another, but that was only one of the difficulties encountered in closing down, in effect, a major regional industry, and Liberal popularity suffered. On the other side of the coin, the government blamed European fleets for reckless overfishing, and claimed for itself the right to board and inspect boats just outside the 200-mile territorial limit. When a Spanish ship was boarded and arrested, the European Union denounced the act as "organized piracy," but federal Fisheries Minister Brian Tobin, from Newfoundland, became a "Captain Canada" hero at home — and also in Britain where fishermen suffering from European competition in what they regarded as their own waters flew the Canadian flag. Two Spanish warships were dispatched to guard their trawlers on the Grand Banks, but before a serious clash could occur, Canada and the EU reached a compromise. Tobin went on to become Premier of Newfoundland, and just before the 1997 election Ottawa decided that cod stocks had recovered sufficiently to permit limited fishing — a move that many suspected of owing more to politics than to conservation.

Concern about violent crime and the spread of guns prompted Justice minister Allan Rock to introduce legislation imposing draconian new controls on guns. He proposed among other things to ban the sale of 21 types; to allow handguns only to collectors and target shooters, and then under tight control; and to require all firearms — an estimated 7 million — to be registered with the police. While warmly welcomed in most urban centres, the controls were resented and resisted in rural areas where hunting was a part of daily life — particularly in the West with its sense of "frontier" tradition. Some social conservatives also tended to see the controls as an attack on civil rights. A prolonged battle in Parliament ensued, but legislation eventually passed.

Under the previous Conservative government, troops of the Airborne Regiment had been sent to Somalia to serve with contingents from other countries to try to bring peace to a country ravaged by feuding warlords. When the shocking news emerged that a few Canadian soldiers had tortured to death a Somalian youth caught in the compound, the military police investigated and courts martial followed. But there were allegations of an attempted cover-up in the Defence department, and the Airborne Regiment was accused of harbouring neo-Nazi racists and permitting brutal and obscene hazing of new recruits. It fell to the Liberal government to respond, and the first action was to disband the regiment, dispersing its paratroopers to other units. Next, a three-man commission was appointed to conduct a public inquiry into all aspects of the Somalia affair, and this produced evidence of poor leadership and administration at the highest military levels, together with suggestions that records had been doctored in an attempt to conceal the truth. But the inquiry dragged on for more than two years, and before it had got to the bottom of the alleged cover-up, the government ordered it to wrap up its work and report. The commissioners protested, the media were outraged, and the Liberals wound up getting the blame, indirectly, for events which had occurred under the Conservatives. The serious outcome was that the military was shown to be in a mess which the government had done little or nothing to correct.

Conclusion

We cannot know how the events outlined above, and many others of less apparent importance during the three-and-half years of Liberal government, influenced the electorate. But it is a fact that the Liberals were still well ahead in the opinion polls when they called the election; in fact, that lead probably persuaded Chrétien to go the country instead of serving for the normal period of at least four years. Another factor of course was that the other parties had failed to make much impact on the country, and none appeared to be an alternative national government in waiting. But instead of romping home as they had expected, the Liberals had a hard fight to maintain a narrow majority. In retrospect, it may be shown that the big loser was Chrétien; he retained the prime ministership but lost any claim to be a national leader acceptable in all regions.

Notes

[1]See *The Canadian General Election of 1993*, by Alan Frizzell, Jon H. Pammett and Anthony Westell, Carleton University Press, Ottawa, 1994)
[2]An excellent account of the education of Paul Martin can be found in *Double Vision: The Inside Story of the Liberals in Power*, by Edward Greenspon and Anthony Wilson-Smith (Doubleday, 1996).
[3]*How Ottawa Spends 1997–98. Seeing Red: A Liberal Report Card*, Carleton University Press, Ottawa, 1987.

Two
Following the Trail of Campaign '97
by Edward Greenspon

Campaigns matter.[1] But so do governments. And so the character of the Liberal Party's 1997 election campaign was very much determined by the events of the first term in office. As Jean Chrétien prepared in early 1997 to go to the polls, his advisers and ministers vigorously debated the type of campaign they should wage. On the one side, the fiscally oriented ministers arrayed around Finance Minister Paul Martin wanted to run on the February 1997 budget, which had stayed the course on deficit reduction but had begun to show that the proverbial corner was close enough to justify renewed spending — they learned from focus groups to call it investment — in selected areas. Overall, the school of thought around Martin felt that the government had maintained a high standing in the polls over the previous several years not in spite of its deficit reduction policies, but in large part because of them. It aimed at making electoral gains in fiscally conservative and fast-growing Western Canada, particularly by embracing the legions of mostly affluent, mostly male ex-Tories who had been attracted to the Liberals by virtue of those deficit policies.

But another wing of the party argued that the budget cuts would come back to haunt the government during the campaign, that Liberals would be bitten to death by a swarm of regional and special interests. It counselled a renewed commitment to a traditional Liberal base, particularly among women and low-income voters and Atlantic Canadians. Pollster Michael Marzolini told the caucus at a special retreat in Québec City in January that these groups were wavering in their commitment, that although the headline numbers of Liberal support remained high that the foundations were weak. Many women in particular had moved from the Liberal to undecided column. They would have to be given a reason to move back.

Prime Minister Chrétien's close advisers struggled with these conflicting viewpoints as they sought to put the party's election platform to bed in the late winter and early spring. The debate was confined to a extremely small circle, people like Eddie Goldenberg, John Rae, Chaviva Hosek and David Zussman — many of them also occupied with running the government from the Prime Minister's Office. Deadlines slipped away as they struggled to define their election messages. Should they run strictly on their record? Was a dose of "vision" required given that the next mandate would most likely cross a millennial divide? How detailed should a government, especially one burned by its 1993 GST and daycare promises, be?

The election advisers were badly divided. They drafted and redrafted the Red Book II, stuck not just on matters of left versus right but also on how far to stick their heads out of their shell. Hosek and Zussman endorsed an activist approach that would set out three to five high-profile "national projects" that the government would undertake in its term. Goldenberg and Rae, not seeing any compelling reason to present a target to their opponents or to set Chrétien up for possible failure in the second term, nixed the idea. Ultimately, their Red Book would be pureed into political porridge. In seeking to be all things to all people, some strategists outside the inner core worried their party could end up being nothing to anybody.

The weeks leading up to the election were unusual even by the standards of pre-writ periods. A largely somnolent government suddenly shifted into hyper-drive. It settled the long-festering Pearson airport lawsuit. It re-opened the cod fishery. It softened the impact on immigrant families of the 1995 right of landing fee. It signed an historic labour market training agreement with Quebec, as well as a host of other provinces. It reached an accord with British Columbia over the regulation of salmon fishing. It rushed through several justice measures aimed at neutralizing growing law-and-order sentiments. Fearful that Prime Minister Chrétien might lose his own seat, the government resorted to the time-honoured ways of pork-barrel politics, getting the Minister of Defence to approve a 6,000-metre armoury for Shawinigan and persuading the Minister of Human Resources Development to dip into a wage subsidy fund for a $600,000 grant to hire construction workers for a local hotel. (Ironically, the money came from one of the programs devolved to Quebec as part of the labour market agreement, meaning that the next time out the Prime Minister would have to try his powers of persuasion on the provincial Parti Québécois government.) Each announcement came with doeful looks of hurt on the faces of ministers as bemused reporters rudely suggested linkages with an impending election call.

But the best laid plans sprang a leak as the Liberal procession marched inexorably toward a late April election call. Flooding in Manitoba precipitated a round of strategic soul-searching over the wisdom of pulling the plug. A decision was made for a prime ministerial visit to the site on Saturday, April 26. Chrétien would play the I-feel-your-pain game. (Although his aides said that he wanted to assess for himself whether to proceed with the election, the Prime Minister himself later conceded that the die had already been cast. There was no turning back.)

The visit proved to be a disaster. A disorderly media scrum along the sandbag lines in south Winnipeg angered local residents. The enduring symbol of the trip quickly became Chrétien's response when a volunteer handed him a sandbag. "What do you want me to do with it?" he asked. The television footage of his half-hearted toss became an icon for Liberal insensitivity.

On Sunday, April 27, Chrétien convened a final meeting of his cabinet and proceeded to Rideau Hall to dissolve Parliament. For months, Liberal operatives and journalists had been exchanging views that the first question thrown at Chrétien would be why he was calling the election. Dutifully, the media pitched the expected fastball. Unbelievably, Chrétien, swinging before the words were even out of the reporter's mouth, whiffed.

He looked down at his notes for the scripted answer. The ghost of Kim Campbell — who in the same spot 43 months earlier was perceived to have flubbed a question on future unemployment trends — hovered in splendid anticipation. "Why now?" he asked rhetorically. "It's because it's the fourth year of the mandate. We had four budgets. Because the success of our... against the deficit. The Canadians have to make a choice — to finish the job and invest in health care, children, jobs for tomorrow. Because for me, it's very important that we go to the people. We're campaigning. Not me as much as my other opponents — they have been campaigning since weeks. And we did not want to have an election that will last like Americans, six months." And on it went, making little sense at all.

Liberals across the country winced. They had debated long and hard about an early election call, fearing they would look arrogant and opportunistic. Their fears had been realized.

The election campaign was quickly drowned out in the media by the drama of the Manitoba flood. Which was really too bad because that first week was, if not terribly elucidating, at least entertaining. Partly this was due to the contortions to which politicians subjected themselves so as to be seen not to be campaigning in Manitoba. Reform Party leader Preston Manning went so far as to propose postponing the election in the province while speaking over an airplane intercom flying over the flood area. He didn't want to be seen on television as exploiting the disaster.

But the week was much more than that. Bloc Québécois leader Gilles Duceppe served as a powerful reminder of the danger of throwing inexperienced or rusty leaders into high-pressure situations like campaigns, as per Kim Campbell and John Turner. Not only was his party deeply divided after the bitter Bloc leadership contest, but he had not yet learned the political art of staying on message or the risks of thinking on one's feet. He toured a cheese factory in a sanitary hair bonnet that, while required by health regulation, presented too tempting a target of ridicule to resist for a media horde. Then, his media bus got lost and so he fired the driver (who protested that he had been given poor directions). None of this was very funny. Pundits had stated self-assuredly that the Bloc could run a clown and still win 50 seats. But under this particular clown, the party's supporters seemed more inclined to vote for the bus driver. Nobody seemed to recognize that the Bloc was, in fact, vulnerable. A large poll taken for the CBC in the days before the campaign found that the Conservatives under Jean Charest enjoyed 25 per cent support in Quebec, in keeping with a steady progression over the previous year or so. Nor were they merely splitting the federalist vote. Charest was drawing support from soft nationalists.

The wheels also appeared to be falling off the Liberal campaign in that first week. In the wake of their stumble at Rideau Hall, the Liberals seized the agenda the following day in Halifax with an announcement that they would roll back planned cuts to provincial transfers to the tune of $6 billion over the next five years. The announcement dovetailed nicely with the overall Liberal message that the sacrifices that had been made in wrestling down the deficit were about to produce dividends of the sort Canadians desired, increased room to spend on health care. Other parties might be dangling tax cuts at voters. But the Liberals offered a different choice: continued deficit reduction accompanied by renewed health care spending. Not that they were against tax cuts. These would come in time.

For reporters travelling with Chrétien, it was all a bit too much. Or perhaps too little, too late. They noted that there was no new spending on health. Instead of continuing the sharp downward trend in transfer payments, the Liberals merely were cancelling the last two passes of the scythe. They would leave health transfers at the same level that the

Charest Conservatives proposed despite their advocacy of deep cuts elsewhere. Even Reform was on the record as favouring increased health care spending. (None of the parties bothered to explain how they would direct money to health given that federal transfers to the provinces are largely unconditional.)

Reporters wanted to know why the measure had not been contained in Finance Minister Martin's budget of two months earlier. They were told that the deficit picture, although well ahead of plan at that point, had improved considerably since then. The Liberals maintained they could now afford what had been out of their reach eight weeks earlier. To the press, it smacked of the worst kind of election ploy. There was Chrétien, flanked both by Martin, the author of the cuts, and David Dingwall, his left-wing health minister, desperate to prove to his native Nova Scotians that the Liberals, the real Liberals, not Paul Martin, were back in the saddle again.

The divisions were readily apparent. Even after the election, Chrétien's ministers were still debating whether the health care announcement had been a winning day for the campaign or, as more fiscally minded ministers contended, a day which had undermined, particularly in Western Canada, three years of messaging that deficit reduction came first.

There was no debate as to the harm to the Liberals of the next major event in the campaign — the premature leak of their platform. Reform, desperate to make inroads in Ontario, had released its platform the previous October, emulating the provincial success of Ontario premier Mike Harris in getting it out early. Like Harris, Reform proposed broad tax cuts and sought to make the case that these would stimulate job creation. The Conservatives also chose against waiting for the election to release their platform. It also called for major spending reductions and tax cuts, although the Conservatives, unlike Reform, proposed the more radical route of cutting taxes even before balancing the budget.

The Liberals privately acknowledged a great deal of respect for the Reform platform, although they did not fear Preston Manning personally. They did fear Jean Charest. For months, Chrétien had exhorted his advisers to prepare strong arguments to use against Charest, particularly to tar him with Brian Mulroney. In the Tory platform, they believed they had found these. The document was a shambles, on the one hand taking a strong policy line, but on the other focussing almost exclusively on Charest himself. It was Jean Charest's plan for the future. Jean Charest this and Jean Charest that. Charest unveiled it before a live audience, including party partisans and journalists, in a television studio in Toronto. It was slick, slick, slick — too slick for some. The Liberals played a tape of his presentation to one of their focus groups. Several compared it to an Infomercial. One indelicately suggested that Charest looked like the hyperkinetic TV exercise personality, Richard Simmons.

But it was the centrepiece of the platform, the tax cut, that gave the Liberals the greatest delight. They thought that Charest and his erstwhile band of Harris Tories — the "little shits" as first *Frank* magazine and thereafter the veteran, centrist Conservatives derided them — had misread public opinion badly. Canadian voters were a cautious lot. Poll after poll showed that they wanted the deficit eliminated first and foremost. They also wanted increased health care spending. Tax cuts came well down the list. Moreover, Ontario's cuts were just beginning to bite. School boards were debating whether to drop junior kindergarten. A health restructuring committee was pronouncing the death sentence on scores of hospitals. The consequences of tax cuts suddenly were all too apparent for the very voters Charest most wanted to win over.

For the Liberals, the cherry on top of the cake was this: Charest's numbers, like the missed deficit targets of the Mulroney years, didn't add up. He said his tax cuts would be financed by spending reductions. But the reductions failed to produce the required savings. Paul Martin was rolled out to drive home the message.

Now, it was the Liberals' turn to release their platform, an event scheduled for the first Thursday of the campaign. Shortly after 6 pm. eastern time on Tuesday, Preston Manning sent a tremor through Liberal ranks by pre-empting the big event. On the tranquil boardwalk in Québec City, he produced the bombshell of a leaked copy of the Liberal platform, a fully bound edition of the type that had not even made it yet to Ottawa headquarters, according to the Liberals.

The origins of the Reform document remain obscure. Manning's aides say it was offered by an unknown source and that they accepted. They flew it across the country to Manning, verified its authenticity and pounced. The Liberals were caught flat-footed. Chrétien was out in Vancouver. He was being hounded by demonstrators. The media, alerted by colleagues in Québec City and editors in Montréal and Toronto, surrounded him for a reaction. He didn't bother trying to contain his bewilderment about who had leaked, or his anger. "If I knew, there would be one employee less," he said menacingly.

The importance of the incident went well beyond upstaging the Liberals. In politics, great stock is put in the manner in which messages are delivered. How is an issue to be packaged or framed? The Liberals had intended to frame their Red Book II as a middle-of-the-road document — staying the course on the deficit fight but setting out modest new spending in priority areas. Its essential balance was to be captured in a core promise that once the deficit was eliminated the future surpluses would be divided evenly — 50 per cent for new spending initiatives and 50 per cent for tax cuts or debt reduction.

But it wasn't the Liberals framing the document. It was Preston Manning. "Goodbye Red Book and hello chequebook. And it is the Canadian taxpayers' chequebook we are talking about," he said in a clip that made every newscast. He characterized the Red Book as a return to old tax-and-spend Liberalism. The platform provided him with plenty of material. The Red Book promised $2 million for a Commissioner for Aquaculture Development and $10 million for new works of art for the 21st century. Liberals campaigning in the fiscally conservative regions of Western Canada shuddered. These were small sums, but symbolically powerful. They flew right in the face of three years of hard-won but far from secured political advances.

In the fast-paced world of electoral politics, the Liberals took forever in trying to regain the initiative. After some hemming and hawing, they moved up the official release of the Red Book to Wednesday afternoon in Saskatoon, hastily assembling a supporting cast of mostly conservative ministers — John Manley, Ralph Goodale, Anne McLellan and Lucienne Robillard — to appear with Chrétien. They tried to maintain a pretense that they had not been trumped, refusing to show their platform to the reporters travelling on the campaign plane until the appointed hour. The journalists were beside themselves — here they were assigned to cover the Liberals and they were the only people in their news organizations without the damn document. The Liberal humiliation wasn't yet complete, though. The ministerial props got stuck between floors in the hotel elevator. They had to be rescued by the Mounties.

The Globe and Mail, summarizing the first week of Canada's 36th general election campaign, commented: "If the Royal Canadian Air Farce had written the election script, could it look any more ridiculous than this?"

Reform, and to a lesser extent the tightly focussed New Democrats, had stolen the show in that first week. The second week had an even more improbable star — former Quebec Premier Jacques Parizeau.

On Wednesday, the Québec City daily, *Le Soleil*, published a story quoting from a forthcoming book by Parizeau. The material appeared to provide compelling circumstantial evidence that Parizeau had intended to unilaterally declare Quebec's independence in the immediate aftermath of a Yes vote, contrary to the commitment of the separatist side that it would first try to negotiate a partnership arrangement with the rest of Canada. Leaving aside for a moment Parizeau's denials and half-denials, which he took more than 24 hours to issue, the apparent admission landed on the campaign like a bombshell.

The separatists were in disarray. Premier Bouchard and Bloc leader Duceppe moved quickly to distance themselves from the hardline Parizeau. One could feel the air being sucked right out of their campaign. First the hair net and bus driver, now this seeming duplicity. The soft nationalists, already heading for the exits, picked up the pace.

Electoral campaigns invariably consist of a mix of a party's own strategies, defences against the strategies of others, and responses to the inevitable emergence of unexpected events. In the 1993 campaign, the Liberals had faced a choice on more days than not between sticking with their game plan or reacting instead to Kim Campbell's latest gaffe. The taciturn John Rae, the Liberal campaign director, confessed afterwards that on some days he felt like a kid in a candy store. More often than not, he abandoned his planned diet of policy announcements in favour of the sweet morsels offered up by Campbell.

This time it was easier to shuck the message of the day since the Liberals didn't have much to say anyhow. The press travelling with Chrétien learned of the Parizeau revelations while in Edmonton. That evening, on a long flight for a morning event in Moncton, he was to stopover briefly in Québec City. Filing times would be exceedingly short, but the Liberals provided a souped up bus, complete with electricity and phones, to carry the reporters from the speech back to the airport. That would allow a quick file.

Chrétien made his point with unusual restraint. He reminded his audience that Duceppe had several days earlier referred to Parizeau as an elder statesman of the sovereignty movement and suggested that Quebeckers could no longer afford to place their blind faith in the Bloc. Some of the reporters felt he had missed a golden opportunity to strike hard against the wounded separatists. His handlers privately countered that Bouchard, Parizeau, Duceppe, and company were in enough disarray. Why shift the focus back to Chrétien?

The next day in Nova Scotia, Chrétien was more forceful. He placed Parizeau's alleged intentions in the context of other suspicious behaviour by the separatists and allowed that he thought there had been a major conspiracy under way to hoodwink Quebec voters. He wasn't going to let Bouchard off the hook. Chrétien reasoned that he had to be part of the conspiracy. Meanwhile, Parizeau was muddying the waters further with a strong denunciation of the interpretation Le Soleil had placed on his words.

The sudden intrusion of Parizeau into the campaign was both a blessing and a curse for Charest. On the one hand, it helped shake loose soft nationalists, the mid-section of the Quebec body politic that was crucial to Conservative growth in the province. It also gave Charest a chance to showcase his major campaign advantage, his own personal leadership, especially when it came to taking on the separatists.

On the other hand, the Parizeau factor placed the full glare of the public spotlight on Plan B, the tough-minded measures such as a Supreme Court reference on the legality of separation that the Chrétien government was putting in place in advance of the next referendum. Charest didn't like Plan B at all. His instincts, like those of many of the Quebec ministers in the cabinet, was to pursue solely a Plan A approach of reconciliation toward Quebec. But Plan B was very popular outside of Quebec. Reporters on the Chrétien campaign dubbed his chartered aircraft Plane B.

Charest, despite his high personal ratings, already had a consistency problem. A passionate advocate of distinct society status for Quebec — a key component of Plan A — he nonetheless had refused to utter the phrase on a swing through Alberta. Over the course of the next few days he was forced to come out strongly against Plan B, and then add his own qualifiers.

The Parizeau intervention had reshaped the campaign as it headed into the debates. A front-page banner headline in *The Globe and Mail* said it all: Unity Becomes Campaign Focus.

The Ottawa-based media had never been terribly comfortable with the jobs issue, which required some economic grounding and a policy orientation. National unity was sexier and, given its heavy reliance on rhetoric, far easier to deal with. The media were secretly delighted at the shift of the campaign. When Chrétien's bus was surrounded at the end of the week in Newfoundland by protesting union activists — upset at the level of support for out-of-work fishery industry workers — the incident was seen as more of a joke or nuisance than a genuine expression of the angst of Atlantic Canadians. The lack of follow-up perhaps explains why everyone was so surprised by the depth of antipathy toward the Liberals expressed in the region on election night. (The bus incident proved the value in campaigns of cellular phone technology. The RCMP would not let reporters off the bus to interview the protesters or their union organizers. Under siege, the reporters conducted their interviews with Canadian Auto Workers president Buzz Hargrove from their cellular phones while looking right at him on the other side of their rocking glass and aluminum trap.)

The New Democrats, the only party running on the left, had good reason to be concerned about the return to prominence of the national unity issue. Leader Alexa McDonough seemed to be making modest strides despite a platform that had to be recalled for recalculation and her public confession that she didn't understand all the economic gobblygook anyhow. Unlike Duceppe, she was an experienced politician, well schooled in the art of staying on message. But nobody cared anymore about her message.

Reform, on the other hand, was delighted. Its strategists had always counted on playing the unity card in the campaign, which they viewed as a so-called wedge issue, one which separated them from all the other parties. The party unambiguously opposed distinct society, in all variations; it felt its opponents embraced the concept. Long before the election, Reform strategist Rick Anderson talked about national unity as an important element in the party's campaign plans. Now it was on the radar screen, and without any effort on the part of Reform, which intended to drive the wedge hard and deep.

On the Monday and Tuesday of the start of the third week of the campaign, the leaders gathered at the government conference centre in downtown Ottawa for the English- and French-language debates. Reporters watched from a large room down the hall from the improvised studio, many of them filing stories to their newspapers and radio stations as the debate proceeded. If election campaigns represent the summit of pack journalism, the debates are its peak. The reporters exchange quips back and forth as the leaders spar, testing their own reactions against those of their colleagues. A consensus begins to form — in plenty of time for the instant analysis and the ubiquitous boxing metaphors. The parties also pack the site with their very best spin doctors, senior strategists who offer up pithy explanations in the moments afterwards about how it was that their leader so exceeded expectations. The NDP even trotted out Saskatchewan finance minister Janice MacKinnon to counter Chrétien's contention that his policies were the same of those of the province's premier, Roy Romanow, and within the tradition of socialist icon T.C. Douglas.

The English-language debate hinged, it seemed in the immediate aftermath, on a single line — Jean Charest's solemn declaration to keep the country intact for his children. At the time, it didn't seem particularly memorable. Who can even remember the precise quote? It lacked the bite of Lloyd Bentsen's famous rejoinder to Dan Quayle — "I knew Jack Kennedy....." But the audience had applauded — spontaneously and in defiance of the rules of engagement. Charest had connected — if not against his opponents, at least with the studio audience. As with the famous CBC town hall of the previous December, reporters, operating in isolation, tended to put great weight in the only real people they could see interacting with political leaders. Charest already seemed to the reporters to be enjoying a strong debate. At times the others seemed to defer to him as if afraid that he might put them away with a quick flick of the tongue if they drifted within verbal reach. The applause clinched matters. It represented one of the few objective facts upon which one could seize. Therefore, Charest was deemed the unanimous winner on points. The media thought so and, polls quickly showed, the public concurred.

Charest also was seen to have performed well the following night in French. But once again, it was the X-factor (perhaps the X-files factor) that stole the show — the collapse of moderator Claire Lamarche just as the debate was turning to the unity issue.

By this point, the polls all agreed that Charest was gaining ground in the vacuum created in Quebec by the Bloc's freefall. The debate furnished him with critical momentum. The Conservatives were buoyed, but they knew that the coming days would be crucial. Could they build on Charest's personal likeability? Allan Gregg, the veteran Tory pollster who was sitting out the campaign, had trouble imagining how Charest could escape an unpopular platform, particularly in Ontario, which also happened to be the province most contented with the Liberal government.

Preston Manning had fought hard to be included in the French-language debate despite his almost total lack of fluency. He used the opportunity to address his core supporters outside Quebec. In both debates, Manning employed a phrase that would spark controversy before the campaign ended — dismissing his squabbling opponents as "Quebec-based leaders." Doggedly, he continued to drive in his wedge.

The polls on the weekend after the debates confirmed that Charest had enjoyed an upward bump. But they were disquieting for the Conservatives in that almost all his growth had occurred within Quebec, where he personally outpolled Chrétien as choice for best prime minister by a margin of two to one. His strategists had spoken earlier in the campaign about the need to establish his credibility outside his native province and then translate that into support inside Quebec. Now they reversed their logic: they would build a bridge from Quebec into Ontario.

Over Victoria Day weekend, the polls suggested that two important trends existed, aside from the Conservative uptick in Quebec. First, Liberal support continued to drip away, slowly but steadily. From the high 40s, the party had dropped to an even 40 per cent, according to the Globe/Environics poll. In Quebec, they were holding their own, but the Conservatives were the ones making inroads among Francophone voters. As well, all the Liberal talk of a major breakthrough in Western Canada appeared to be for naught. Indeed, the real surprise of the polls was not the Conservatives, but Reform. Outside of Quebec, they were leading the

Tories by 23 per cent to 21 per cent. They had re-established their 1993 base in Western Canada, going in the space of six weeks from 25 per cent to 36 per cent, enough to dominate the region.

The key now for Reform, which desperately wanted to win the mantle of Official Opposition, was stopping a Conservative surge. If Charest did well in Quebec and successfully built his bridge into Ontario, he could deny Reform second place and position himself as the true national alternative to the Liberals. Reform needed to bomb that bridge. Ontario, with its 103 seats, had been key from the start for both parties. Now that was even more so. It was clear the next week would be about Ontario, with the Conservatives laying down a barrage from the east and Reform from the west.

The town of Orangeville in the riding of Dufferin-Peel-Wellington-Grey exemplified the state of the campaign. Orangeville displayed a block of economically satisfied but almost mute Liberal supporters, a hardcore of establishment Tories, and a band of energetic, even impassioned Reformers. A Liberal strategist compared the Reformers to Pentacostals in their fervor. The Tories were Church of England and the Liberals United. Not a single person interviewed independently raised the subject of Charest's strong debate performance. That was last week's news. Even more striking was the number of voters who volunteered that they had had their fill of leaders from Quebec. Preston Manning had been pressing the theme all week, including during a breakfast meeting in Orangeville. (That was 36 hours before his famous ad about Quebec-based leaders.) It seemed to be resonating. In the town of Burlington the tone was somewhat more restrained, but many residents also brought up without prompting their fatigue with Quebec leaders. They seemed resigned to more Chrétien, for whom they evinced little enthusiasm despite widespread, but not unanimous, satisfaction with the state of the economy. What about Charest? That's when they would raise the Quebec issue.

The Liberals were still hammering away at Charest. A televised ad featuring Paul Martin decrying Conservative arithmetic was getting extensive airplay. Organizers in Western Canada, apoplectic about the Reform surge, complained bitterly to headquarters about its insensitivity to their regional needs. By this point, the Liberals had pretty well given up on expanding the Western base and were working to hang on to their small 1993 beachhead. That meant drawing a defensive perimeter around the major cities, particularly Edmonton and Vancouver.

In the middle of that week, the Liberals played one of their wedge cards — gun control. They chose to do so in Montréal, scene of the 1989 massacre of female students at the École Polytechnique. Their gun control message took dead aim at Charest, whose platform, in attempting to woo rural Ontarians, promised to scrap the Liberal gun registry. The decision to raise the profile of the gun control issue also spoke to the diminished expectations of the Liberals in Western Canada. If they thought themselves competitive in Western seats with sizable rural populations, they would have been far more reluctant to talk about their controversial legislation. But once those seats weren't going their way anyhow, the strategists felt free to use the issue.

Indeed, the Liberal Western strategy now depended strongly on galvanizing urban women and, to some extent, seniors. They began running an attack ad, only in the West, decrying Reform's record on health care.

Nobody in the media took much notice. The only ad that mattered as week four drew to a close was the Reform ad suggesting that Quebeckers — it seemed to equate Lucien Bouchard and Gilles Duceppe with Jean Chrétien and Jean Charest — had almost lost the country and that perhaps the time had arrived for a non-Quebec prime minister.

It was clear by this point that Reform had gained control of the election agenda. The public campaign, waged via the leader tours and through the media, revolved around Manning and Reform. He began to attract loud protests along with his fervent audiences. He led the newscasts. Even in Quebec, where the party was not a factor, Reform had stolen the spotlight. Commentators concluded that its ads had offended soft nationalists, who, ironically, were reconsidering their shift toward the Conservatives. The beneficiary was the Bloc Québécois, who had also turned to, of all people, Jacques Parizeau, to help persuade hard nationalists to turn out on voting day.

Reform now served as the prime target for nearly all the other parties. It seemed to me that its surge was well underway before the anti-Quebecker ad made its brief appearance on the airwaves. Whether the ad was necessary, let alone helpful to Reform, remains to be proven. But Reform had some momentum and, at the end of week four, it seemed possible the party might snag four to six seats in the 519 and 705 telephone regions well beyond Toronto. As for the famous 905 suburban belt, not to mention the metropolitan area itself, those seemed safely Liberal.

Week five began curiously. Chrétien was to spend the early part of the final week trying to stave off elimination in Alberta and British Columbia. Throughout the campaign, he had studiously avoided (other than the debates) situations that could conceivably spin out of control, such as radio hotline shows or town halls. But on the eve of his Western swing he granted interviews to the English- and French-language services of the

CBC in which he stated that he would not accept the result of a 50 per cent plus one vote in a Quebec referendum even if he participated in writing the question. The comment was provocative. Indeed, the same question had been directed at Chrétien in the French-language debate, but the collapse of the moderator prevented him answering. In the follow-up debate, nobody had bothered following up. Now, Chrétien himself appeared to be going out of his way to make sure the matter was raised.

Clearly, it was a message that would play well in the West. On this particular matter, Chrétien took a harder line than Manning, who always said that Quebeckers should be aware that if they voted to get out, then they would be out. For him, 50 plus one was sufficient to break up the country. But Conservative strategists attributed even darker motives to the intervention. They reasoned that he was trying to polarize the vote within Quebec, to squeeze out Charest by driving soft nationalists back to the Bloc Québécois while federalists rallied around the Liberal flag. The Conservatives could offer no concrete evidence of such a nefarious plot, but the end result would be consistent with their assertions. The Bloc clawed back enough of its support to again gain the lion's share of seats in Quebec, helped along by reminders of why it was that many Quebeckers feel they need to send people to Ottawa to promote their interests as much as to defend them.

The New Democrats entered the last week deeply frustrated by all the attention being accorded Reform and particularly its fixation with the unity agenda. Reform was drawing away NDP support in the West. Alexa McDonough escalated her attacks on Manning, whose views she suggested could lead to a civil war. The NDP continued to talk jobs — to what it considered the profound indifference of the national media. Polling showed little life in the NDP camp. The party strategists claimed that national polling wasn't sensitive to their highly targetted campaign — by this point they were concentrating on a little more than 20 ridings. So they leaked their polling to *The Globe and Mail*, which treated it with kid gloves.

At the start of the last week, it was obvious that the hazy, lazy Liberal campaign had failed to light a fire. The fractured nature of their Opposition made anything but governing status impossible to contemplate, but their majority could no longer be taken for granted. A poll by Ekos Research Associates showed them on the knife's edge at 38 per cent. The unanswered question was whether their slow slide had abated or not?

Throughout the campaign, the Liberals had been frustrated by what they called the by-election syndrome. By that they meant that voters felt so sure of another Liberal victory that they felt able to cast their ballots to send a message without fear of actually defeating the government, as often happens in by-elections which have no chance to unelecting governments. Out West, embattled MPs found many voters anxious to vote Reform if for no other reason than to deny Official Opposition status to the Bloc Québécois once again.

Now Chrétien sought to use strategic voting considerations to his advantage. Told by his pollsters that Canadians preferred a majority government, he began appealing for one as he travelled the West. That he had been reduced to such measures spoke volumes not just about Reform's strong campaign in Western Canada, but about Liberal mishandling of the region. It came back to the fact that government, as well as campaigns, matter.

The Liberals had always expected to drop seats in Atlantic Canada, a region hard-hit by the harsh austerity measures of the Martin budgets. But they counted on making up for these losses, and any in Ontario, with gains in Quebec and, particularly, the West. Chrétien had spoken bravely about snaring a majority of British Columbia's 34 seats and making major inroads in Alberta, including the previously hostile Calgary.

To some extent, his government had a case to make for itself in the two provinces. Natural Resources Minister Anne McLellan had bested successive environment ministers on behalf of the Calgary oil patch and had delivered a royalty regime favourable to oilsands development. Chrétien had put tremendous effort into building trade ties with Asia and had made a major priority of reaching pre-election agreements with BC Premier Glen Clark on a number of fronts.

But the Liberals had booted as many files as they had fielded smoothly, including their infamous bobble of the regional constitutional vetoes in late 1995, when Chrétien had steadfastedly refused, until the final moment, to consider British Columbia a region in its own right. Less profoundly but perhaps more tellingly, Justice Minister Allan Rock not only had pressed ahead with the gun registry, but he had failed to address in timely fashion the use of the so-called faint hope clause by serial killer Clifford Olson. In stark contrast, he was fast off the mark when Quebeckers had agitated against biker gangs. The late attention to the Olson matter — by the time the Liberals moved to restrict the clause, it was too late to apply to changes to BC's most notorious murderer — cost the Liberals dearly. The Canadian Police Association highlighted the failure in mid-campaign with shocking billboard ads, playing to Reform's strength on law-and-order.

Still, the Liberals were satisfied that their anti-Reform health ads and their call for a majority would be sufficient to hang on to most of their urban seats in the two provinces. But Western Canada certainly could not be counted on to compensate for losses elsewhere, a fact that continued to befuddle Chrétien even after the campaign. In a press conference on June 4, he expressed an understanding of the voting behaviour of Atlantic Canadians, whom he figured had lashed out at a government that had cuts its benefits. But he couldn't fathom why Western Canada, with its strong economy and fiscal conservativism, had failed to grasp his party to its bosom. With his analysis, Chrétien confirmed himself to be an economic determinist in matters political. But his problem in Western Canada was far more culturally driven. The Liberals were so clearly from somewhere far away; whatever one may have thought of Reform, they enjoyed home-team status.

The majority would be won or lost in Ontario. The Liberals won a break. The furious counterattack on Reform for its anti-Quebec ads was causing many voters to have second thoughts about the party. Reform needed to reach beyond its diehard supporters in order to win seats in the province. But it suffered a serious image problem. Manning himself was viewed as a highly negative figure in a country and particularly a province that prefers upbeat politicians. As well, the party still suffered from an image for intolerance that had taken hold over the previous Parliament.

Now the Quebec ads reinforced those impressions. Manning tried to counter with a dramatic shift toward more positive messaging, surrounding himself with Canadian flags and rousing himself to some passion for the country he sought to lead. But it was probably too late. Even a week earlier in Orangeville, when he had enjoyed the wind at his back, voters had tempered their enthusiasm for Reform policies with reservations about taking such a radical leap. Many voters said that while they liked Reform, they remembered having taken a flyer on Bob Rae and the NDP, a gamble they had come to regret. Reform was a young party and its hard messages may have frightened off some of its potential supporters. On election night, Manning would not be able to hide his disappointment about being shut out in Ontario. Even a small success there would have helped him claim status over the Conservatives as the national alternative. Now he would have to put up again with being denigrated as a Western regional rump.

For the Conservatives, the final days were agonizing. They had failed to build their bridge from Quebec and, without an organizational foundation in Quebec, support was crumbling there, too. Atlantic Canada, where they had shucked their platform and ran from the left of the Liberals, promised to produce a harvest of seats. But even on election day, one of the most senior Tory operatives could do no better than predict anywhere from 10 to 30 seats. Ten would not be enough to provide official party status.

The New Democrats also were wringing their hands as Canadians headed to the polls. On election night, an emotional Alexa McDonough would be as surprised as anyone by the length of her coattails in Nova Scotia and by the downfall of Doug Young, the right-wing Liberal minister from New Brunswick. In the days before the election, her party had pulled campaign workers out of ridings they figured lost in order to concentrate their forces in those they considered winnable. Several of these abandoned constituencies actually went NDP on election night.

Indeed, the Liberal collapse in Atlantic Canada was greater than expected — helping vault both the New Democrats and Conservatives back into official status. The Liberals hung on to just 11 of their 31 seats. Afterwards, journalists would question themselves about having misread the depth of anger and despair in the region. They were in good company. Liberal pollster Michael Marzolini expected at least 16 seats. He was as shocked as anyone on election night when Health Minister David Dingwall went down to defeat.

I spent election night in *The Globe and Mail* newsroom in Toronto. Deadline pressures forced us to pre-write large portions of our stories. We could make adjustments on a rolling basis throughout the night, but the tilt of the stories assumed a narrow Liberal majority. As the early results came in from the east coast, we all held our breath. If the trend carried through to Ontario, we were looking at a minority at best. But Ontario saved the Liberals, and a lot of last-minute rewriting on our part.

The 72 hours following the election were as instructive as the campaign itself. A vigorous debate broke out among Liberal backbenchers and ministers about the precise meaning of the result. Many chose to focus on the party's rejection in Atlantic Canada, and take that as a sign that the party had to restore its reputation for compassion and social activism. For them, the election was a warning to steer to the left.

But others preferred to focus on their unfulfilled ambitions for major gains in Western Canada. Why had they failed? This group, largely on the right of the party, complained that the campaign, with its pre-writ spending blitz and all-things-to-all-people Red Book II, had undermined the government's main success of restoring its 1950s and 1960s reputation for competent economic management. They counselled staying the course on the deficit and argued that British Columbia alone has more seats than the entire Atlantic region.

The Quebec result was also subject to differing interpretations. Chrétien argued that his party had increased its representation and that the sovereigntist vote had fallen below 40 per cent for the first time since

1973. The Prime Minister's detractors muttered, though, that for the third time in a row — the 1993 election, the 1995 referendum, and now the 1997 election — he had failed to deliver the Francophone majority in his native province. Any gains made at the expense of the separatists were owed to Jean Charest, not Jean Chrétien.

While Chrétien privately boasted to colleagues that he was the first Liberal since Louis St. Laurent to secure a second consecutive majority and that his feat was actually the more impressive because he had dropped fewer seats in the process, pundits already had begun their countdown to a Liberal leadership race.

The election over, the mandate of the incoming Liberal government promised once again to produce interesting times. A party that had essentially run without a program now was condemned to developing a consensus while in government. Part of that consensus would involve whether they had emerged from the 1997 general election campaign as clear winners or near losers.

Notes

[1] Thanks to Hugh Winsor of *The Globe and Mail* for comments on a draft of this chapter.

Three

Securing Their Future Together: The Liberals in Action[*]
by Stephen Clarkson

The Liberal Party's campaign in 1997 may well be remembered as among the most puzzling in the annals of Canadian electioneering. The basic conundrum was that, although Jean Chrétien and his team pulled off the historically rare triumph of returning to power with a second majority government in a row, this feat was treated as a virtual failure. Viewed from outside the frenzy of the struggling combatants, the enigma of the Liberals' campaign can be broken down into six queries.

1. Why, when the Liberal government had coped brilliantly with the heavy fiscal legacy left them in 1993, did it bring its mandate to a close under increasing public discontent?
2. Why, when the leader's team of managers had been so capable both in campaigning and in governing, did they show no flair for political generalship when it came time for re-election?
3. Why, when the government, and especially its finance minister, had already redefined liberalism for the 1990s, was the party's policy direction anything but clear?
4. Why did the long underestimated but shrewd Jean Chrétien seem both overconfident and underachieving when he returned to the hustings?
5. How did the media, which consistently indicated Chrétien would win handily, help facilitate the Liberals' slide?

---

[*] This chapter benefited enormously from research carried out by a special team of my students: Katherine DiTomaso, Franca Fargione, Isher Kaila, Sharoni Sibony, and Priya Suagh.

6. How did the well-prepared and competent campaign organization fail to achieve some of the party's most basic objectives?

Answering these questions should help us understand the evolving character of the Liberal Party of Canada as it struggles to hang on to its historic role as the country's "government party."

1. The record

In the summer of 1995, as the Liberals contemplated the approaching second anniversary of their electoral triumph, Prime Minister Jean Chrétien and his entourage had reason to be happy. In Parliament they were in a politician's heaven, since no party offered an immediate threat to their hold on power. The Official Opposition, le Bloc Québécois (BQ), was a separatist party with no pan-Canadian mandate. The Progressive Conservative Party, the only rival that could expect to replace the Liberals because of its deep roots in every province, had been reduced to two seats, leaving in third place the western right-wing Reform Party and in fourth place the New Democratic Party. The forthcoming referendum in Quebec seemed to show the federalist side in a good position to beat the sovereigntists.

Despite having performed lamentably as Leader of the Opposition up until the 1993 election campaign, Jean Chrétien had been transmogrified by power into an effective prime minister. His staff was loyal and sage. He ran his competent cabinet judiciously, giving his ministers free enough rein to let them get on with their jobs of managing their departments and doing their best to implement the many promises made during the campaign in their famous "Red Book."

One of these promises — bringing the escalating deficit and runaway national debt under control — had been taken on as an overriding goal by the finance department. However reluctantly, the government as a whole then bent to the dictates of deficit-cutting policies, managing to carry out more drastic amputations of government programs than their Conservative predecessors had dared essay. More astonishing still, in cutting the various social and cultural programs which had been the Liberal Party's greatest pride and his own father's enduring political legacy as a welfare Liberal, Finance Minister Paul Martin had managed to inflict the pain of restraint and at the same time become the government's most popular politician.

A striking confirmation of Martin's magic was the friendly attitude which English Canada's "national newspaper" adopted towards the party of whose policies it had long been a relentless critic. For *The Globe and Mail* the Chrétien government had become "responsible, frugal, and in control," its character pragmatic and prudent, its integrity high since — productive, fiscally responsible, hard-working — it was "rapidly fulfilling its promises."[1] When the government published *A Record of Achievement: A Report on the Liberal Government's Thirty-Six Months in Office*, the *Globe* gave the Liberals' self-evaluation more space than the opposition politicians' critique.[2] The view cumulatively established by the chief organ of Canadian conservatism and capitalism suggested not only that the Liberals were unbeatable but that they deserved to be re-elected: Chrétien had done well as prime minister and performed satisfactorily at G-7 meetings and in other capacities abroad. Only he could speak for Canada.[3]

The Liberal government had indeed proven generally competent, with only two ministers having to resign over issues that exuded not even a whiff of scandal. While a formal inquiry into military misdemeanours during the armed forces' peacekeeping mission to Somalia in 1992 caused it prolonged embarrassment, the general impression the government had created by 1995 was one of success. Luck helped: the decline of interest rates allowed it to accelerate its deficit reduction schedule so that the finance minister could validly claim to have more than exceeded the 3 per cent of GNP target set by the Red Book.

Although the Chrétien team had run a down-to-earth government of the type to be expected from an experienced group, it also committed two major blunders, first in Quebec and then in the media. Ever since Jean Chrétien had misjudged the constitutional mood of Quebec in 1990 when he had opposed the Meech Lake Accord, his political nose for his home province had been unreliable. As prime minister he was still so traumatized by his vilification in the Quebec media and the hostility expressed to him on the street that he rarely ventured into the province and, when he did so, travelled there without alerting the press, lest he give reporters another chance to vent their scorn on him. His poor understanding of the Québécois political sensibility was demonstrated for all to see by his insouciant handling of the 1995 referendum on Quebec sovereignty, a campaign that was directed so badly by the federalist forces that it came within 50,000 votes of losing. Even an otherwise supportive *Globe and Mail* suggested that Chrétien had become the wrong person to speak for Canada.

A year later it also seemed that he was the wrong person to speak for his party. In a televised "Town Hall" meeting orchestrated by the CBC he took a verbal beating from the well-primed audience, one member of which flailed him for having broken the Liberals' promise made in the

1993 campaign to eliminate the Goods and Services Tax (GST). Overnight Chrétien's image was transformed. The straight-shooting patriot of unblemished integrity had become just another evasive politician, alternately defensive and aggressive, charming and pitiable, denying the fact that was patent to all: he had broken his promise to eliminate the roundly hated sales tax.[4] As speculation in the media turned to the next election, Chrétien looked out of his depth, his skills rusting. How else to explain his incapacity to reframe the image of broken promises into one of contracts kept, the appearance of failed generalship into one of effective leadership? Part of the answer lay in the team he had around him.

2. The tacticians

The Prime Minister's entourage was seasoned and smart. From his octogenarian mentor Mitchell Sharp, whose long and distinguished career was rooted in Mackenzie King's post-war government, to Peter Donolo, his youthful communications manager, Chrétien's principal advisers had been with him through the worst times in opposition and turned out to be adept at handling the best times of running a majority government. They kept him out of trouble, rallied the caucus and cabinet behind Paul Martin's tough-love deficit cutting, and helped orchestrate a very substantial record of achievement across the broad range of government policies and ministries. But since they were also human, they were not exempt from that most common of political maladies, hubris.

Excited in the early days of 1997 by their continuing high poll numbers and heartened in the weeks that followed by the Bloc Québécois's self-destructive leadership campaign (see Chapter Seven of this volume), the Liberals decided to precipitate an early election despite three obvious reasons for patience. First there was the "Peterson factor." In 1990, David Peterson, the Liberal premier of Ontario, basking not just in his legislative majority and high poll numbers but in the psychic high that power had engendered, called a surprisingly early election, only to be soundly punished by the voters for provoking an unnecessary campaign. Second, there was much unfinished business. The government's battle to reduce the national deficit was going its way but was far from won. In a year it would be on the point of balancing its books and on much firmer ground for seeking a mandate to implement a new program. Finally there was the question of sovereignty. Since the Parti Québécois's threatened next referendum could only be held following a new provincial election and since Premier Lucien Bouchard would not want to issue the writs before the next federal election, holding off the national campaign would prolong the period during which the PQ would be forced to make federalism work in Quebec and possibly Bouchard might run into political difficulties of its own making.

Overconfidence, which had brought the Chrétien team to the brink of disaster in the October 1995 referendum, still prevailed in the Prime Minister's Office in the early months of 1997 when it was felt that the newly shortened campaign period would favour a cautious, front runner's return to office. The BQ's disarray promised Liberal gains in Chrétien's home province.[5] Besides, why wait four months for the opposition to get more press, for the media to get tougher?

The decision may have been wily but its execution was wobbly. In the spring of 1997 campaign preparations had been going on for many weeks. Nominations were held; candidates were appointed in specific ridings where Chrétien wanted a female or minority representative; constituency workers were trained; policies were prepared. In response, the opposition parties had geared up their own pre-writ activities. The preparatory process developed such a momentum that its creators seemed unable to stop it. Not even an act of God — the rising waters of the Red River that threatened to flood southern Manitoba — was enough to give the Liberal high command serious pause. It simply flew the PM out to Winnipeg to throw a sandbag on a dike for the TV cameras on Saturday April 26 in time to fly him back to Ottawa so he could call on the Governor General the next day and start the race. But when quizzed by the media about the reason for holding an election after just three-and-a-half years in office, the Prime Minister looked unsure of himself. "We are in the fourth year, and I believe it is important that we take the summer to prepare for the launch of the new government in September," he offered, implying that an election was a disagreeable diversion from the more enjoyable business of continuing to govern.

No sooner had Chrétien given his campaign such a lacklustre launch than he became embroiled in Western anger at this intrusion of politics into Manitoba's calamity. Then, when he took to the hustings, he gave confusing signals. Despite claiming credit for three years of tough deficit cutting and government restraint, he dropped a spending promise — $200 million for AIDS research. He followed this good-times electoral gift with another cash promise, though one with a difference. It was a commitment not to cut the Canadian Health and Social Transfer to the provinces by the further $2.1 billion envisaged for the next two fiscal years. Voters presumably were to be grateful not to have more pain indirectly inflicted on them via reductions in their provincial services.

While producing these manifestations of traditional campaigning, Chrétien was being kept in a cocoon. CBC's National Magazine was refused a conversation with the Liberal leader although the other party chiefs were lining up at interviewer Hana Gartner's studio door. The isolation of Chrétien was so complete that it was not until the last day of Week 1 in the campaign that Canada's great man-of-the-people politician was to be seen glad-handing with voters. But the greatest confusion of all for the Liberal campaign in its early days was the bizarre prospect of the Reform Party calling a press conference for Preston Manning to brandish before the media a leaked copy of the Liberal platform. The Liberals had lost control — ironically enough with that part of their campaign agenda generally most amenable to complete management, the articulation of its policy.

3. The platform

There is nothing new in an electoral organization being deeply divided over how to present its platform. Whatever the party's ideology, there are bound to be partisans who lean more to the left arguing with fellow workers who lean more to the right, activists versus minimalists, idealists confronting pragmatists. There is nothing new, either, in compromises having to be made in the interests of presenting a united front to the public. What characterized the 1997 backroom exercise in Liberal platform making is how driven it was by considerations of electoral manipulation.

Those Liberal insiders arguing that the party should champion some real nation-building projects were deriving their proposals from poll data showing the public wanted some sense of vision from its politicians. Their aim was to reassemble the lower- to middle-class coalition including women and ethnic voters, who had been repelled by the Liberals' drastic cuts in social and economic programs but who might be lured back by the promise of new social initiatives. Those arguing for a minimalist program of staying the course of restraint believed their party should appeal to the wealthier and more conservative voters across the country who had already been attracted by the Liberals' deficit-cutting achievements. With the Prime Minister's concurrence these tactical realists purged the visionaries' prose from the proposed drafts,[6] causing a platform to be published that was as long in verbiage as it was short in content.

Many are the times that the Liberal Party has successfully campaigned on the left, only to govern on the right. The challenge for the Liberals in 1997 was whether to try to repeat the stunt. The political context created a delicate problem. In 1993 the Red Book had been a serious exercise in policy analysis that provided intellectual context, reasoned analysis, and specific promises, all of which were carefully costed and professionally packaged. The platform's actual exploitation had centred less on the party leader explaining its policies than on his brandishing the slickly designed book as a talisman, constantly asserting that he wanted the public to hold him accountable for carrying out its undertakings.

The 1993 Liberal campaign had proposed governing along the two putatively parallel tracks of fiscal caution and economic stimulation. Upon taking power the Chrétien team proceeded to implement their promises up to the point that their inner contradiction appeared. Once it finally understood the full magnitude of the burgeoning national debt, it could no longer stay on both tracks. To reduce the deficit required cutting programs, not expanding them. Paul Martin's mildly restrictive 1994 budget was followed by draconian budgets in 1995 and 1996. Cutting 45,000 jobs from the civil service and $16.5 billion from program spending was simply not compatible with the 1993 campaign's commitment to create jobs and improve social services. With a new election in the offing, the finance minister delivered a budget in the spring of 1997 in which the second track was officially rehabilitated. Now the deficit would continue to come down as a portion of gross domestic product, but certain new expenditures put some rouge back on the cold blue face of the Grit government.

The Liberal Plan — 1997. Securing Our Future Together: Preparing Canada for the Twenty-First Century was a carefully compiled text. The presentation was so similar to its 1993 model that it was quickly dubbed "Red Book II." Much of the analytical material had been pulled from *A Record of Achievement: A Report on the Liberal Government's Thirty-Six Months in Office* which had put the most positive spin possible on the interpretation of how the Chrétien government had implemented the 1993 promises. Cutting and pasting many items from the 1997 budget into this document created the impression that the government party was simply filing a report to its stakeholders about its performance. As for the new promises, many were put forward tentatively: their implementation would depend on provincial agreement and participation.

The document was coherent. The promises were costed in an appendix. As an exercise in political positioning it seemed to have the political wisdom of King Solomon. The government would stay the course in bringing the deficit down to zero. Once a surplus was achieved in the government's accounts, one-half would be used to pay down the national debt and/or cut taxes; the other half would be used to enhance social programs targeted for children in poverty, the health care system, and job creation. In one stroke Red Book II made Reform and the Progressive Conservatives on the right seem recklessly irresponsible in calling for premature tax cuts and the NDP on the left hopelessly idealistic in urging increased government spending. No figures seemed necessary to justify such an eminently sensible solution. All that was needed was for this program to be communicated.

Interestingly, however, the story of *Securing Our Future Together* was all show, no tell. Despite being twice released — once by Preston Manning in his scoop, next by Jean Chrétien — the document disappeared from public view. Its circulation was perfunctory. It was available on the party's web site, but few were expected to wade through its 102 dense pages. And its propositions seemed to be the last thing that the party leader wanted to discuss, even though almost all the concrete proposals that might prove embarrassing to him either on the campaign trail or when returned to power had been deleted. He who campaigned in 1993 urging voters to hold him accountable for his platform wanted neither to discuss the original document nor to elaborate on the new one lest, perhaps, it perpetuate the impression that his government had broken more promises than it had kept. On the one occasion that Chrétien did highlight a campaign promise, the idea of Pharmacare, questioning reporters found him to be unsure about the costs of such a program, how much provincial governments would contribute, or when it might be implemented.

4. The leaders

The Pharmacare incident revealed how the Liberals managed to turn their assets into liabilities. Even though their cautious policy was consistent with the spirit of the times, it seemed of little value in their campaign. The Chrétien who had surpassed expectations as prime minister became a salesman who managed somehow to diminish his product, a generally inferior campaigner who appeared to have lost the self-confidence, the charm, the common touch that had once endeared him to both his own party and the country. His engagements were confined to events from which the public was generally excluded. If a protest demonstration developed at a campaign stop, the visit would be cancelled from his schedule or postponed in order to keep him away from the protesters.[7] Requests for appearances at Newsworld's daily press conference or for an interview on MuchMusic were turned down, ministers from the "auxiliary team" being dispatched to take his seat.

The one rendez vous that Chrétien could not avoid was the leaders' debate. This nationally televised event had become too entrenched in the public's consciousness for the Liberal leader to boycott. In the first encounter, staged in English, he looked uncomfortable, reading his opening statement somewhat haltingly and answering questions posed to him by the journalists in a flat, unforceful style. He blamed the opposition parties for having precipitated the early election. He woodenly apologized for the government's cuts to social programs. In the cut and thrust of the leaders' exchanges he defended himself somewhat better, even demonstrating some energy when attacking Gilles Duceppe of the Bloc Québécois: "You are not interested in any solution because you are a separatist."[8]

In the next evening's debate in French, Chrétien was more confident, counterpunching with some assurance. Even though he had nothing memorable to say, his stance was more statesmanlike. While refusing to get into slanging matches with his opponents, he was still able to convey both his negative message (Quebec's economic problems were caused by the political instability resulting from the threat of another referendum) and his positive message (the government's tough fiscal management was working, having produced low interest rates).

When cornered by the difficult question about how he would respond to Quebeckers voting by 50 per cent plus one ballot in favour of a clear question or sovereignty, he was taken off the spot by the debate's moderator collapsing and crashing to the floor.

Being saved by the bell on TV was not the only example of Chrétien's good luck. *Fortuna* mainly took the form of his opponents' mistakes, which were frequent enough to buoy up the plodding Liberal campaign and keep it out of trouble. After a dismal Week 1 for the Liberals, former PQ Premier Jacques Parizeau gratuitously entered the campaign by publishing a book in which he made it clear he would have made a unilateral declaration of independence following a successful referendum result in 1995. The pandemonium this embarrassment caused in the BQ's own halting campaign rescued the Liberals for several days. When they were again in trouble following the debates from which Jean Charest had emerged as the media's articulate, passionate, and youthful darling, the Progressive Conservative leader himself offered Chrétien an opportunity: "Mr. Chrétien seems not to originate from Quebec. [His policies] demonstrate that he is from Ottawa."[9] Pumping up his moral indignation, Chrétien tried to turn this rather banal criticism into a blood insult as he had done in 1993. This was an ethnic slur, Chrétien expostulated, and completely unacceptable. "It's been done to me several times. It's hard to take... because I was elected nine times by Quebeckers in a riding that is 98 per cent francophone."[10]

His enemies' attacks had a tonic effect. When in Week 2 Charest burned the Liberal Party's platform at a barbeque, Chrétien used humour to dismiss this as "childish" behaviour showing they are "the same old Tories — just like Mulroney: they're cooking the books again."[11] Attempting to offset Charest's success in handling the national unity issue, Chrétien became more aggressive. He accused the Conservative of leading a one-man parade, of hiding his party, of taking different stances in different regions, of opposing the Liberals' tough gun control legislation. To Preston Manning's attacks, Chrétien made some effective ripostes. When the Reformer implied he was too old, Chrétien responded. "I'm old enough to know how divisive and irresponsible this brand of politics is and I'm old enough to know how it hurts our country. And I'm old enough to know it's wrong — absolutely wrong — to pit region against region."[12] When Reform tarred Chrétien in a TV commercial with the same brush as Lucien Bouchard and Gilles Duceppe he felt personally insulted but claimed the high road in response. He excoriated regional divisiveness: Manning was the prince of darkness, appealing to a nostalgia that never was.[13]

In the panic of the last week, when the Liberals knew from their party's pollster that they faced the real possibility of coming back to power as a minority government (see Chapter Ten of this volume), Chrétien pleaded for strong government so that Canada could stay the course of deficit reduction because "we have built an example for the world."[14] Revving up tired rhetoric of this kind showed how unfocused his campaign had been. His advisers had not seemed able to decide what image Chrétien was to project. The campaign had produced a confusion of Chrétiens, some negative, some positive. The competent statesman at international summits, the captain of Team Canada was little to be seen. Instead viewers were reminded more of his referendum persona, the inarticulate, insecure, out-of-touch leader who was graceless and testy under pressure. He may have seemed to some to be mature, "a man among the girls and boys" in the debate telethon[15] but he also appeared, in Charest's vivid phrase, disconnected. The Liberal ads presented him close up as an average, hard working man competently doing a tough job because of his long experience. But the *petit gars de Shawinigan* seemed so discombobulated that he staged his own nomination in St. Maurice surrounded by all seventy-four other Quebec candidates as if he needed their protection to run in his home riding. The Liberals wanted him to be the agent of hope, the leader of the people unifying regions. Ironically, there was a good deal of truth to these desired projections: Chrétien could be optimistic and express positive messages; he had been a very strong party leader with a firm grip on such key inner party functions as its nomination process. However, he ended the campaign a moral loser, his standing diminished everywhere except in Quebec where it was too low to fall much further.

The Chrétien tour's passive approach of waiting for situations to arise before dealing with them was best exemplified by the hoary issue of national unity. Even though the political situation in Chrétien's home province was the chief reason for the Liberals to precipitate the early campaign and though the BQ campaign obliged them with a series of disasters — the new leader was untried, his tour was accident prone, and the separatist camp was openly squabbling over fundamental policy issues — the Liberals were unable to exploit its disarray. They even helped the BQ remedy it. At the outset, national unity was the principal issue the Liberals wanted to avoid lest it remind the public of their fumbled referendum performance and give the BQ a way to rally its soft supporters. National unity could also play into the hands of Reform which needed an issue since the Liberals had appropriated deficit reduction as their own. No sooner had Jacques Parizeau caused consternation among the sovereignists with his avowal of duplicity over a unilateral declaration of independence than Chrétien weighed into the brouhaha, slurring all sovereignists as anti-democratic and claiming that Parizeau's avowal of premeditated unconstitutionality justified the controversial federal court challenge concerning the legality of separation.[16]

Having once encouraged the national unity genie to stay out of its bottle, Chrétien proved unable to turn it to his own advantage during the debates. It was Charest who managed to take the attractive middle ground between the tough federal line and the sovereignists. Claiming he could sell reconciliation to both camps, he struck such a chord in the francophone media that his popularity rocketed up in the polls. Although Chrétien had been saved during the francophone debate from having to declare himself on the validity of another referendum vote, he first rejected then accepted a reprise engagement that necessarily would focus on national unity. When the debate was restaged he remained ambiguous about his position. It was only a few days later and in a carefully chosen venue (an interview on the francophone news service RDI) that he stated clearly that a majority Yes vote of 50 per cent plus one would not be enough to legitimize Quebec's separation.[17] The statement had been considered, and so, presumably, were the consequences. In an apparent effort to shoot down the Charest rocket, Chrétien offered the BQ, aided by Premier Bouchard who denounced Chrétien as an "adversaire de la démocratie," a perfect target against which to mobilize its supporters. With his carefully staged intervention Chrétien managed to polarize the francophone vote at the expense of the Conservatives, but without great benefit to the Liberals. *Le Devoir* expressed outrage at Ottawa's interference. Even the moderate columnist Lysiane Gagnon criticized Chrétien's statement in *La Presse*. The party with its ascribed role as historic national conciliator, the bridge between the two founding peoples, showed in the crunch that it preferred to have separatists rather than rival federalists elected in Quebec and preferred the possibility of having Gilles Duceppe as Leader of the Opposition than Jean Charest, even though the latter's support had been crucial in saving the last referendum and his contribution would be essential once again in the next.

The Chrétien group was equally ineffective on the national unity question in responding to attacks from Reform. While Preston Manning's aggressively anti-Quebec stance did give Chrétien the opportunity to present himself as the incarnation of national unity, tolerance, and acceptance of Quebec as a distinct society, Reform maintained the offensive. Whatever Chrétien's counterattacks, they failed to put the Western populist on the defensive, guaranteeing Manning his coveted status as Leader of the Opposition.

Failure to control the national unity issue illustrated a broader problem, the Liberal incapacity to work out a general strategy for their electoral battle. Since Chrétien and his intimates prided themselves on their rejection of grand schemes in favour of an incrementalist, nuts-and-bolts approach to politics, whether in governing or in campaigning, it is not surprising that no strategy document was communicated to the party as a whole. The campaign was designed mainly to avoid mistakes. In the end the campaign seemed to be largely improvised, and reactive, responding to attacks more than delivering a specific message.

Beyond the national unity confusion (the Liberal Party stood for national reconciliation but was taking a tough stand on Quebec), Chrétien and his team talked tough economically (discipline was needed to stay the deficit-reduction course) and soft socially (child poverty was their prime concern). Having been unable to give a reason for precipitating the campaign in the first place, Chrétien nevertheless ended it by talking vaguely about "a Liberal vision for a better future."[18] Government can be a force for good, he repeated, yet the Liberals had cut back the federal government more drastically than any of their predecessors. The leader himself was tightly scripted in his performance but was meant to show his passionate love for Canada. He was offering hope for Canada, but there were no grand plans in Red Book II. Chrétien was a strong leader but he let his ministers speak for him whenever possible. These contradictions did not escape the deeply sceptical pack of reporters.

5. The media

Even if the Liberals had managed to decide on an effective strategy with a clear message, they would still have suffered from a number of handicaps in communicating it to the public. They could not enjoy the benefit-of-the-doubt treatment which had been the corollary of the media's gleeful destruction of the Conservative campaign in 1993. Nor could they receive the generally favourable treatment they had benefitted from in government. Once campaigns begin newspaper, radio, and television editors consciously attempt to achieve balance among the contesting parties. Less overt is their tendency to hold the likely victor to a higher standard. Promises made by Alexa McDonough did not rate as careful a vetting as statements made by Chrétien since there was no chance she would be able to implement her policies. The Liberal communications chief summed up the dilemma nicely: "Being a front-runner is always trouble; being an incumbent front-runner is double trouble."[19]

Further trouble resulted for a pan-Canadian centrist party trying to compete with parties which appealed to different regions' sense of alienation. Speeches claiming credit for cutting the deficit did not have the same hot-button newsworthiness as anti-Quebec statements or attacks on Chrétien's broken promises. Without being overtly hostile, the Liberals' coverage in print and on television was palpably unfavourable. In quantitative measures the Liberals were given slightly more CBC television exposure than any other party, getting 16.3 per cent of the items on the National, ahead of Reform (14.7 per cent), the BQ (11.8 per cent), the PCs (9.5 per cent), and the NDP (8.3 per cent).[20] But it was not just a question of having its name spelled right. Sixty-two per cent of the items reporting on the Liberal Party could be considered unfavourable, compared to 24 per cent neutral and only 14 per cent favourable.[21] Similarly, while The Globe and Mail gave almost as much front page coverage to the Liberals as to the other four parties combined, quantity did not make up for quality. Fifty-five per cent of these items were unfavourable compared to 30 per cent that were neutral and just 15 per cent favourable.[21]

Having fallen to below 10 seconds in 1993, the leaders' sound bites clocked in between 2 and 3 seconds in 1997 — leaving the bulk of the television news items to the editorial whim of the particular reporter. In one of its "reality checks" the CBC on Day 13 of the campaign had Neil MacDonald appraising Chrétien's record of new job creation with the dismissive comment, "Chrétien is right, if you're interested in one meaningless, raw number."[23] CBC television news' comment on the Liberals' campaign at midpoint was "plodding and predictable, and above all as safe as possible. Factory tours are safe — Chrétien does a lot of them,"[24] implying that he feared interrogation from the media and the voters. Emphasizing Chrétien's reluctance to engage in interviews with the media or the public, the same broadcast treated its viewers to an image of Chrétien waving goodbye from inside his campaign bus. The clip was the message: the Liberal leader in an enclosed, protected, and inaccessible space leaving the scene of the sign.

Chrétien's advance men must have felt that the CBC was dedicated to unmasking their best laid plans rather than delivering the message they had worked to set up. This pattern was exemplified by CBC's treatment of the Prime Minister's visit to the dike building operation to save Winnipeg from the rising Red River. Rather than just showing the Prime Minister participating in the effort by tossing a sandbag, it aired the prior few seconds which caught Chrétien's question to his handlers: "What do you want me to do with this [sandbag]?"[25] The message, of course, was that Chrétien's demonstration of concern was staged and opportunistic.

All the Liberals could do in the face of media cynicism was buy space for their own commercials to be broadcast unmediated by journalistic spin. Here too the governing party's apparent advantage proved of minor value. Although the election legislation formula gave the Liberals 118 minutes of commercial media time compared to 51 for Reform, 43 for the BQ, 34 for the PCs, and only 26 for the NDP, an Alberta Court of Appeal ruling removed the cap, so that each party could buy extra time if it wished. Given the regional concentration of the other parties, the Liberals felt at a disadvantage since they were constrained to buy commercial time on the national networks whereas their opponents could buy cheaper, regional ads that targeted only the areas where their prospects were best.

Chrétien had governed as if taking a cue from former Ontario premier William Davis's winning formula: "bland works." Applying the same approach to their ads, the Liberal advertising team had Chrétien make such comforting, non-controversial, and sunny remarks as "This country is much stronger than it was a few years ago," or "People in this country are starting to dream again." As a mild counterattack on the right he said in another ad "Over and over I ask Canadians what is important to them — a strong economy or a tax cut before they can afford one. They told me a strong economy."[27] The blandness of the advertising reflected the campaign organization's obsession with minimizing risk.

In both quantitative and qualitative terms the Liberals' treatment in the Quebec media was mixed. On Le Téléjournal the Liberals had received the most coverage of all the parties. In *La Presse* they came third. Judged in terms of content 39 per cent of the Liberals' coverage on Le Téléjournal was unfavourable, 49 per cent neutral and only 12 per cent favourable. For *La Presse*, however, 50 per cent of the front page coverage of the Liberal Party was neutral, 33 per cent favourable and 17 per cent unfavourable.[27] The Liberals nevertheless suffered from the same media cynicism as they had received in the anglophone coverage. At the end of Week 1 Le Téléjournal showed Chrétien signing autographs in a crowded market but the reporter went on to say that his advance men had come earlier in the week to remove all the "For Rent" and "For Sale" signs in this usually deserted site.[28] The Liberals could console themselves that their treatment had not been as bad in the hands of the francophone media as in the rest of Canada — largely because the Bloc's pratfalls had drawn reporters' gleeful attention away from the duller, safer Liberal campaign.

6. *Organization*

However inept the leader's tour appeared, the Liberals' electoral organization was a formidable machine. In March, long before being willing to admit that an early election was to be called, it had mounted campaign colleges around the country, providing election seminars complete with a check list of riding readiness deadlines for candidates and their chief constituency personnel to meet between March 17th and April 24th. Party organizers were in the field to help ridings in difficulty. Advice was offered on fund raising and technical services. A logo and other paraphernalia from national headquarters were provided to demonstrate visual consistency between the candidates' local efforts and the national campaign. Ottawa could produce for each constituency a whole brochure for distribution complete with a photograph of the candidate with the leader. Also available were draft letters that candidates could send to voters concerned about specific issues such as gun control. Candidates turned to the national campaign office for political-cum-legal advice on how to deal with such dirty tricks as billboards linking Liberal MPs with killers who had been let out of prison or the National Citizens' Coalition commercials attacking Liberal MPs' generous pensions.

A near daily fax from Ottawa, *Talking Points*, sent the ridings a continuous digest of information based on the party's platform or the government's record that candidates could use at constituency all-candidates meetings and for media interviews. To help ensure that the 301 local campaigns sang from the same hymn book, lines were prepared to help candidates respond to the other parties' stances and explain Chrétien's statements. However brazen, the message would be consistent from coast to coast: the government that had made deep cuts to the provincial health and education programs faxed its candidates the message that:

> We have been remarkably successful in bringing spending and the deficit under control. We have initiated the biggest spending cuts since the end of World War II. Ensuring a continued commitment to fiscal responsibility, all spending commitments in the Liberal platform fall within the framework of existing deficit reduction targets. This is necessary to ensure the sustainability of key social programs like health care.[29]

Partisanship exceeded the bounds of the acceptable when one *Talking Point* referred to Jean Charest as "the separatist who shamefully questions the birthright of those who disagree with him," necessitating an apology when the text was leaked to the media.[30] The regional organization in the provincial capitals and the national organization in Ottawa strove to maintain the morale of the troops on the ground and keep the local campaign "on message." The problem in the ridings — as in the country as a whole — was to know what that message was. "It is a challenge to pinpoint one specific strategy," observed one rural Ontario campaign worker who served on an MP's re-election committee. "Rather I think it would be safe to say that for the most part, the [party's] strategy was to some extent without effort or premeditation. At times the set strategy seemed to arise from internal forces or causes. Throughout the election, the strategy was not set in stone, but [was] rather flexible, to deal with any issues that arose daily or weekly."[31]

Table 1. Percentage by which the Liberals won/lost in all 301 ridings in the 1997 federal election

RIDINGS WON   RIDINGS LOST

Province	Total %	0-4.9%	5-9.9%	10-14.9%	15+ %	Total %	0-4.9%	5-9.9%	10-14.9%	15+ %
P.E.I.	4	2	1	1	–	0	–	–	–	–
Newfoundland	4	2	–	1	1	3	–	2	1	–
Nova Scotia	0	–	–	–	–	11	3	4	1	3
New Brunswick	3	1	–	2	–	7	1	2	1	3
Quebec	26	3	2	6	15	49	2	10	5	32
Ontario	101	5	2	11	83	2	1	–	1	–
Manitoba	6	–	1	1	4	8	2	–	1	5
Alberta	2	2	–	–	–	24	–	2	2	20
Saskatchewan	1	–	–	1	–	13	–	2	3	8
B.C.	6	–	2	1	3	28	–	6	3	19
N.W.T.	2	–	–	–	2	1	–	1	–	–
CANADA (Total)	155	15	8	24	108	146	9	29	18	90

*As tabulated from election results in *The Toronto Star*, June 3, 1997 and *The Globe and Mail*, June 3, 1997

The results

Before the campaign started the Liberal Party's pollster Michael Marzolini had warned that the voters might rebel against an early election call. Once the polls closed on June 2nd it quickly became apparent that this predicted rebellion had taken place but in a peculiarly restrained form in which the government party was thoroughly chastised without being dismissed. Periodic opinion polls suggesting the Liberals would be returned at the very least with a comfortable minority may well have created among voters the understanding that they could register their displeasure without worrying that the consequence of their actions would be the defeat of the government. Indeed considering the results on a regional basis confirms that 1997 was more like a series of regional by-elections than a general election.

The **Atlantic Provinces** had voted massively in 1993 for the security of being on the winning side and for the party that made job creation its top issue. But Liberal government turned out to mean radical cuts to social programs and the virtual closing of the fisheries. In 1997 Atlantic Canada clearly felt betrayed and refused to heed counsels of prudence. In their Week 5 panic the Liberals managed to persuade their three Maritime premiers — Brian Tobin of Newfoundland, Frank McKenna of New Brunswick, and John Savage of Nova Scotia — to rally to the cause. As the *Halifax Chronicle-Herald* put it on May 27, "Premiers swarm Charest ... Atlantic Canada's Liberal premiers on Monday accused federal Tory leader Jean Charest of wanting to cut $100 million annually out of funding for health, education, and social services." This damage control did not save the party from the public's wrath. Nor did it soften scorn for the Prime Minister who had been insensitive enough to express sympathy with the plight of the chronically unemployed in the area by saying that he too had been unemployed — for a month after he finished law school when his wife was pregnant. As one Nova Scotian put it, "What he said is enough to make me sick.... If he really wants to know what unemployment is, let him walk in my shoes for a long period of time."[32] For his part Jean Charest ran his Atlantic campaign to the left of the Liberals, attacking their cuts to government services, and was rewarded with enough seats (thirteen) to regain official party status for the Conservatives, a prize that was also awarded the NDP under Alexa McDonough, the former party leader in Nova Scotia who found willing listeners to her call to "wake up the Liberals" and "send a message to Ottawa."

It was in her home province that the Liberals received the clearest

Figure 1. Support for the federal Liberal Party in Atlantic Canada

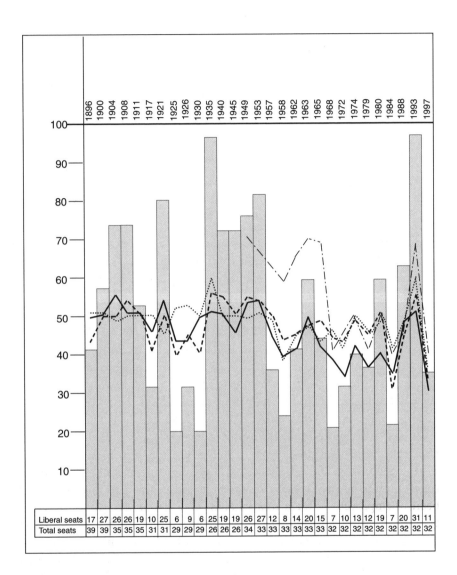

The following data appears at the bottom of the chart:

	1896	1900	1904	1908	1911	1917	1921	1925	1926	1930	1935	1940	1945	1949	1953	1957	1958	1962	1963	1965	1968	1972	1974	1979	1980	1984	1988	1993	1997
Liberal seats	17	27	26	26	19	10	25	6	9	6	25	19	19	26	27	12	8	14	20	15	7	10	13	12	19	7	20	31	11
Total seats	39	39	35	35	35	31	31	29	29	29	26	26	26	34	33	33	33	33	33	33	32	32	32	32	32	32	32	32	32

▢ – Percentage of seats won by Liberals

– – – Percentage of votes received by Liberal candidates in New Brunswick

— – Percentage of votes received by Liberal candidates in Nova Scotia

–·– – Percentage of votes received by Liberal candidates in Newfoundland

····· – Percentage of votes received by Liberal candidates in P.E.I.

message, falling to zero from a full house of eleven seats in 1993 and from their highest vote in forty years (52 per cent) to their lowest on record (28 per cent) and third place. New Brunswick was the next worst result for the Grits who lost six of their seats and 23 per cent of their 1993 vote, coming second in votes and seats after the PCs. They fell even further in Newfoundland's popular vote, from 67 to 38 per cent, and lost three of their seven seats, but managed to stay one seat and 1 per cent ahead of the second place Conservatives. Prince Edward Island's results suggest that part of the Liberals' fall from the voters' good graces elsewhere in the East had to do with public anger at Liberal provincial governments. Charlottetown being the only Atlantic provincial capital not under Liberal control, the federal Liberals kept PEI's four seats for a third time in a row — their single holdout against the Maritime tide.

The Eastern Canada vote constituted the Liberals' most dramatic rebuke of election night. The Liberals were generally acknowledged in media editorials as the best party for the nation, but they were not seen by the voters as best serving the interests of the region. The Tories and New Democrats, in contrast, campaigned specifically to defend the interests of the Atlantic region and carried off twenty-one of its thirty-one seats. Still, as Figure 1 shows, the results were less a calamity than a correction. The previous election had given the Liberals 97 per cent of the area's seats for just over half the vote. In 1997 the Grits received a more appropriate one third of the seats in return for one third of the votes. As Table 1 shows, however, even this second-place position is tenuous: almost half the Liberals' Atlantic seats were held with margins of less than 5 per cent.

Quebec had appeared in the spring to be fertile ground for solid Rouge gains and the Liberals had exerted themselves there with determination during their campaign. Chrétien initially spent more time in his home province than in any other, even though he remained widely unpopular there. The party was considered to have fielded a good team of francophone candidates. Indeed team was the leitmotif of their approach. Finance Minister Paul Martin, of whom Quebeckers were twice as likely to have a good as a bad opinion, was used throughout the province, as were caravans of ministers in the "auxiliary team" who went out on six or more daily tours into different regions of the province. The slogan was "agir ensemble" and, together, Chrétien's ministers came to Montréal to let the city know how many goodies the government had provided during its previous mandate.[33] Even anglophones such as Allan Rock (spelled Roch for the French media) dropped in to extol the virtues of his tough gun control legislation.

Figure 2. Support for the federal Liberal Party in Quebec

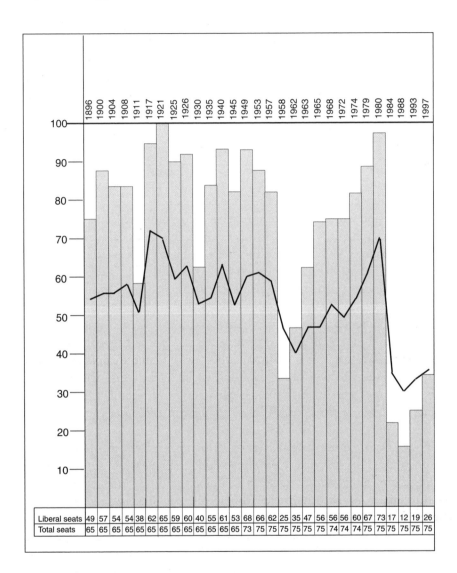

□ – Percentage of seats won by Liberals

— – Percentage of votes received by Liberal candidates

This concerted effort had not prevented Jean Charest from appropriating national unity as his issue during the leaders' debates and, thanks to the public's enthusiasm for his eloquence and the media's approval of his conciliatory approach to sovereignty, turning the Quebec campaign into a three-way race. It was Charest's appeal to soft nationalist BQ supporters that induced the Liberals to polarize the national unity issue with a tough, 50-per-cent-is-not-enough stance. This allowed Premier Bouchard to recycle his outrage at the diabolic combination of Jean Chrétien and Preston Manning ("the couple from hell") and consolidate the BQ's vote. Far from responding to the federal issue of the economy's management, the largest number of Quebec voters seem to have decided how to vote on the basis of which party would best defend the regional interests of Quebec in Ottawa.

The BQ did suffer a setback probably suffering from their association with the provincial government whose popularity was in decline; it fell 11 per cent from its 1993 results and lost ten seats. It lost its status as Official Opposition, but still retained a commanding majority of the province's seventy-five seats. Charest's 22 per cent of the vote yielded five MPs for the Tory caucus. After all their exertions the Liberals only raised their vote from 33 to 36 per cent. This was enough to win twenty-six seats (seven more than 1993) giving them, as Figure 2 shows, roughly one third of the available seats for one third of the votes. While they won by large margins in their urban stronghold, they lost heavily elsewhere: of the forty-nine seats where they were defeated, only two were lost by less than 5, most by over 15 per cent. (Table 1) Condemned by the concentration of their vote in the Montréal area to remain in second place in the province, the Chrétien Liberals have little prospect for returning to their historical norm of garnering four fifths of Quebec's seats.

Ontario has replaced Quebec as the Grit fortress, making it possible for Jean Chrétien to boast of being the first Liberal since Louis St. Laurent to deliver back-to-back majorities. The heartland of the country was nursing no particular federal grievance so there was no major "Ontario" flash point to prevent the Liberals from repeating their coup of 1993 — capturing all but one of the province's seats for about half of its votes(Figure 3).[34] Their vote dropped 4 points to 49 per cent, but the Liberals' sweep of the province was still overwhelming. Eighty-three of the Liberals' 101 seats were won by over 15 per cent margins (Table 1), enough to deny Reform national legitimacy as more than a Western protest party and to stymie Charest's attempt to come within challenging distance of the government party.

Figure 3. Support for the federal Liberal Party in Ontario

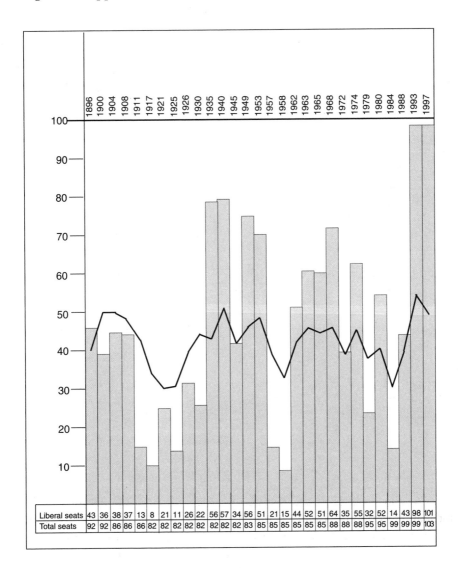

	1896	1900	1904	1908	1911	1917	1921	1925	1926	1930	1935	1940	1945	1949	1953	1957	1958	1962	1963	1965	1968	1972	1974	1979	1980	1984	1988	1993	1997
Liberal seats	43	36	38	37	13	8	21	11	26	22	56	57	34	56	51	21	15	44	52	51	64	35	55	32	52	14	43	98	101
Total seats	92	92	86	86	86	82	82	82	82	82	82	82	82	83	85	85	85	85	85	85	88	88	88	95	95	99	99	99	103

□ – Percentage of seats won by Liberals

— – Percentage of votes received by Liberal candidates

Chrétien attacked Charest more aggressively than he criticized Manning in Ontario, but it was Premier Michael Harris who clinched the Ontario election for the Liberals by rejecting the notion of entrenching Quebec's status as a distinct society. Even though this was Chrétien's position, it was also Charest's. In undermining Charest, Harris was implicitly supporting Manning, and so helping ensure that the right-wing vote divided evenly between Reform and the Progressive Conservatives at 19 per cent each. (In twenty-five constituencies the combined Reform and PC vote would have beaten the Liberal candidate.)

Ontario's results were consistent with the electoral trend to regional protest. The major issues on the Ontario agenda in the spring of 1997 were the radical cuts in public services (especially the threatened closure of hospitals) executed not by the federal Liberals but by the Conservative government of Michael Harris in Queen's Park. To the extent that they were protesting, Ontario voters were objecting to the Conservatives in what one observer called a "mid-term assessment of Harris."[35] They also acted distinctively from other regions, but with their customary Ontario twist. It was the national economy, national programs, and national unity based on a traditional accommodation with Quebec that dominated the province's electoral discourse and were seen to be the province's interest — in reaction against Jean Charest's platform cloned from Harris's Common Sense Revolution and against Preston Manning's perceived anti-Quebec bigotry. In the face of a threat to Ontario mainstream values many New Democratic sympathizers seem to have voted strategically for the Liberal Party in order to shut out Reform, leaving the NDP with just 11 per cent of the ballots.[36]

The **Prairie Provinces**' behaviour was as distinct as every other region's. In Manitoba prophecies of a Griterdämmerung were not fulfilled. Natural catastrophe in the Red River did not turn into the anticipated political catastrophe for the Liberals. Despite the flood, despite the four Western premiers publicly denouncing the Liberals for undermining health care, despite the aggressive Reform campaign, the Liberal vote fell only 10 points from 45 to 35 per cent. Massive flood relief funds channelled into the province by Chrétien's seasoned cabinet minister, Lloyd Axworthy, plus some eight thousand troops dispatched to help build the dikes and guarantee security had put the federal government in a favourable light. As a result the Liberals held onto six of the province's fourteen seats; the remaining eight split among the NDP (four), Reform (three), with the PCs, the party of the provincial government, only winning one.

Figure 4. Support for the federal Liberal Party in the Prairie provinces

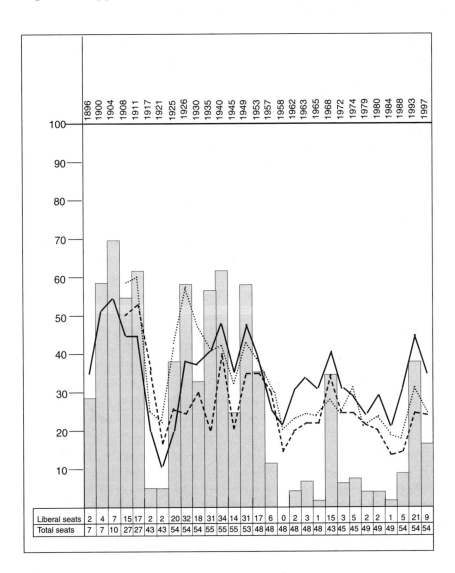

	1896	1900	1904	1908	1911	1917	1921	1925	1926	1930	1935	1940	1945	1949	1953	1957	1958	1962	1963	1965	1968	1972	1974	1979	1980	1984	1988	1993	1997
Liberal seats	2	4	7	15	17	2	2	20	32	18	31	34	14	31	17	6	0	2	3	1	15	3	5	2	2	1	5	21	9
Total seats	7	7	10	27	27	43	43	54	54	54	55	55	55	53	48	48	48	48	48	48	43	45	45	49	49	49	54	54	54

■ – Percentage of seats won by Liberals

— – Percentage of votes received by Liberal candidates in Manitoba

- - - Percentage of votes received by Liberal candidates in Alberta

····· – Percentage of votes received by Liberal candidates in Saskatchewan

Further west the Grits did much less well than they had expected. In Saskatchewan they fell from first place (five seats) to third (one seat). In only three of the other thirteen ridings did the Liberals finish in second place. Since Premier Roy Romanow fully supported Chrétien's 50-per-cent-plus-one statement, the Saskatchewan vote can also be seen as an expression of protest, "a rejection of the national party and the governing party," as David Smith put it.[37] Editorial comment during the campaign emphasized the province's tradition of protest. As the *Regina Leader-Post* reflected, it sends to "Ottawa voices to oppose the central government rather than be a part of it... This is truly the Saskatchewan way."[38]

In Alberta, the birthplace and stronghold of Reform, the Liberals went from a poor second-place position (25 per cent of the vote) to a poorer second-place position (24 per cent of the vote). They only managed to salvage two of their four seats (with margins of under 5 per cent) thanks to Paul Martin campaigning hard there in the final days before the vote. If Chrétien's 50-per-cent-plus-one statement had been aimed at challenging Reform's primacy on the national unity question in the West, there is no evidence it succeeded. The pronouncement received no editorial or news coverage comparable to its treatment in the Ontario and Quebec media. Instead Alberta's media presented the campaign as a battle between Manning, the hometown boy, and Chrétien, the man from Ottawa. When on May 27 the *Edmonton Journal* wrote "the Reform Party's platform on national unity is a genuine contribution to the debate on the issue," it was evident that Chrétien's attacks on Manning for divisiveness had fallen on dry ground in the West. Quebec's disproportionate influence in Ottawa is a long-standing Western grievance, and Manning's promotion of equality among the provinces was an attractive position for those in a relatively prosperous Alberta who were enraged that Ottawa pays it so little heed. Far from being intolerant bigots, Reformers were seen in the region as intelligent federalists. In the words of the *Edmonton Journal* on the morning after the balloting, "the election made Canada better.... Her Majesty's Loyal Opposition will be formed by a party committed to federalism."

Receiving proportionally fewer seats than votes on the Prairies has been the fate of the Liberal Party for half a century, as Figure 4 reminds us. The graphic also suggests that the Liberals may be down but they are far from out. Canada's national party still harvests one quarter of the ballots cast in protest country.

British Columbia proved frustratingly resistant to the Liberals' charms. As in other regions, editorialists commended them for their fiscal

Figure 5. Support for the federal Liberal Party in British Columbia

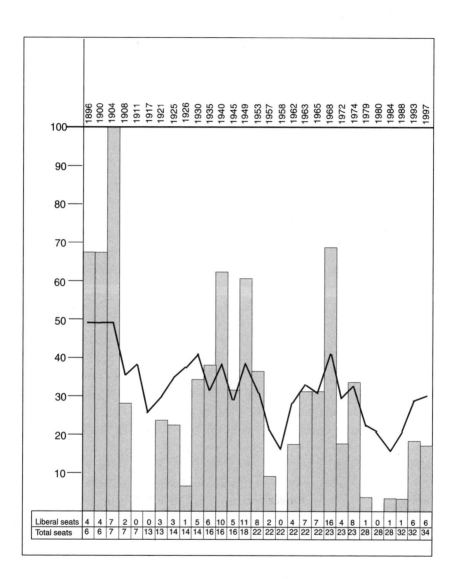

	1896	1900	1904	1908	1911	1917	1921	1925	1926	1930	1935	1940	1945	1949	1953	1957	1958	1962	1963	1965	1968	1972	1974	1979	1980	1984	1988	1993	1997
Liberal seats	4	4	7	2	0	0	3	3	1	5	6	10	5	11	8	2	0	4	7	7	16	4	8	1	0	1	1	6	6
Total seats	6	6	7	7	7	13	13	14	14	14	16	16	16	18	22	22	22	22	22	22	23	23	23	28	28	28	32	32	34

▨ – Percentage of seats won by Liberals

— – Percentage of votes received by Liberal candidates

management and national unity positions, while nevertheless favouring a protest vote. Thus the *Vancouver Sun* could write on May 30, "Canada needs a party that represents all regions and can steer a middle course;... when it comes to national purpose, Liberals are best" and at the same time could promote Reform as "a Western-based party willing and able to give voice to Western grievances and aspirations. That is no small thing in a country that has been constantly governed by parties rooted in Central Canada and, for the last 30 years, obsessed with Quebec." The Liberal Party, in other words, was good for Canada, but Reform was better for BC. And since the former were going to win in any case, British Columbians could vote for the latter, however flawed, without fear of repercussions. Like their counterparts in other provinces, British Columbians opposed the federal wing of the provincial government, the NDP getting only 18 per cent of their vote.

The Liberals had hoped for a share of the thirty-four available seats proportional to the 30 per cent of the vote that they could expect. But, as Figure 5 shows, this kind of equity eluded them once again. Chrétien's effort in the final days to persuade British Columbia to be "part of the solution not part of the problem" and his appeal "to the good side of people" — in contrast to Reform's attack on Liberal MPs for being soft on crime — had little impact. Their vote edged up one point from 28 per cent but their catch remained constant at six seats. Reform had outfought them with a classic Western protest campaign that brought in 43 per cent of the votes and, thanks to the electoral system, four times as many (25) seats.

The first-past-the-post, single-member ridings may have favoured Reform in BC and Alberta, the Bloc in Quebec, the NDP in Nova Scotia, and the Conservatives in New Brunswick, but on balance, thanks to Ontario, it had benefited the Liberals the most. As Figure 6 demonstrates, they formed a majority government party again because they managed to make the winner-takes-more principle work for them once again.

Conclusion

Did the campaign, which started with only one really national party, end with none, turning the Liberals into the country's fifth regional formation? Certainly, Chrétien's boast from 1993 to have a caucus with members from every *province* of the country now had to be adjusted to every *part* of the country. But the party had run second in every region outside Ontario and had come second in 104 of the 146 ridings it lost, indicating that it was still competitive from coast to coast.

The campaign had reinforced rather than changed the political

Figure 6. Support for the federal Liberal Party in Canada

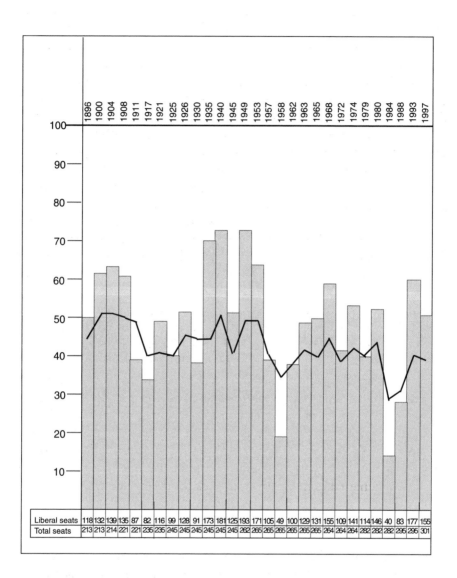

Liberal seats	118	132	139	135	87	82	116	99	128	91	173	181	125	193	171	105	49	100	129	131	155	109	141	114	146	40	83	177	155
Total seats	213	213	214	221	221	235	235	245	245	245	245	245	245	262	265	265	265	265	265	265	264	264	264	282	282	282	295	295	301

☐ – Percentage of seats won by Liberals

— – Percentage of votes received by Liberal candidates

landscape that the 1993 election had altered so dramatically. With the Office of the Leader of the Opposition held by Reform, the geographical balance in the House had shifted westwards. Although the Bloc Québécois had lost seats and votes, the sovereignists remained a coherent force, facing the Chrétien Liberals with the prospect of another referendum to come. With Reform and the BQ having the second and third largest caucuses, the 1997 Parliament will turn out to be as capable of voicing regional grievances as the one following the 1993 federal election. Ideologically, it is more evenly balanced. With a majority of the members of the NDP and PC caucuses hailing from the have-not Atlantic provinces, these parties can be expected to make the case for sustaining social programs. And with these partisan groups restored to official parliamentary status, the new Liberal government can expect to be under more substantial pressure from the left to abandon its one-track deficit-cutting obsession in favour of a genuine two-track support for economic development and social programs. Apart from having a severely reduced majority, the Liberals thus find themselves in a dream position for a second time in a row.

The Liberals had lived up to the title of their campaign platform, *Securing Our Future Together* — it was their *own* future they had secured. They were able to take the summer, as Chrétien had anticipated, to prepare for the launch of the new government in the fall. The campaign had shown that this new government would be much like the old. Its vision would be limited by the imperatives of fiscal prudence, its administration would be cautious, and its handling of Quebec problematic. Without any clear guidelines emerging from Red Book II and with ambitious candidates for the succession already starting to plan their leadership campaigns, it remained to be proven how secure Canada's future would be — together or divided.

Notes

[1] Edward Greenspon, "Liberals practice practicality," *The Globe and Mail*, 15 January, 1994, A 1, 4.
[2] Susan Delacourt, "Liberals brandish vow keeping record on modest goals." *The Globe and Mail*, 25 October, 1996, A 13.
[3] Delacourt, *ibid.*
[4] Gordon Gibson, "Jean Chrétien loses a crucial bit of teflon," *The Globe and Mail*, December 17, 1996, A 19.
[5] Peter Donolo's comment on "The Unofficial Story," CBC television, June 1997.

[6] Edward Greenspon, "Wanted: a national agenda," *The Globe and Mail*, 5 July, 1997, D 2.

[7] The National, 9 May, 1997 and 30 May, 1997.

[8] James Travers and David Vienneau, "National unity sets off sparks in leaders' debate," *The Toronto Star*, 13 May, 1997, A 1, 11.

[9] David Vienneau, "PM denounces Charest's unacceptable comment," *The Toronto Star*, 15 May, 1997, A 12.

[10] Tu Thank Ha and Anne McIlroy, "Chrétien counterpunches Charest jab," *The Globe and Mail*, 16 May 1997, A 8.

[11] Tim Harper, "Chrétien accuses Charest of hiding from his Conservative heritage," *The Toronto Star*, May 7, 1997, A 16.

[12] "Chrétien calls Reform policies divisive," *The Globe and Mail*, May 7, 1997, A 9.

[13] David Vienneau, "Deep in Reform country, PM slams Manning," *The Toronto Star*, 27 May, 1997, A 1, 11.

[14] David Vienneau, "Chrétien pleads for tolerance and unity," *The Toronto Star*, 30 May 1997, A11.

[15] In Mark Kingwell's phrase on TV Ontario's Studio Two, May 30, 1997.

[16] Anthony Wilson-Smith, "The Unity Bomber," *Maclean's*, 19 May, 1997, p.14.

[17] Réseau de l'Information, 25 May, 1997.

[18] *The Toronto Star*, 27 May, 1997.

[19] Interview with Peter Donolo by Sharoni Sibony, August 19, 1997.

[20] Sharoni Sibony, "Television and the Liberal Party in the 1997 Canadian Federal Election Campaign," unpublished essay, 1 August, 1997, Table 2.6, p.15.

[21] *Ibid.*, Table 4.2, p.19.

[22] *Ibid.*, Table A 1, p.41; table C 1, p.43.

[23] The National, 9 May, 1997.

[24] The National, 22 May, 1997.

[25] The National, 20 May, 1997.

[26] Scott Feschuk, "Voters cynicism greets campaign ads," *The Globe and Mail*, 12 May, 1997, A 8.

[27] Sibony, *op.cit.*, Table 4.1, p.19.

[28] Le Téléjournal, 3 May, 1997, cited in *ibid.*, p.24.

[29] Liberal Party of Canada "The 1997 Liberal Platform: Fiscal Responsibility," *Talking Point*, 1 May, 1997.

[30] Edison Stewart, "Liberal fax calls Charest separatist," *The Toronto Star*, 17 May, 1997, A 12.

[31] Letter to the author, July 31, 1997.

[32] Brian Underhill and Cameron MacKeen, "Unemployed Offended by

PM's Parallel," *Halifax Chronicle-Herald*, 31 May, 1997, A 1.

[33] Karen Unland, "Liberals give Montréalers pointed reminder," *The Globe and Mail*, 21 May, 1997, A 8.

[34] Formally the Liberals received 101 of 103 seats, but one of the missing ridings was lost (by a mere 3 per cent) to John Nunziata, a renegade Liberal who, claiming to be an independent, ran a campaign that was Liberal in all but name. Even the Liberals' loss of York South had less to do with support for the Conservataives than with voter revulsion at the scandal over the credentials of their 1993 MP, Jag Bhaduria.

[35] Dalton Camp, "Reform's reckless rhetoric didn't sell east of Manitoba," *The Toronto Star* 4 June, 1997, A 21.

[36] While opinion research did not focus on this kind of strategic voting, evidence gathered from NDP candidates suggests this was a factor, at least in Toronto.

[37] The University of Saskatchewan political scientist is quoted in Mark Wyatt, "Saskatachewan maintains tradition," *Regina Leader-Post*, 3 June, 1997, B 2.

[38] Murray Mandruk, "Saskatchewan won't decide the election," *Regina Leader-Post*, 31 May, 1997, A 4.

Four
On the Ropes Again?: The Campaign of the Progressive Conservative Party in the 1997 Federal Election
by Peter Woolstencroft

On December 6, 1993, six months to the day after losing to Kim Campbell at the Progressive Conservative leadership convention, Jean Charest became the interim leader of the party. Few offered congratulations. That October's election had been such an unqualified disaster for the Tories that, despite their history extending to pre-Confederation days, they were politically marginalized and faced possible extinction. After two successive majority governments in the 1984 and 1988 elections, rare accomplishments in Canadian politics, the party was reduced to two seats and lost "official party status" in the House of Commons. The party's financial situation was dire (it had a debt of over $7 million) and many of its constituency associations also were encumbered by heavy debts as a result of their candidates failing to reach the 15 per cent vote threshold which produces a 50 per cent rebate of allowable election expenses. Demoralized party activists feared that the collapse of Brian Mulroney's electoral coalition of the 1980s — manifested in the rapid rise to electoral prominence of the Reform Party of Canada and the Bloc Québécois — was irreversible. Reform, in particular, was looking to expand, and one potential growth area lay in the 16 per cent of the electorate which had supported the Tories in the 1993 election.

Yet, by the time the writ was dropped for the 1997 election, a considerable number of people believed (more within the party, to be sure, than in the wider public) that the party would make significant gains; if the Liberals stumbled, perhaps they could even become the Official Opposition. While the Liberals had held a commanding lead in the polls since the 1993 election, the other parties, Reform, the NDP, and the Bloc Québécois, seemed to be in electoral trouble. Each of them, depending on the region, was the leading competitor with the Tories for anti-Liberal votes. Furthermore, the Tories were the second choice of many voters, especially those leaning Liberal. The same polls reported that many voters held Jean Charest in high regard, despite the party's low profile since 1993. For one thing, his highly charged pro-Canada speeches during the 1995 Quebec referendum were widely recognized as energizing the federalist forces; for another, his easy expressiveness, especially on television, and fluid bilingualism gave him an appeal far greater than the reach of his party.

By the time of the election call, the Tories had put themselves on firm financial footing; had successfully restructured their political processes; and had gone through an extensive policy development process. Party strategists calculated that there was a strong anti-government sentiment in Atlantic Canada that could only rebound to their advantage. Charest was by far the most popular federalist leader in Quebec. There were strong Progressive Conservative provincial governments in Manitoba, Alberta, and Ontario, where the Tories remained popular despite sustained controversy over their "Common Sense Revolution" package of tax cuts, spending cuts, and massive reorganization of municipalities and school boards. A recent victory in Prince Edward Island augured well. Even the Calgary area, Reform leader Preston Manning's home territory, held promise.

For the PC party, then, the election results — 20 seats and an increase in the popular vote of almost three per cent from the 1993 mark of 16 per cent — were bittersweet. The party had some positive talking points, official party status, and the election of MPs in six provinces. But it was also true that Preston Manning had become leader of the Official Opposition (though the Tories would point to Reform's failure to elect MPs east of Manitoba). The Tories were merely the fifth largest party, their very standing after the 1993 election. The campaign, then, was more failure than success, and, given the expectations that the party had before the election, it was the campaign in Ontario that provided its biggest disappointment and its biggest failure.

This chapter traces developments within the party after the 1993 debacle; considers the party's pre-writ preparations; discusses the strategy employed in the election campaign; and analyzes why the campaign, in large measure, failed. It will be argued that the campaign's messages were inconsistent; that the opportunity presented by Jean Charest's performance in the leaders' debates was not seized; and that, in the last weeks of the campaign, the leader was reacting to the other parties rather than driving the agenda by speaking to his platform. At the highest levels of the Tory campaign team, debate raged over a number of issues throughout the election: Emphasize the platform or Jean Charest? Focus the attack on the Liberals or Reform? How to handle the flashpoints of national unity? Internal indecisiveness reflected on the party's image and reduced its potential vote.[1]

The rebuilding of the party

Jean Charest's task as the new leader of the party required boldness. The PC party had to be reorganized, its debt paid down, and its optimism and sense of purpose revived. Decisions arising from the financial crisis facing the party after the 1993 election led to dramatic staff reductions at its national headquarters, closing of almost all field offices, and severe operating budget reductions. If, however, the Tories were to move beyond the deep-seated antipathy that Brian Mulroney had engendered in the last years of his second mandate as prime minister and the pervasive internal demoralization in the aftermath of the 1993 election, then an assertive and expansive reconstruction strategy was imperative.

In the Mulroney years, despite trappings of participatory democracy, such as leadership conventions and policy conferences, the party was organizationally top-heavy and many members perceived it to be dominated by the leader and his close advisors, with members being little more than "cheerleaders and fundraisers."[2]

One of Charest's first initiatives as leader was to establish The National Restructuring Committee with a mandate to examine all aspects of the party's operations.[3] The proposed remedies were structural change, new processes (particularly in the area of policy development), and an open, "grassroots" attitude. These were intended to create a new image for the party and lead Canadians to associate the future instead of the past with the PCs.

At its first meeting after the 1993 election — in Hull, Quebec in April of 1995 — the party amended its constitution in a number of important ways under the "3-Rs" rubric of "Restructure, Rebuild, Return." Believing that democratizing their processes would enhance their appeal and following the lead of other federal and provincial parties, and with the eager support of Jean Charest, the PCs adopted the "one member–one vote" method of leadership selection.[4] Jean Charest heralded the new system for making the Conservatives "the most modern political party in Canada."[5] Another issue that the party confronted resulted from a lack of control over its finances in the 1993 campaign. After that election, the party discovered that unrealistic expenditure and revenue projections, along with lack of controls, had created deep financial problems.[6] To address the issue of accountability two important changes were put in place. First, the party established a National Council comprising the leader, party officials, and constituency presidents which would meet annually to discuss party affairs, provide direction, and approve budgets, including those for elections. The National Council was given non-delegatable powers, such as being able to initiate the leadership selection process. Second, the party established a Management Committee, chaired by the party's National President and composed of representatives of various parts of the party, and charged with the responsibility of general management of the party and reporting annually to the National Council.[7] Another innovation was the National Membership Program by which people could directly join the national party instead of just their local constituency association.[8] This was an important step in the evolution of the party as it meant that for the first time it could communicate directly with party members.

A program of policy development predicated on inclusiveness was put in place. In August, 1995 the booklet *Developing a Conservative Agenda for Canadians: Asking the Right Questions*, prepared by the party's Policy Advisory Committee, was circulated to party members. The idea was that Conservatives, guided by the booklet, would meet first in riding and regional caucuses, then in provincial meetings, culminating in a national conference.[9] One strategic theme running through the policy discussions was how would the party position itself in the next election. Tory partisans knew about underground and some public discussions about merger with Reform. Some thought the party had to develop policies that would appeal to Reform voters; others said that the next election would be determined by the PCs' ability to attract Liberal supporters. One idea that the party considered at the urging of Jean Charest was the flat income tax, which was finding some favour in Republican circles in the United States and had attracted the interest of Reform. In December, 1995, the party held a one-day conference on the topic, but the idea generated little sustained support.

In August, 1996 the party met in Winnipeg. One driving force was the party's large, well-organized and vociferous youth wing, especially on the issue of taxes. The Policy Advisory Committee reported that "members of the party clearly want tax reductions" but that there was no agreement about the timing of tax cuts "in relation to necessary deficit and debt reduction."[10] The PC youth pushed for a 20 per cent reduction in federal personal and corporate income taxes within the first mandate of a Conservative government, but were persuaded by Jean Charest that he and the party needed sufficient flexibility to respond to events (especially Liberal budgetary initiatives) and to be able to develop a balanced platform. Even with this compromise before the convention, however, the party was divided by what many saw as a right-wing move away from traditional Conservative thinking. After forceful interventions in opposition to any tax cuts by John Crosbie, a former finance minister, and in favour of compromise by Hugh Segal, often identified as a "Red Tory", the convention voted to cut income taxes by 10 to 20 per cent over the course of five years. In January of 1997 the party released the pamphlet *Designing a Blue Print for Canadians* which summarized the resolutions passed at the Winnipeg policy conference.

Jean Charest's goals for the most part had been reached by December 1996. Contrary to what many had predicted, the party's debt was close to being retired so its election planning would not be constrained by nervous bankers. Party activists were generally satisfied that the democratization initiatives addressed the deep disquietude that they had had about internal decision-making, part of the Mulroney legacy. And the policy development process for the first time in the life of the party had successfully involved thousands of Conservatives in extended discussions which would determine the parameters of the party's policy directions and set benchmarks for the development of the campaign platform. Parties in opposition, especially those ousted from office, often rebuild by bringing heretofore marginalized activists into the party's central processes; the danger, especially in terms of policy is that single-minded groups will take the party in directions that are ideologically satisfying but are electorally cumbersome. The party in Winnipeg had Ontario very much on its mind: Harris's provincial Tories had made tax cuts the central piece of their successful election campaign in 1995 and were still popular. The question: Did tax cuts lock the party into a position that would make it difficult for it to convince voters that increased spending on health and education as well as deficit reduction was possible?

All of Charest's successes in reorganization had had little impact on the public. The Tories were still mired in the low teens in the public opinion polls, although Charest's events were generally well-attended and enthusiastic. As it became clearer and clearer that a June election was likely, not just possible, the question of the party's pre-election preparations, which had started in the summer of 1996, became the new imperative. However, even by 1997, while many of the negative effects of the 1993 debacle had been attenuated, the party had not recovered from the exodus of volunteers, both in the constituencies and at the national headquarters, which followed the 1993 defeat. In the constituencies, the rebuilding process was very uneven, with some parts of the country, but especially Quebec, showing few signs of life.[11] And many of the difficulties that the Tory campaign was to suffer flowed from the fact that numerous people in the inter-election period had declined Jean Charest's request for their time, energy, and commitment.

Pre-election developments: four decisions

In the pre-election period, four decisions shaped the campaign of the Progressive Conservative Party. The first concerned the scope of the party's campaign: Would the party be a national entity or something less than that? While the question was not seen to be of primary importance, the answer had a significant impact throughout the pre-election period and the election itself. Tory strategists were deeply worried about the party's marginalization in Parliament and its low profile in the mass media. Once the election was called, in a nominal five-party contest, would the media consign the Tories to oblivion? How could they establish themselves as the only national alternative to the Liberals? Strategists reasoned that it would be hard for the media to treat the party as a mirage if it presented candidates in every constituency. If the Tories could claim to be a national party with candidates representing the diversities of Canada, then they would be able to draw a telling contrast with Reform. Despite being in existence for 10 years, it was not expected to nominate candidates everywhere. Reform's inability to attract support in francophone Quebec ridings would be a serious weakness, especially in the eyes of Ontario voters concerned about national unity, if the Tories had a full complement of candidates.

The commitment made in the summer of 1996 to run candidates in every constituency required the allocation of considerable but scarce organizational resources. In several regions — British Columbia, parts of the prairie provinces, strongly separatist regions of Quebec and the anglophone ridings of the Montréal area — the party had little with which it could work and little promise of electoral growth. The poor condition of the party extended into Ontario, where only about a third of riding associations were viable; another third had a coterie of activists but little sustained life and few financial resources; and the last third essentially were shells with, at best, one or two activists.[12] Yet, in the province which was thought to be the crucial election battleground, in the inter-election period of 1993–1997, severe financial constraints caused the party to rely on only one paid party organizer working out of her home. As the party realized that a 1997 election was highly likely, four organizers were hired in the late fall-early winter before the election call.[13]

Nationally, the party talked about having one hundred candidates nominated by the end of 1996 but, in fact, only about 35 nomination meetings had been held and just seven candidates had been selected in Ontario. By the time the election was called, the party had nominated about 200 candidates. In Ontario, despite the organizational weakness of the party, a herculean effort resulted in 96 of a possible 103 nominees in the field before the writ was dropped; 57 nominations occurred in April. The party was hardly primed for the race. Nonetheless, many nominations were contested at well-attended meetings, and the party had attracted a number of credible candidates, most notably recently-retired General Lewis Mackenzie in Parry Sound–Muskoka. Throughout the nomination meetings in the pre-election months, it became evident that most of the Atlantic constituencies were active, but that ridings in other parts of the country, especially Saskatchewan and British Columbia, were organizationally weak. And Quebec was a big problem, with many constituencies having no organization whatsoever and, in the days just before the close of nominations, the party resorted to parachuting candidates into about half of the province's 75 ridings.

The commitment in the post-1993 period to broaden the participatory life of the party led to a decision to bring more people into leadership roles in the campaign at a time when the party was having difficulty getting key people to commit themselves to fill important positions in the campaign organization. Under the leadership of senators David Tkachuk and Pierre-Claude Nolin, who had been appointed campaign co-chairs in July of 1996, the decision was made to decentralize the campaign. Instead of following the traditional pattern in which a few people ran the campaign, in the name of inclusiveness broadly-based campaign committees were established in the provinces. The "provincial partners," as they were called, took a leading role in terms of provincial tours and management of the nomination process; the central campaign committee was responsible for the development and delivery of campaign strategy and messages. Broadening participation had the merit of bringing more people who had useful knowledge of local circumstances into the heart of the process; but the problem of achieving coordination was evident as well since the "provincial partners" did not always share the central campaign's understanding of the campaign's message.[14]

Others played significant roles in the election campaign. Pierre

Fortier, the president of the party, took on a much more active role than had his predecessors. Conservative senators, of which there were quite a few as a legacy of the Mulroney years in government, also took on more tasks than ordinarily was the case, helping to replace the corps of young lawyers, public relations people, and businesspeople commonly volunteered by their employers. The National Council in late February approved the election budget in macro-terms. The party's Management Committee, which was involved in the development of the budget, also had to approve deviations from the approved budget. In one instance, because the approved budget was thought to be light in terms of media advertising, the Management Committee approved a change.

The absence of personnel began to show its effects. The state of the party's electoral preparedness in the month leading up to the election call was seriously deficient in many respects. For example, decisions about sign artwork and logos were not finalized; commercials were not ready for the beginning of the paid advertising period; communication operational issues were unresolved; and various aspects of the national campaign were seriously understaffed, especially the national tour. A room for tour organizers had been provided, but without phones, computers, and desks. And one considerable concern was that the Progressive Conservative Canada Fund, the party's fundraising arm, had fallen behind in its projections for the first quarter of 1997. What would happen to the party's fundraising in the election? The party could not survive a repeat of the campaign of 1993 when donations plummeted as the party dropped in the polls in the last weeks of the campaign.

The third, and most important, decision was made in the fall of 1996. Leslie Noble and Alister Campbell were recruited to prepare the federal party's platform.[15] Despite their youth, they had been active for a long time in Tory circles, particularly with the Ontario Progressive Conservative Party. They were central figures in the development of *The Common Sense Revolution*, a decidedly right-wing document that in the 1995 election surprisingly and very much against the odds had taken Mike Harris to the premiership of Ontario.[16]

The approach taken by Noble and Campbell was to extract major themes from the Winnipeg policy resolutions and develop a few defined policies rather than produce a "soup to nuts" collection of positions on an enormous range of issues.[17] The federal party's research carried out in the period from mid-summer 1996 through the mid-winter 1997 revealed that Canadians were greatly concerned about jobs and economic security, the deficit and the economy, the declining quality of health care, education, and the future of social security programs such as the Canada

Pension Plan. Canadians' biggest fear was separation; but that did not extend to interest in mega-constitutional reform projects which might be designed to prevent it.

The product of Noble's and Campbell's work, originally intended for release in January, was delayed — partly to take into account the Liberal government's last budget before the anticipated election. It was released in late March. Following on the themes of the party's 1996 policy conference, *Let the Future Begin*, a document of 61 pages, outlined the Tory plan for the next 10 years, focussing on job growth, prudent spending, and rebalancing the federation. Its major points were:

- phase in a 10 per cent reduction in federal income tax; reduction in corporate tax rates from 28 per cent to 24 per cent; and reduction in small business rates from 12 per cent to 8 per cent; and reduction in Employment Insurance payroll taxes by $5 billion;
- reduce planned cuts to the provinces in spending for health, education, and welfare;
- negotiate for one year with the provinces to eliminate interprovincial trade barriers; failing agreement use Ottawa's constitutional powers over trade and commerce to remove barriers;
- negotiate with the provinces to establish a "Canadian Covenant" which would set benchmarks for health care, post-secondary education, and inter-provincial trade;
- work with the provinces to establish national standards in education and commit to use federal dollars to establish a Canadian Education Excellence Fund and a National Testing Institute;
- reform of the appointments process, with the effect of reducing the role of the prime minister by increasing the role of the provinces for some appointments to the Senate, and giving an all-party parliamentary committee a central role in major appointments for Governor-General, ambassadorial posts, the Supreme Court Chief Justice;
- repeal of the Firearms Bill (Bill C-68) and increases in mandatory penalties for use of a firearm in the commission of a crime;
- balance the budget by 2000, to be effected by large spending cuts to some departments.

As the party went through the last stages of developing its election platform, a decision had to be made about the time and manner of its release. As had been the case with the nominations of candidates, Tory strategists were conscious of being almost invisible in the last Parliament and receiving only sporadic media coverage. Since there was danger that the short election campaign with five parties competing for attention would mean the party would not get its message out, it was necessary for the Tories to jumpstart the process. This was done in two ways. First, on March 18th the party launched its platform, highlighted by an elaborate electronically-connected six-site release in Ontario. Second, a million-dollar television advertising campaign was run in March and April. Futuristic in tone and youth-oriented, the TV ads focussed on Jean Charest, his plan for Canada's future, and his platform's health-care guarantee. Viewers were encouraged to phone in for CD ROM versions of *Let the Future Begin* or access the party's website. These commercials were run in Ontario, the Atlantic Region, and, to a lesser extent, Alberta, but not in Quebec, as a result of a decision by the Quebec campaign committee.

The fourth decision was made in early April. Jodi White was appointed to the national campaign team with the title of "campaign director." A long-time Tory activist and Jean Charest's campaign manager in the 1993 Conservative leadership race, White had served on the party's platform committee and had been involved in the discussions leading to the development of *Let the Future Begin*. In the short timeframe available to her the task was to put the campaign on its best footing; and, indeed, by the time of the election call many of the deficiencies in election preparedness were addressed. The "provincial partners" model was for the most part put aside and central campaign committee took on more decision-making and initiative. But one important question remained unanswered: How would Jean Charest and the Tories campaign? That this question was still being debated in April provides considerable insight to what happened in May!

The electoral strategy of the Tory election platform: Charest, ideas, television

Political developments between 1993 and 1977 had the effect of giving the Conservatives little space on the right of the Canadian ideological spectrum. Spending cuts to reduce the deficit had pulled the Liberals to the right of their 1993 platform; most of the country, especially voters in Ontario, seemed to accept the way in which the Liberals were handling the politics of deficit management and expenditure reductions. Only in

Atlantic Canada was anti-government sentiment palpable, driven by the Liberal failure to produce jobs for the region and exacerbated by resentment over the harmonization of the GST and provincial sales taxes. But so long as Paul Martin was Finance Minister it seemed that the Liberals were going to "stay the course," leaving little room for the Tories to distinguish themselves. For its part, Reform clearly had its eyes on Ontario; its "fresh start" platform, called for (amongst other things) tax cuts and a partial restoration of health care funding. The Reform platform reflected its attempt to move away from the negative images that it had accumulated since the 1993 election and to lose its regional identification arising from its large contingent of MPs from Alberta and British Columbia. From the PCs' point of view, Reform's major themes looked very much like the PC platform.

The Progressive Conservative Party's limited electoral strengths, according to its polling, were in Ontario, Atlantic Canada, and amongst older voters; Charest was popular and well ahead of other opposition leaders in terms of the "who would make the best prime minister" question, but was not well-known, especially compared to Jean Chrétien. Opportunity was present among the many voters who expressed concern about the government's record. The party's polling indicated that between 40 and 50 per cent of voters thought that the Liberals were on the wrong track, especially about jobs; and over 50 per cent thought that major change, not tinkering, was required. However, people saw the Liberals as being fixated only on being re-elected, not in longterm planning. On the basis of that information, the strategy developed by Tory strategists was to focus on the Liberal record and appeal to "soft Liberals," voters claiming to be supporters of the government but with misgivings about its record and doubts about its leadership for the future.

Ontario would be the primary battleground for the Conservatives. Its large number of ridings of course would always make the province the centrepiece in a national election, but in the 1997 election the province would be strategically essential for the Tories. The 1993 election in Ontario had produced one seat and 57 second-place finishes for Reform. It would be disastrous for the Tories if Preston Manning was able to expand Reform's beachhead and establish itself as the alternative to the Liberals in Ontario.

Two considerations structured how Noble and Campbell looked at the political situation in the province. The first was that Ontario in 1995 had elected a PC government committed to both extensive spending reductions and tax cuts, policies consistent with Reform's platform; and although it was true that the new government was running into much opposition as it implemented its program, it was also the case that the provincial Tories had maintained their support levels — and were much more popular than their federal counterparts. The second was that Preston Manning — and Reform itself — were highly unpopular in the province; their 1993 vote was seen as a simple protest against the Mulroney heritage of the Tories. As memories faded Reform's support base was withering. These two considerations suggested that the right appeal would produce seats for the Tories in Ontario. In addition, it was hoped that Premier Mike Harris would support the federal party, an uncertain prospect to be sure, despite his approval of the taxcutting plank. Harris hesitated partly because of his longstanding opposition to "distinct society" for Quebec, to which Jean Charest was irrevocably committed and Preston Manning's Reform was adamantly opposed. Moreover, the Reform Party had stayed out of the 1995 provincial election, thus conceding the right of the spectrum to the Tories, whose re-election prospects would be hurt if Reform decided to enter the fray. Tactically, it made sense for Mike Harris not to get embroiled in the feud between the federal Tories and Reform.

Leslie Noble's position was that the party had to establish that it was the only alternative to the Liberals, to capture dissatisfaction with the government by stressing that it had ideas to which it was committed, ideas that would address the core concerns of voters. True, there were many similarities between the parties, but there were definite points of differentiation, especially on issues that mattered to voters. The choice for Noble was straightforward. A winning strategy required a focussed iteration of the message, as specified in *Let the Future Begin*, throughout the campaign and the party; a losing strategy would not have faith in the message.[18] The plan was that the initial weeks of the campaign would set the stage for the Tories. Repeated iterations of the platform in Charest's speeches and in the party's advertisements would produce improving poll results for the Tories, especially in Ontario. Prospects for seat gains in Ontario — 10, 20, even 30 seats — coupled with anticipated gains in Atlantic Canada as a result of hostility would generate attention in Quebec. As the Tory numbers improved, Quebec voters, already attracted to Charest himself, would vote for the party in sufficient numbers to produce seats in the province. Such was the optimistic scenario of the Conservative strategists.

Candidates attending "campaign schools" in the weeks preceding the election were told they were to direct their efforts to bringing wavering voters into the Tory fold. The themes of the campaign were job creation, job security in the future, restored funding for health care, and preparation of Canadians for global competitiveness through federal-provincial cooperation in the development of national education standards. It was made clear to candidates that the national campaign would not talk about national unity or attack Preston Manning and Reform. There was good reason for the Tories to be cautious on the national unity issue. Voters were not keen on "distinct society" or any other formulation that would imply constitutionally embedded differentiation between Quebec and the other provinces. The platform's national unity plank called for Ottawa to use its resources — constitutional and the spending power — to provide national standards in health care, set the stage for the establishment of national standards in education, and abolish inter-provincial trade barriers. But did voters appreciate what the Tories were talking about? Were they interested in "rebalancing the federation"?

"We have the momentum — but where are the votes?"[19]

The campaign period, from April 27 until June 2, from the perspective of the party was divided into three parts. The first ran from the day of the election call until the first debate between the leaders and the beginning of paid advertising; the second was the post-debate period to the time that Reform began to raise the national unity issue; and the third encompassed the last 10 days of the campaign.

The first part did not go well for any of the parties. The public, not very keen on the call of the election, was much more preoccupied with floods in Manitoba than the party leaders' tours and exhortations. The Tory strategy in the initial phase of the election was to highlight each day different aspects of the campaign platform in events that provided an appropriate setting. For example, at a site close to the University of Waterloo, Charest talked about education and preparation for a computer-based global economy in the context of youth underemployment and unemployment; near an H&R Block office tax cuts were the topic; and close to the Nova Scotia and New Brunswick border he talked about barriers to interprovincial trade. However, if media coverage was the indicator, the national tour was almost invisible in terms of media coverage. Although organizationally the party had come a long way from the first week of April, some operational aspects of the tour were problematic and required rectification. More seriously, Charest was ill throughout the first week and his need for rest and recuperation meant he could not maintain a full schedule. And he was out of public view for some time because he was filming commercials. But the fundamental problem was what the media were doing. The PCs' fifth place standing and poor prospects resulted in skimpy media coverage, with the party especially not "getting its share of voice" on television," with many accounts of the campaign giving the Tories only a snippet at the end of their five-party coverage.[20] Party organizers were bothered that their internal polls showed no movement in Ontario and began to be concerned that the major themes of the platform were not resonating well with voters. Candidates were told that now the party expected little movement in the polls until the debate and the start of paid advertising.

Continuation of the first phase of the election saw the stirring of the national unity pot. The media reported that former Quebec premier Jacques Parizeau was going to reveal in a forthcoming book that he had been willing to make a unilateral declaration of independence if the Parti Québécois had won the October 1995 referendum. Tory organizers did not welcome the emergence of the national unity issue despite Charest's clear avowal of his views on a range of issues such as the Supreme Court reference, distinct society, and Plan B. The party had been given ample notice that no one should imagine that national unity was the "sleeper issue" waiting to emerge. Peter Lougheed, former Premier of Alberta, and Joe Clark, former prime minister, in speeches to the National Council meeting at the first weekend in March had warned that the issue could not be ignored. And Brian Mulroney in a mid-April Toronto speech called for resumption of high-level constitutional discussions. The problem was that there was no polling data to suggest that the issue would pull voters to the Tories; indeed, there were reasons to think that Reform was the party with the most to gain by playing the national unity card. The Covenant part of Let the Future Begin, however attractive an antidote to the decentralist thinking of Reform it might be, was too complicated to swing votes to the Tories without having an extended gestation period. Nonetheless, on the Thursday of the second week, Charest, at a speech in London, Ontario devoted the bulk of his time to the issue, attacking both the Bloc and Reform for sharing similar views, as he saw it, and Jean Chrétien for almost losing the referendum.

The second stage of the campaign centred on the English- and French-language debates. Jean Charest's performance in the debates, particularly the English language event, was superb in the view of almost every observer. There was no strategic complexity to the party's planning: Charest's job was to speak directly to Canadians and not get involved in scraps about minutiae. For his part, Charest feared that the media had generated unrealistic expectations that would make his job impossible; and given the presence of five party leaders and the structure of interactions between them, the media's preoccupation with thinking that there would be a defining moment or knockout blow in the debate would divert the media from focussing on the differences between the Tories and the other parties.

Within moments of the close of the first debate Charest (despite a nervous beginning) was declared the winner by media commentators and focus groups (see Chapter Eleven of this volume). Internal Tory tracking polls reported a noteworthy uptick in Conservative voting intentions and a concomitant Liberal decline; focus group testing showed that Jean Charest's campaign was seen as moving positively. Public polls appearing after the first two debates recorded that Charest had made a considerable impact. A national poll conducted by the Strategic Counsel for *The Toronto Star* and CFTO Television showed that the Tories had made some gains, especially in Quebec, and that the Liberals and especially Reform had slipped. For example, voters were more favourably disposed to see the Conservatives as best able to handle whatever they thought was the most important issue. While nationally Jean Charest was in the high 20s on the "which leader would do the best job as Prime Minister?" question, he was far ahead of his opponents in Quebec. In terms of perceived "momentum" (that is, "which political leader/party is doing a better job of campaigning?" and "which party is gaining in popularity?") the Conservatives leapt well in front of the other parties. On the negative side, the Liberal lead on "which party is best able to deal with specific issues?" was only slightly reduced across the nation, except that the Tories were ahead in Toronto and Quebec on the issue of "keeping taxes as low as possible" — the problem was that voters did not rank tax cuts as a very important issue.[21] And it was of considerable irony, given the PCs' election strategy, that it was in Quebec, not Ontario, that there was increased interest in the Conservatives.

What did the Conservatives do with the opportunity that the debate had given them? Very little, as it turned out. The tour schedule worked against Charest, as he went to Atlantic Canada after the abbreviated French language debate; the scheduling of the lost portion of the French debate on the Sunday forced Charest to cut short trips to Ontario and Quebec. At the top of the campaign team, the uncertainty over the effectiveness of the platform began to become evident in how the party presented itself in its advertisements. The first set of commercials reflected the major themes of *Let the Future Begin*: they were hard, comparative, and starkly put (with some reminiscent of the hardhitting "T-Bar" Conservative commercials in the 1995 Ontario election that graphically differentiated party positions). But while the polls showed growing interest in the Tories, Jodi White thought that there was no polling evidence that suggested any issue had any "traction," in the sense of pulling voters into their camp.[22] Leslie Noble, who was not directly involved in the campaign until its third week, thought that the party had not established clearly and consistently the link between tax cuts and job creation, as had happened provincially in Ontario in 1995.[23] White's judgement was that the 1997 federal election was a different strategic situation than the 1995 Ontario election. In the latter case voters wanted to turf out Bob Rae and the New Democrats. Once they determined that Lyn McLeod and the Liberals were not what they wanted, they voted for their only other option, Mike Harris and the Progressive Conservative Party. But in 1997, voters were not eager to expel the Liberals (and, indeed, by large margins they expected their re-election); and the regional character of political competition complicated the options available to any one party.

In White's mind, a platform is not a strategy, and simple reiteration of its major points would not be enough.[24] In the end her strategic analysis carried the day. In the post-debate period "softer" advertisements were run: Charest was given greater prominence, stressing his personality and style, in settings such as on a bus and in a committee meeting. In the last part of the election, the party ran "leadership" commercials, in which Charest focussed on the choice that voters had. If they were dissatisfied with the status quo, then they should vote for him as the agent of change. The difficulties that the Tories had in their search for the right package of Charest, ideas, and television advertisements is evidenced by the number of ads run by the nationally-oriented parties: 8 for Reform, 8 for Liberals; 9 for the New Democrats, and 15 for the Conservatives.[25]

But as the second phase of the campaign closed, the energy of the Tory campaign dissipated. Candidates sensed that the positive reaction in the post-debate week began to disappear. In the riding of Kitchener-Waterloo, for example, in the four-day span after the Victoria Day long weekend requests for lawn signs dropped monotonically (32, 16, 8, and 4) and never recovered. As the polls showed the Tories falling, the party responded with endorsements from Ralph Klein, premier of Alberta; Gary Filmon, premier of Manitoba; Pat Binns, premier of Prince Edward Island,and Bill Davis, who had retired as premier of Ontario in 1985. But Davis's endorsement had the effect of emphasizing that Mike Harris had steadfastly refused to endorse any party leader, most notably Jean Charest. A Harris endorsement presumably would have energized the Tory campaign. Without it, despite the fact that many Ontario provincial cabinet ministers publicly supported Charest, it appeared that Mike Harris had no problem with Preston Manning and the Reform

Party. Whatever positive effect the endorsements produced surely was negated by an erroneous press report in the second last week that Jean Charest regularly sought the advice of Brian Mulroney.

Ten days before the vote, Reform ran a graphic television spot focussing on the national unity issue and Quebec politicians including Jean Charest. For a few days there was no reaction from the Tories but in the latter half of the last week Charest accused Manning of "bigotry." In his last campaign stop in Ontario, in Markham, the leader devoted all of his speech to the national unity question and spoke not one word about *Let the Future Begin*. That week, as strategists looked at the stalled then falling numbers for the party, they debated and rejected a proposal not to go into Ontario in the last week and to go to western Canada instead. In Quebec, voter interest in the Tories, which started in the week after the debate, began to falter, and there was little organizational capacity to mobilize whatever support the party had. Certainly, there was a considerable drop in Conservative voting intentions in Quebec polls released on the second last weekend of the campaign to the actual vote received on election day. White interpreted the last week as "the big squeeze." Reform, desperate to be the Official Opposition, played to anti-Quebec sentiments with its "Quebec-based politicians" commercial. The Liberals, with Chrétien's statement that he would not accept a "50-per-cent-plus-one" result, polarized opinion in Quebec and hurt the Conservatives as soft nationalists returned to the Bloc Québécois which eagerly exploited one of the few good things that had come its way.[26]

Conclusion

The Progressive Conservative Party did better in the 1997 election than many would have imagined prior to the election, but not as well as the campaign itself promised. The campaign's main events — Charest's sparkling performance in the debates and the playing out of the national unity issue in the last weeks of the campaign — were not handled in such a way as to bring "soft Liberals" into the Tory column. Instead of keeping to the plan — focussing on the platform's themes of jobs, health care, education, and tax cuts — by the end of the campaign the party was embroiled in a running feud with Preston Manning over the national unity issue. The party's weakness was that national unity, despite being Mr. Charest's passion and one of his strengths, was not the kind of issue that attracted a large number of voters to them, given the negative public feelings about the national unity initiatives (the Meech Lake and Charlottetown agreements) of the previous Conservative government. For some voters the prospect of a minority government, with either the Bloc or Reform as the official opposition, was sufficiently unpalatable that voting Liberal was their best course. Generally, the Tories were unable to move away from the memory of Mulroney and did not offer enough to dissuade large number of voters from voting Liberal.

In the post-election period, Conservatives comforted themselves with the knowledge that, in Ontario and Quebec, they had polled about one million more votes than had Reform; that Jean Charest had much greater popular appeal than had any other opposition party leader; and that their official standing in the House of Commons would lead to greater visibility and financial resources than had been afforded them after the 1993 election. The campaign's fundraising appeals had met projections as a result of a heavy inflow of donations in the post-debate period. Overall, however, because of less-than-projected revenue in early 1997, the party was looking at a post-election debt of about $6 million compared to the break-even situation predicted when the budget was presented to its National Council in March. The party's better showing resulted in considerably fewer candidates (109) losing their deposits and not receiving election expense rebates than in 1993 (144). Most of the improvement occurred in the province of Quebec.

In the end, the Tories experienced a middling result. The party avoided extinction. But its main competitor, the Reform Party of Canada, was not only stronger, but became the Official Opposition party. The Conservative caucus is now anchored by a large contingent of Atlantic-based MPs with political attitudes apparently less right-wing than the platform on which they ran (and the party has to contemplate the possibility that the platform moved many Atlantic voters looking for change away from them to the New Democratic Party). In some parts of the country, talk of merger with Reform is inevitably in the air as partisans ponder the unappetizing prospect of a third election with the PCs and Reform fighting each other. But, with Jean Charest and Preston Manning holding disparate views on the national unity issue, such a merger seems very unlikely as long as both lead their parties.

While the prospects for the Conservatives in the West are not likely to improve significantly by the time of the next election, Reform's big move into central Canada, especially Ontario, has failed. Although the contest between Reform and the Progressive Conservatives is more than the "fight for the right" portrayed in much of the media, nonetheless there are important ideological and spatial factors underlying the 1997 election results. Canadians in Atlantic Canada and Quebec clearly chose the Tories over Reform; Western Canadians just as clearly aligned themselves with Reform. But Ontario, with its massive number of Liberal seats, was a saw-off for the two right-wing parties, as it had been in 1993, with the Tories this time feeling better — but only a little — about things than did Reform. Given the regional strengths and weaknesses of the two parties, each must look to Ontario for electoral gains in the next election. Failing a merger, it appears that the Progressive Conservative and Reform parties face another knockout round before they — and Canadians — know which party can seriously challenge the Liberals.

Notes

[1] I am indebted to the many people who were interviewed in the preparation of this essay. Those who asked not to be quoted have had their confidence respected. A number of people were willing to be identified and my gratitude is evident in their appearance in the essay. I am grateful to The Strategic Counsel Inc. for allowing access to their election surveys. The author attended many election post-mortems, as well as every national meeting of the party between 1993 and 1997. His wife was the Progressive Conservative candidate in the riding of Kitchener-Waterloo. Statements of fact or interpretation are my responsibility.

[2] See Peter Woolstencroft, "The Progressive Conservative Party of Canada, 1984-1993: Government, Party, Members," in Hugh Thorburn, ed., *Party Politics in Canada*, 7th edition (Scarborough: Prentice-Hall, 1995), 280-303.

[3] *Ibid*, 298.

[4] John Courtney, *Do Conventions Matter?: Choosing National Party Leaders in Canada*, (Montréal: McGill-Queen's University Press, 1995), 255.

[5] Quoted in John Courtney, *Do Conventions Matter?*, 264.

[6] Although the financial situation was operationally very pressing, the party's situation was eased by the existence of the Bracken Trust (between 3 and 4 million dollars). While not available for operating expenses, it provided collateral for the party's borrowing.

[7] *Constitution*, Progressive Conservative Party of Canada, April 1995, Section 8.

[8] *Ibid*, section 5.

[9] An important distinction was drawn between "policy, developing our positions on major issues and the subject of this material, and platform — the specific programs and initiatives by which the policy will be implemented — which should follow policy development." *Developing a Conservative Agenda for Canadians: Asking the Right Questions*, Working Document # 1 (August 1995), 4.

[10] *Report*, Policy Advisory Committee (July 1996), 26-8.

[11] One measure of party activity is completion of the constituency reorganization process after the 1996 electoral redistribution. By the end of February, 1997, 59 of 301 PC constituency associations were not organized; 51 were in Quebec.

[12] Rod Phillips, interview, July 21, 1997. Mr. Phillips was co-chair of the Ontario campaign.

[13] Financial constraints precluded engaging a full complement of political organizers. It was not until the late fall that people in the party began to think that a spring election was highly likely.

[14] In election post-mortems, participants in general expressed their satisfaction with the structure of the campaign, and there was interest in developing sub-provincial campaign committees for the next election.

[15] Other people centrally involved in the writing of the Tory platform were John Williamson, active in the party's youth wing; Gary McKeever, a party vice-president from Ontario; John Perenack, a business associate of Noble's; and Mark Mullins, a private sector economist, who had been closely associated with the 1995 Tory election campaign in Ontario.

[16] See Peter Woolstencroft, "Reclaiming the 'Pink Palace': the Ontario Progressive Conservative Party Comes in from the Cold," in Graham White, ed., *Government and Politics of Ontario*, fifth edition, 1997 (Toronto: University of Toronto Press), 365-403.

[17] Leslie Noble, interview, June 26, 1997.

[18] Leslie Noble, interview, June 26, 1987.

[19] Jodi White, interview, July 21, 1997.

[20] Jodi White, interview, July 30, 1997.

[21] The Strategic Counsel Inc., *A Presentation to The Toronto Star and CFTO Television, Election 1997, Survey #1*, May 24, 1997.

[22] Jodi White, interview, July 30, 1997.

[23] Leslie Noble, interview, June 26, 1997.

[24] Jodi White, interview, July 30.

[25] Jodi White, interview, July 30, 1997; two of the commercials were carryovers from the party's pre-election advertising campaign; figures for other parties come from *Marketing Magazine*, June 23, 1997 which reported that the Tories ran 17 commercials.

[26] Jodi White, interview, July 30, 1997.

Five

Alexa McDonough and Atlantic Breakthrough for the New Democratic Party
by Alan Whitehorn

The federal elections of 1988 and 1993 were the best and the worst of times for the New Democratic Party.[1] Whereas the veteran parliamentarian Ed Broadbent had guided the NDP to its electoral peak in 1988, the 1993 campaign under the leadership of Audrey McLaughlin, a new and largely untested federal leader, produced the party's worst ever result. In votes, the NDP was a dismal fifth place, with most ridings in Canada giving the party less than the 15 per cent required to receive financial reimbursement. Every single province had seen a decline in the NDP vote. Perhaps most significantly, the NDP also dropped below the threshold number of seats necessary to be recognized as an official party in Parliament. The NDP was left with only a Western rump of 9 MPs.

Since the NDP had been created to overcome the limited appeal and skewed regional profile of the CCF, many began to reconsider the party's future after the 1993 result. Massive layoffs at the party headquarters occurred and urgent meetings were held concerning the party's grave financial crisis. The leader and her staff were criticized extensively, and McLaughlin eventually resigned. A new leader would be selected, but who would chose to run and what format would be employed? Organizationally, it was not clear how well the NDP could rebuild in Central Canada. Bob Rae's provincial NDP government (1990–95), with its controversial social contract legislation, had alienated trade union allies and precipitated major divisions within the labour movement. After the NDP's federal election setback in 1993, the Canadian Labour Congress, one of the founding partners in the creation of the NDP, began an election post-mortem and commenced a formal re-assessment of its relationship with the party.[2]

There was a consensus that the federal NDP was in crisis,[3] and that any possible political recovery would require major reassessment. Accordingly, commencing in 1994[4] a number of broadly-based renewal conferences were launched to examine socialist ideology, the party's platform and organization, and its ties to various social movements.

In step with the mood of renewal and in an effort to generate much needed publicity and funds, the NDP opted in 1995 for an untried, hybrid, two-step process of leadership selection. While a number of other provincial parties had experimented with new leadership selection procedures,[5] this was the first attempt by any party at the federal level and possessed the added complication of involving both individual and affiliated NDP members. It combined a non-binding, direct ballot primary and convention. The unique two-step approach involved first a direct ballot in five regional primaries which were open to all NDP constituency members and one national primary amongst affiliated union members. The combined result would determine the threshold for entry into the leadership convention in Ottawa. Of the four candidates (left intellectual Herschel Hardin, former Nova Scotia provincial leader Alexa McDonough, former Saskatchewan MP Lorne Nystrom, and BC maverick MP Svend Robinson), McDonough would prove to be victorious, becoming the party's first federal leader from Atlantic Canada.

Alexa McDonough was an experienced and highly respected provincial leader from Nova Scotia. Her family's political roots dated from the early CCF era. Her father had been a legendary figure, a factory owner supporting the socialist movement in Atlantic Canada. Many party veterans and strategists had hoped previously that McDonough would contest the 1989 leadership race, which she might have won. For personal reasons, she had declined to run at that time. By 1995, however, she was prepared to leave Nova Scotia and move onto the national stage.

Despite McDonough's extensive legislative experience, the harsh reality was that she had no experience in the federal Parliament. She was also handicapped in coming from one of the weaker sections of the party. However, as a region with Canada's highest levels of unemployment and poverty, it was a potential area of growth for the NDP, unrealized so far.[6] In addition, after Audrey McLaughlin's tenure as leader, many activists, particularly males, speculated whether the party and the electorate at large were willing to embrace another female federal leader.

The federal NDP's prospects in the last two elections have been greatly affected by the popularity or lack thereof of NDP provincial governments. The provincial victories in Ontario in 1990 and British Columbia and Saskatchewan in 1991 meant that in the early 1990s half of the country's population had provincial social democratic governments. Initially, these victories seemed an asset, but the mounting unpopularity of the Rae government in Ontario[7] and the Harcourt government in British Columbia hindered Audrey McLaughlin's efforts as federal leader in the 1993 federal campaign. By contrast, the popularity of the Romanow government assisted the federal NDP in collecting 5 of its total 9 seats in Saskatchewan.

Prior to the 1997 federal election, all three NDP provincial governments went to the polls. In 1995, Bob Rae's NDP government was soundly defeated, but the loss did not heal fully the wounds amongst party and union activists. The fiscally prudent Romanow government, by contrast, cruised to yet another Saskatchewan NDP victory in 1995. In BC, Premier Harcourt was unable to adequately handle a financial scandal which had involved the party over a decade earlier. Harcourt's indecision and growing unpopularity led him to announce his resignation.[8] His successor, Glen Clark, was able to win the provincial election in May 1996, but not without subsequent controversy and decline in public support over the twin issues of honesty and accuracy of government finances. Within a few short months the Clark government became a liability for federal NDP election prospects in British Columbia. On a positive note, the election of Piers McDonald and his colleagues in September, 1996 saw the NDP form the government in the Yukon territory.

After McDonough's narrow leadership victory, there was considerable pressure by the media and even party activists for her to seek a seat in Parliament as soon as possible. When Deputy Prime Minister Sheila Copps resigned over her credibility on the GST, a by-election was called in Hamilton East for June 1996, but McDonough chose not to run so far from her home base. Nevertheless, the NDP placed a strong second, campaigning in opposition to the GST and for fairer taxation.[9] Meanwhile, the NDP won her old provincial riding of Halifax-Fairview with 65 per cent of the vote. While national polls still had the NDP much lower than the governing Liberals, the NDP was showing signs of being competitive with most of the other parties, a significant improvement from 1993.

NDP election organization and committee structure

Normally, between NDP conventions, the Federal Executive and Federal Council are the principal decision-making bodies of the party. Technically, the Strategy and Election Planning Committee (SEPC) is a committee of the Federal Executive. However, immediately prior to an election campaign, the SEPC becomes the pre-eminent organ of the party. Working closely with its working group and platform committees, the SEPC designs the strategic election plan. The implementation of the plan is left to the federal secretary, operating as the campaign director, and senior party staff.

In preparation for the 1997 campaign, the SEPC was composed of the chair, the party leader, two associate chairs, all members of the federal executive including the federal treasurer and the federal secretary, an MP representing caucus, the principal secretary to the leader, CLC political action director, chairs of the POVM (Participation of Visible Minorities), Aboriginal, POW (women) and Youth committees for a total of about 35 persons. The SEPC started preparing for the campaign just over a year before the election was called, meeting four times in total. Given the size of the full SEPC and the diverse regional composition of the committee, it is not surprising that a smaller body existed, almost all of whom were members of the SEPC proper. The Working Group involved about 18 persons, with federal staff from Ottawa assigned to assist. This group met more frequently to plan the campaign and oversee the operation once the election began. The Platform Committee, a sub-committee of the SEPC, culled the hundreds of resolutions passed at previous party conventions, and strove to draft a coherent policy platform that would maximize the party's electoral appeal. Its key publication was a 53 page document entitled A Framework for Canada's Future, a draft of which had been presented to the party's federal convention in Regina.

During the actual campaign, a series of groups supervised and, where necessary, modified the election strategy. At the pinnacle of the decision-making hierarchy was the inner circle of campaign strategists (federal secretary, SEPC chair and co-chairs, and various section directors) who met early each morning. The SEPC Working Group, often involving many individuals from the daily group, met once a week for several hours each Saturday afternoon, to assess the previous week's events and plan the next. The committee discussed modification to the leader's tour, daily tracking of polling results, focus group findings, ongoing testing of campaign slogans and phrasing, the final changes of the ads and when to replace one round of ads with subsequent ones, and preparations for the leaders' debates.

NDP election finances and party income

On the eve of the campaign,[10] the proposed budget was $6 million, lower than 1993 by about $1.5 million, and even 1988. Increasingly, the largest expense for a political party in modern elections is for mass advertising. The NDP media budget for 1997 was set at $1.5 million. In the recent past, the largest amount of NDP advertising has been allocated to the powerful medium of television (ranging from 58 per cent to 80 per cent over the years 1979 to 1988)[11] and 1997 was no different. The leader's tour, the second largest portion of the campaign budget, was projected to cost $1.05 million. The remainder of the campaign expenditures were primarily for public opinion research and organization. Funds for the campaign were to be raised in the following manner: central rebate ($1.35 million), labour ($1.1 million),[12] riding rebate ($900,000), direct mail ($600,000), non-cash goods and services ($2.05 million).[13]

Polling

In 1993, polling had been directed by the Winnipeg-based Viewpoints Research. That company had been instrumental in the NDP provincial electoral victories in Ontario in 1990 and BC in 1991. However, the ill-fated 1993 federal campaign broke the company's string of successes, and after the death of Dave Gotthilf, the co-founder of Viewpoints, the NDP selected another polling firm to guide the 1997 campaign. Jim Matsui of Comquest had polled for the Ontario and Saskatchewan NDP, both in power on the eve of the 1995 provincial elections. Reflecting the smaller overall campaign budget, about $350,000 (a considerable amount of the $200,000 pre-election budget) was allocated for survey research in 1997. This was a significant decline from 1993 ($525,000).[14]

NDP election polling fell into two categories. The baseline surveys conducted prior to the campaign (commencing in the fall of 1996) tended to be more in-depth and were designed to build a national data base from which comparisons could be made at a later time. Amongst the topics explored were voting intentions, party identification, perceptions of the parties and party leaders and ranking of issues. During the campaign itself, the party opted for shorter surveys, posing questions regarding party standings, the evaluations of leaders, most salient/effective messages and phrasing, and the viability of party commercials and literature.

Given the very tight budget constraints of the party, polling commenced later and was less extensive than in the past with a rolling sample of 200 persons daily. In addition, a modest attempt was made during the campaign to poll nationally for two consecutive days each week to provide a rough overview of the Canadian electorate at large. Because the 1997 election of necessity focused on re-achieving official party status (i.e. 12 seats), the surveys conducted during the campaign targetted the ridings in which the NDP was thought to be competitive. These included incumbent ridings and others selected as most promising (e.g. the seats previously held between 1988 and 1993 and seats where there had been strong provincial successes and potential carry over to the federal level).[15]

Over time the total number of ridings selected for polling declined. The most dramatic adjustment occurred after the full impact of the leaders' debates was assessed; at that time the number was cut by half to 26, with larger samples drawn from this narrower band of ridings. Growing support for the NDP in Atlantic Canada and Nova Scotia, in particular, gradually led the party to poll more in this region. In the last week, the number of different questions posed was also reduced, thus enabling the sample in each riding to become even larger (50 to 80 per day) and more accurate.

In addition to conducting mass surveys, the NDP made use of small focus groups in selected cities (e.g. Vancouver, Saskatoon, Regina, Winnipeg, and Halifax)[16] where participants were drawn into discussion about party ads and where the various arguments for and against voting NDP were tested. The computer-assisted predictive dialing system used in the 1993 federal campaign was not repeated in 1997;[17] instead a more traditional telephone bank operation was employed to both monitor opinions and persuade voters in key ridings.

NDP strategy

The disappearance of Social Credit from the House of Commons by the 1980s left the Western protest vote by default to the NDP. However, with the birth of the right-wing Reform Party, the NDP, like its predecessor the CCF, was once more challenged by another Western populist party. Increasingly political allegiance in the West has appeared to shift to the Reform Party. Part of the Reform Party's strategy was to contrast itself with the "three old-line parties" (i.e. the New Democratic Party was no longer portrayed as "New"). Given that the bulk of NDP incumbent seats were in the West, the Reform Party was a formidable foe for the NDP. Nevertheless, post-1993 election analysis had reported that most of the NDP vote in that election had drifted to the Liberals.[18] Accordingly, the NDP chose to target Liberal voters in the 1997 campaign. NDP polling showed that the greatest potential expansion of NDP support would be among "soft" Liberal voters. The budget cutbacks by the Chrétien government made the Liberals vulnerable to a social democratic critique. In addition the NDP targetted women, labour, youth, and members of multicultural communities.

In some ways the 1997 campaign strategy was a continuation of the last days of the party's 1993 campaign. The NDP was still fighting for official party status in Parliament, and the goal was quite straightforward — to win at least 12 seats this time. Only six incumbents chose to run again. Just prior to the campaign, the NDP labelled 46 ridings as either priority "A" (incumbent or must win) or "B" (potential gain). Of these, 12 were located in BC, 8 in Saskatchewan, 7 in Manitoba, 1 in the Yukon for a total of 28 in the West, where the party had traditionally been strong. By contrast, only 12 were in Ontario, where the greatest number of seats were available and where the largest number of affiliated unions were located. Given McDonough's roots in Atlantic Canada, 6 ridings were targetted in Nova Scotia and 1 in Newfoundland.[19] No priority ridings were listed for Alberta, Quebec, PEI, or initially New Brunswick. The latter is ironic given that the NDP won two seats in the province. By the end of the campaign, the number of targetted ridings was reduced to 26 (largely the "A" priority ridings, except for Saskatchewan where "B" ridings were also included). Party strategists focused their resources in ridings where there was the best hope of success.

In candidate selection, the federal NDP reiterated its priority to implement its mandatory affirmative action plan for women and visible minorities. Led by its second feminist leader, the federal NDP nominated far more women (107) than any other party. Eight would be successful, all newly elected.

Those planning the campaign were confronted with several image problems. The first was that relatively few voters recognized the NDP's new leader and even fewer listed her as their top choice for prime minister.[20] In the 1988 federal campaign, the NDP had been able to tap the popularity of its veteran leader, Ed Broadbent. In 1997, as in 1993, the NDP had a new female leader who was not very well known. One question lingered: "Would Alexa McDonough perform as poorly as her predecessor Audrey McLaughlin?" To make matters worse, some members of the public still confused the two female leaders.

The lack of Official Party status and a small caucus in Parliament had contributed to the party's weak performance in the House of Commons and low media profile over the past three and a half years. Given low leader recognition and low party standings (11 per cent in the NDP's own baseline update in February), the NDP was forced to place more emphasis on the local candidates.[21] In effect, the NDP planned its campaign as 48 by-elections. However, unlike the Reform Party, it ran a full slate of candidates.

Given the sustained high rate of unemployment, the issue of jobs was ranked by Canadians as most important. For the NDP, job creation was a better economic issue than the debt. Nevertheless, NDP polling found that the topic of job creation worked best when tied to a medley of issues (e.g. concerns about government cuts to health care and education) that concerned left-leaning Liberals and social democrats. In contrast to 1988, no NDP strategist in 1997 spoke of a major campaign in Quebec. The party was quite vulnerable on the issue of national unity and sought to focus on other topics wherever possible. This strategy did, however, make it more difficult to challenge the Reform Party's stand on national unity.

Advertising

The advertising campaign was co-ordinated by Vancouver-based Now Communications, headed by Ron Johnson and Dennis McGann. One of the first tasks the advertising team completed was to change the party's logo to one which utilized the Canadian flag and the party's acronym. Given the NDP's small advertising budget of only $1.5 million (down from $3 million in 1988 and $3.28 million in 1993),[22] the campaign was frugal and more regionally focused than in the past. The largest sum of TV advertising ($578,000) was earmarked for British Columbia, the second largest ($371,000) for Ontario, with Atlantic Canada receiving $184,000. Initially, no TV ads were planned for Alberta, Quebec or New Brunswick. According to government regulations, no ads are allowed in the first week. The NDP purchased some ads in the second week, employed most of its free time telecasts in the third week, and sought its heaviest buy in the last week. In line with its strategy to target primarily soft Liberal voters, the first NDP television ad entitled "Snores" employed a newscaster's voice outlining high bank profits, unemployment and continuing corporate tax loopholes against a backdrop of snoring MPs. The final message was to vote NDP "this time" and "wake up the Liberals". The amusing ad sought to grab media attention and make the party appear competitive. The TV ad was accompanied by a related pamphlet distributed to households. Continuing the anti-Liberal theme, the "Wrong Crowd" suggested that Liberals were running with too many right-wingers and cutting programs too much. "What You Got" was also a negative ad pointing out the 1993 Liberal Red Book's promises, but noting their subsequent cuts to education and health care, continued high unemployment, and a Liberal government acting more like the Conservative and Reform parties. When the Liberal Party tried to counter suggesting it was, in fact, a defender of Canada's medicare system, the NDP responded with "Health Care" which reminded the viewers of the historic Liberal cuts. In "Priorities" the NDP suggested that if government could set targets for reducing the deficit, it should also do so for unemployment.

Whereas the NDP's primary national target in 1997 was the Liberal Party, NDP strategists belatedly expressed growing concern about the Reform Party in the West. Accordingly, a television ad for BC and Saskatchewan was hastily made warning that the Reform Party is too extreme. "No Wonder" suggested that the Reform Party favoured tax breaks for the rich, a two-tier US-style health care system and the abolition of the Canada Pension Plan. As in 1993, the NDP strategy seemed somewhat tardy in addressing the potential loss of Western NDP votes to the Reform Party.

Historically, campaigns often try to end on a positive note. "Social Conscience" reminded Canadians that as a people we have a social conscience and that Parliament needed one too. In addition to paid advertising, Canadian parties are allowed free-time telecasts. "Your Canada" was a blend of an inspirational speech by Alexa McDonough from the NDP federal convention in Regina, combined with positive colourful images of the different regions of Canada. It reminded Canadians that while the NDP never formed the federal government, it always made a difference.

Several possible weaknesses in the long range campaign strategy existed. One was the polling-based assumption that the Liberals should remain the primary focus of its campaign. As a result, the Western-based Reform Party was ignored far too long. The NDP's 1997 campaign was intended to have a large Western component, but ironically the campaign proved more effective in the East. One reason for this was the fact that the Liberals as the primary target were more vulnerable in the East where they had more seats. Near the end of the campaign the party relied extensively on local radio ads in Nova Scotia, the area where the party did best. This suggests the utility of greater use of radio, particularly in an era of fragmented television markets.

The NDP campaign and the leader's tour

Given the low profile of the NDP over the previous several years, the pre-election campaign was even more important than usual, hence the rationale for attempting to hold a federal convention in Regina on the eve of the federal election. Despite the financial and labour costs for the party headquarters, local ridings and affiliated unions, the convention was seen as a key national media forum for the relatively unknown Alexa McDonough. Because of the importance of the leader to modern campaigns, the leader's tour was perceived as a major vehicle for communicating the party's national election message. Usually, in a federal election the party leader endeavours to travel to as many regions as possible in order to give the party the greatest media profile. However, given the low expectations for the NDP, the 1997 tour was targetted to the priority regions and ridings. Initially, the party considered not chartering a jet to save money, but the logistics proved impractical.

Ontario had 103 seats; the leaders' debates were to be held in Ottawa; national media interviews often were done in Toronto or Ottawa; and the SEPC working group was based in Ottawa. Therefore, McDonough spent the largest amount of her time in Ontario. Nevertheless, like the Reform Party, the NDP would end up with zero seats in this key province. Since the new leader's home riding was in Nova Scotia, not surprisingly the tour spent more time in that province than had past NDP campaigns. The electoral results suggest the wisdom of that choice to McDonough as both leader and candidate. Due to historic flood levels in Manitoba, she visited that province only in the later half of the campaign and less than planned given the party's optimistic goals there. The time allocated to Quebec, with one quarter of Canada's population, was virtually non-existent. The party was fighting for its survival and attention was focused where there were realistic goals of electing MPs.

This campaign was marked by several changes from the past that would affect the leader's tour. First, it was a shorter campaign (36 days vs. previously 47). The second was that there was more media pooling due to financial cutbacks amongst the press. As a result, fewer media personnel were aboard the leader's tour. Echoing a format employed in the last BC provincial election, CBC Newsworld introduced a daily live press conference for each of the parties. In a sense, the entire campaign period would see a morning debate amongst key party spokespersons; the NDP increasingly used this forum for its leader. Throughout the campaign, the party produced two internal daily publications: "In the News" was a summary of the media coverage, while "The Campaign Daily", sent out to all candidates, was the party's spin on the day's events.

The first week of the campaign (April 28–May 4) saw the release of an Environics poll which placed the NDP at 11 per cent and in 4th position. McDonough lagged behind her party and was selected by only 7 per cent of the public as best person to be prime minister. While "jobs" was by far the top issue, national unity reappeared as the second (at 14 per cent), and was a potentially catalyzing issue, particularly between Reform in the

West and the other parties. McDonough suggested that instead of Plan A or B, Plan C, based on "compassion" and "caring" were essential to win over Quebec. However, the NDP did not wish to emphasize the national unity issue because this topic was less effective than "jobs" in gaining support for the party.

McDonough opened the campaign asserting that under the Liberals Canadians were worse off. She noted that it was the longest extended period of high unemployment since the 1930s and was highly critical of the cuts to unemployment insurance. She also listed the broken Liberal Red Book promises. By contrast, the NDP's vision for Canadian society was outlined on May Day in a 53 page booklet *A Framework For Canada's Future*, a detailed blueprint calling for significant cuts in unemployment, greater government spending on social programs, expansion of medicare to include prescription drugs and home care, eliminating child poverty, and closing of tax-loopholes so that corporations, banks and the wealthy, paid their fair share (e.g. establishing a minimum corporate tax). It advocated a halt to the harmonization of the GST with provincial sales taxes and proposed the gradual phasing-out of the GST. Based on higher rates of employment, the analysis projected a better deficit reduction rate. 100,000 copies of a two-page summary version of the "Framework" were distributed at the same time, and about 30 "Fact Sheets" on a variety of topics were also issued. In contrast to the past several years, the party received a reasonable amount of media attention, and at the end of the week, commentators generally believed that the new NDP leader had done well. The long awaited Labour Party victory in the UK was perhaps a positive omen, as might be the victory of French socialists later in the campaign.

Week two (May 5–11) saw McDonough criticize the Liberals for cuts in an area where historically the Liberals have been praised, health care. She also pointed out that the Liberals had been excessively generous to foreign multinational companies possessing drug monopolies. News that the unemployment rate had climbed to 9.6 led McDonough to point out a corresponding rise in bank profits. Noting the growth in child poverty, she claimed the Liberals were making the wrong choices about our future. Much of the week, however, focused on former Quebec Premier Parizeau's statement about a Unilateral Declaration of Independence (UDI) had a "yes" vote occurred. National unity still dominated much of the newscasts, to the NDP's chagrin.

The most important events of week three (May 12–18) were the leaders' debates. Unlike in previous elections, the debates occurred quite early and the English language debate preceded the French one. In the 1980s the NDP had shared the TV spotlight with only the Liberals and

Conservatives. Parity in television status was a major factor in the growth of NDP support in that era. From 1993 onward, the Reform Party and the BQ participated in the leaders' debates and this meant the NDP was not guaranteed even third party status. The dynamics of a five-leader debate greatly lessened the likelihood of the NDP achieving a knockout blow.

The May 12 English language debate was extremely important for the NDP, and strategists hoped that McDonough, as an experienced provincial leader, would perform as well as she had at a recent CBC Townhall meeting. The debate was divided into five segments and party officials hoped that Chrétien would be vulnerable on the jobs issue. In her opening statement McDonough suggested that there were two different visions for the country. She indicated that jobs were not the priority of the male leaders to her political right. McDonough appeared a bit nervous in the opening round and made several verbal slips. She did better when the talk turned to health care and social programs; she noted with dismay that Liberals, despite past election promises, cut program spending like Tories and Reformers. On the topic of the economy, she showed a copy of the "Alternate Budget" as an example of a more responsible economic path. Later, she was questioned on an error in the party's newly released platform document. Unfortunately, the effectiveness of her verbal comments were undercut by the fact that she had spilled ink over one hand. It was a distracting visual image. Things did not improve when the all important topic of national unity arose. Manning accused Chrétien of almost blowing the referendum while McDonough chose to talk about jobs and social programs as a way to lessen the country's divisions. Charest, however, stole the show with his passionate pledge to his children to make the country work. The NDP, by contrast, appeared almost irrelevant on the national unity debate.[23] However, in the last segment on Parliamentary representation, McDonough reminded Canadians that the NDP has always made a difference. In her closing statement, McDonough continued her attack on the Liberal record and reminded viewers that in the last election they didn't vote for cuts to social programs, high unemployment, and Reform and Conservative policies. She implored the listeners "To vote NDP this time".

The French language debate occurred the next night, so there was little time to prepare. McDonough had made great strides in learning French, but she was still not fluently bilingual, and thus was at a significant disadvantage. The main focus was on the three Quebec-based leaders. Manning, so adamant in denying distinct society for Quebec, demanded and got special status to speak primarily in English. By contrast, McDonough spoke entirely in French, a fact that was positively noted in the French media. The NDP leader was seen as a distant finisher in the

French debate, though it was far less important than her placement in the English debate. However, the main image of the evening was the dramatic collapse of the moderator and the postponement of the much anticipated segment on national unity. This had the result of prolonging the media pre-occupation with national unity, a topic NDP strategists had sought to avoid. When the debate resumed, McDonough tried to point out that Canadian unity must involve other issues such as social programs, jobs, and common values.

By most accounts, McDonough did not excel in the key English debate (see Chapter Eleven of this volume). Post-debate public opinion polls showed that NDP support had dropped to 10 per cent. More ominously, internal NDP polling also showed a significant decline in the party's priority ridings. To make matters worse, the candidate had lost her voice. However, like the veteran politician she was, she pressed on.

Week four (May 19–25) witnessed a greater intensity and effectiveness in the language employed by McDonough. Manning too opted to be more forceful in his comments, and at one point challenged Chrétien and Charest to debate as a threesome on the issue of Canadian unity. To leave out the BQ and the NDP seemed the height of arrogance, hardly in keeping with his proclaimed populist style. McDonough responded by suggesting that Manning would lead Canada to civil war. On May 22, the Reform Party commenced to air its highly controversial "anti-Quebec ad" which many, including McDonough, perceived to be racist. To add fuel to the nationalist fire, Chrétien stated he would not accept a "50 per cent+1" referendum vote as the basis for the breakup of Canada. The topic of Quebec was centre stage and the Reform Party was setting much of the agenda by focusing on the "hot buttons" of national unity.

Attempting to redirect political debate to the NDP's preferred agenda, McDonough shouted "It's about jobs, stupid." She wondered why the Liberal government would target reducing the deficit, but not unemployment. She called Liberal backbench MPs a "flock of sheep" and cabinet minister Doug Young a "political thug." The tougher language seemed to be more effective in drawing media attention and refocussing the debate back onto the economy and social programs.

As the only female leader, it was deemed imperative for McDonough to participate in the NAC women's televised debate on the CPAC channel in the final week of the campaign. It was the first such debate in thirteen years. Not surprisingly, McDonough did very well and received a standing ovation. She accused the Liberals of abandoning national standards for social programs and fostering the feminization of poverty.

She added that the other parties suffered from "deficit dementia." The closing NDP ads reminded the viewers that the Liberals had not kept their Red Book promises and that the previous Parliament had suffered from the lack of a strong presence of NDP MPs. The NDP campaign wound up with a traditional major rally in Windsor attended by many NDP notables. A final poll showed the NDP at 11 per cent,[24] exactly the same as on the eve of the election. Would it be enough to win 12 seats and regain official party status?

Election results and analysis

On June 2, the NDP rebounded and did so in a manner and degree which surprised many commentators. While it did not equal its best ever showing of 1988, it did win 21 seats with its 11 per cent of the vote. Despite a lower vote than the Conservative Party once again, the regional bias and quirks in our electoral system led to the NDP to remain ahead of the Conservatives in Parliament with a fourth place finish. The increase from 7 per cent to 11 per cent of the vote was the highest increase of any party. This fact, combined with more than doubling their seats and regaining official party status, meant the campaign was a success overall. However, there were some disappointments, particularly in Ontario and the West.

Of the 21 victorious NDP candidates, Nova Scotia led the way with six out of a possible 11 seats (taking all of the metropolitan Halifax-Dartmouth region and all of Cape Breton).[25] McDonough achieved a resounding personal victory, and along the way NDP candidates defeated two high profile Liberal cabinet ministers, Doug Young and David Dingwall (both vulnerable due to federal government cuts to the unemployment insurance program). The two seats won in New Brunswick (in Acadia) were a first for the federal NDP. Together the gains in these two Atlantic provinces marked a long-awaited historic breakthrough for the NDP in a region with such high unemployment.

To the West, Manitoba provided 4 seats, an increase of three,[26] British Columbia 3 seats, a gain of only one, and Saskatchewan with 5 seats, remained unchanged. Following McLaughlin's departure from Parliament,[27] the NDP narrowly retained its Yukon seat. These Western gains were a disappointment compared to initial expectations. Sixteen of the NDP's targetted seats in the West were won by the Reform Party and only two by the Liberals. By contrast, all of the NDP's targetted ridings lost in the East (mostly Ontario ridings) were won by Liberals, an enduring legacy of Bob Rae's NDP government and its social contract legislation.

Quebec has always been exceedingly difficult terrain for the CCF–NDP. The presence of two separatist parties with a social democratic stance on social and economic policy (the PQ at the provincial level and the BQ at the federal level) precludes the NDP acquiring the left nationalist protest vote in that province. In contrast to 1988, the NDP ran only a token campaign in Quebec in 1997. The stark fact that Quebec federal NDP candidates received just under 2 per cent of the votes cast is an indication of the marginalization of the party in that province. The consequences of this are not limited to Quebec; the lack of a viable presence in Quebec undermines the party's stature nationally and its ability to project a distinct social democratic perspective on the key issue of national unity.

The 1997 campaign, like the 1993, owed a great deal to the involvement of organized labour (e.g. New Brunswick) and the outcome saw almost half of the elected NDP MPs have some formal union background. This may well be the highest ratio of unionists elected to the federal caucus. It is also probably a sign of the growing politicization of labour, reacting against the neo-conservative and neo-liberal agendas of governing parties. As the party most committed to affirmative action (with 107 female candidates) and the only federal party to have had two female leaders, 8 of the 21 elected NDP members are women. It is the best ratio achieved in the federal party's history.[28] All, including the leader, were newly elected and half come from Atlantic Canada.

Acquiring 15 per cent of the vote in any constituency is a crucial plateau necessary to receive financial reimbursement. Most ridings in Canada gave the NDP less than 15 per cent of the vote. Still, the party significantly increased (from 48 in 1993 to 87 in 1997)[29] the number of ridings where the party qualified for financial reimbursement. This will help the party financially in the difficult post-election period.

Conclusion

The primary goals of the 1997 NDP campaign were to regain official party status and elect the new leader Alexa McDonough to Parliament; both were achieved. In addition, the party made historic gains in Atlantic Canada, while increasing slightly its seats in the West. Part of the reason for the success was that during the campaign, the party made significant adjustments organizationally in its focus on winable ridings, concentrating at the end on only two dozen. Despite a smaller budget, the polling in 1997 proved quite effective in targetting these ridings.

While polling data repeatedly suggested that "soft" Liberals were the prime source for potential NDP votes, the party seems to have seriously underestimated in both the 1993 and 1997 elections the growth potential of the Reform vote at the expense of the NDP in the West. In both campaigns, NDP strategists had to develop last minute ads attempting to thwart, not very successfully the rising support for the Reform Party. If there was any doubt in 1993, the 1997 election confirmed that in the West (particularly BC), the NDP has been significantly displaced by the right populist Reform Party.

If gains had been less than expected in the West, the breakthrough in Atlantic Canada was a stunning change in fortune at the other end of the country. The Atlantic region, with Canada's highest rate of unemployment, had been hit hard by the Liberal government's cuts to the unemployment insurance program. The NDP's election message regarding the need for a more activist government committed to creating jobs resonated amongst voters of the region.

As in 1993, the central Canadian industrial heartland of Ontario and Quebec has no federal NDP representation. The NDP was created in 1961 precisely to overcome the limited appeal and skewed regional profile of its predecessor, the CCF. In 1993, two strongly regional parties (the BQ in Quebec and Reform in the West) eclipsed the NDP in seats. The year 1993 witnessed the most dramatic realignment of the party system in Canada's entire history, and the 1997 results echoed those of 1993 — we now have an official five party system and a more Balkanized polity. One obvious consequence of the greater regionalization of representation is that the NDP,[30] like its rivals, will have difficulty reflecting each region in the federation.

In the immediate future, the federal NDP, now having regained official party status, will be able to participate more fully in Question Period. With its expanded caucus, it seems likely that the media will have to pay more attention to the NDP. The 1997 campaign projected Alexa McDonough's image across the country. Prior to the campaign she was relatively unknown, but by the end, more viewers recognized and liked her. As with Ed Broadbent in his earlier years, McDonough seems to have the potential to grow in popularity. Unlike her predecessor Audrey McLaughlin, who inherited Broadbent's caucus in 1989, the 1997 NDP federal caucus, with 8 Atlantic MPs, is very much McDonough's. The new MPs from Atlantic Canada owe a great deal to her profile and performance.

Ultimately, the experience of the federal party and that of the NDP provincial governments brings into focus another, and perhaps more crucial, issue facing the NDP. Like so many social democratic parties (e.g. Tony Blair's "new" Labour Party in Britain), the NDP must consider what policy direction to take into the next millennium.[31] On the eve of the new century, social democrats must increasing reflect upon their ideological course and direction. One thing, however, is clear. National unity and the future of Quebec are issues that will not go away. The NDP must address these urgent topics better if it is to have a major say in the survival of the federation.

Notes

[1] I wish to thank the members of the NDP Strategy and Election Planning Committee (SEPC) and the Saturday election working group for allowing me to observe their meetings and who consented to interviews. Many staffers in the federal office provided assistance, and I particularly thank David Woodbury, Peter Julian, Leslie Kerr, Judy Randall, Carmel Belanger, and Audrey Moey who responded to my requests for information, as did Pat Kerwin of the CLC. I am also grateful for funding from the Douglas-Coldwell Foundation.
[2] See Alan Whitehorn, "Some Preliminary Reflections On the Labour Movement and the New Democratic Party," paper presented to the Canadian Labour Congress, Ottawa, 1993; *Report of the CLC-NDP Review Committee* (CLC, Vancouver, 1996); Keith Archer and Alan Whitehorn, *Political Activists: The NDP in Convention* (Toronto, Oxford, 1997) chapter #4.
[3] I. McLeod, *Under Siege: The Federal NDP in the Nineties* (Toronto, Lorimer, 1994).
[4] See Canada's New Democrats, *Ottawa Renewal Conference*, August 27-28, 1994.
[5] See S. Hayward and A. Whitehorn, "Leadership Selection: Which Method?," paper presented to the Douglas Coldwell Foundation, Ottawa, April 1991; Archer and Whitehorn, *Political Activists* #5; J. Courtney, *Do Conventions Matter? Choosing National Political Leaders in Canada* (Montréal\Kingston, McGill Queen's, 1995: 233-253; L. Preyra, "Plebiscitarian Democracy and Party Leadership Selection in Canada" in H. Thorburn, ed., *Party Politics in Canada* (Scarborough, Prentice-Hall, 1996).
[6] The 1996 election of the NDP's first-ever MLA in Prince Edward Island and the fact that as of December 1996 all four Atlantic Canada provincial NDP leaders were sitting members in their respective legislatures attested to a growth in the NDP's electoral prospects in this region, but most

political commentators missed the growing evidence of socialist gains in a once traditional region.

See G. Ehring & W. Roberts, *Giving Away a Miracle: Lost Dreams, Broken Promises and the Ontario NDP* (Oakville, Mosaic, 1993); S. McBride, "The Continuing Crisis of Social Democracy: Ontario's Social Contract" *Studies in Political Economy*, 1996, #50 (summer); P. Monahan, *Storming The Pink Palace: The NDP in Power: A Cautionary Tale* (Toronto, Lester, 1995); L. Panitch & D. Swartz, *The Assault on Trade Union Freedoms: From Wage Controls to Social Contract* (Toronto, Garamond, 1993); B. Rae, *From Protest to Power: Personal Reflections on a Life in Politics* (Toronto, Viking, 1996); T. Walkom, *Rae Days: The Rise and Follies of the NDP* (Toronto, Key Porter, 1994).

[8] See D. Gawthrop, *Highwire Act: Power, Pragmatism, and The Harcourt Legacy* (Vancouver, New Star, 1996), M. Harcourt, *Mike Harcourt: A Measure of Defiance* (Vancouver, Douglas and McIntyre, 1996).

[9] The party conducted a general pre-election campaign campaign and distributed 400,000 "fair tax leaflets" in selected cities.

[10] April 25-26, 1997 SEPC Working Group. At the time of the writing of this chapter, final accounting by the NDP was not complete. Thus the numbers represent only preliminary estimates.

[11] A. Whitehorn, *Canadian Socialism: Essays on the CCF-NDP* (Toronto, Oxford, 1992) p. 216; see also Whitehorn, "Dashed Hopes" in Frizzell et al., *The Canadian General Election of 1988* and Whitehorn, "Quest For Survival" in Frizzell et al., *The Canadian General Election of 1993*.

[12] The Steelworkers, Autoworkers and CUPE were each to donate $100,000. The labour movement had funded the leader's office for much of the critical inter-election period and played a pivotal role in providing guarantees for the election loans. Some estimates had labour providing half the income and volunteer services. It should probably come as no surprise that a party intent on criticizing excessive bank profits has little goodwill amongst the major banks in Canada. Despite a stellar record of paying off its previous election debts, the NDP had significant problems securing bank loans for its campaign both in 1997 and 1993.

[13] The income from the leader's tour was calculated differently in 1997, but was estimated to be $250,000.

[14] Whitehorn, "Dashed Hopes", p. 45; Whitehorn, "Quest For Survival", pp. 45-46.

[15] Almost all of the priority ridings had some daily tracking but there were a few exceptions (eg. Yukon and ridings which were late additions.)

[16] Viewpoints did some additional focus group testing in B.C. However, there was no such testing whatsoever in Montréal, a sign Quebec did not

weigh heavily in the election calculations.

[17] See Whitehorn, "Quest for Survival" p. 47.

[18] Whitehorn, "Quest For Survival"; Pammett, "Tracking the Vote" in Frizzell et al., *The Canadian General Election of 1993*; Archer and Whitehorn, *Political Activists #3*.

[19] The February 1997 regional breakdowns showed that the NDP was not running particularly well even in the priority ridings in British Columbia (19 per cent), Saskatchewan (21 per cent) and Ontario (13 per cent). Only in NS (37 per cent) and Manitoba (34 per cent) did the NDP appear highly competitive. SEPC, Working Group, March 1997.

[20] A Comquest NDP poll in February found that McDonough was selected first by 2-6 per cent in BC, Saskatchewan, Manitoba and Ontario vs. 23 per cent in her home province of Nova Scotia (SEPC, WG, March 10, 1997).

[21] The NDP's initial finding that its candidates were ahead of the party and the leader in popularity was a reversal of normal public opinion literature and past NDP history where the ranking had the local candidate last. (See chapter thirteen in this book.) In Nova Scotia where McDonough was better known and where the greatest level of dissatisfaction with the Liberals was present, the other factors played a greater role.

[22] Whitehorn, "Dashed Hopes" p. 45; Whitehorn, "Quest For Survival", pp. 45-46.

[23] Part of the reason for the NDP's poor profile was the lack of attention to this topic at the renewal conferences.

[24] The best region for the NDP according to public polls were 1) Atlantic at 21 per cent 2) Manitoba/Saskatchewan 20 per cent and BC at 16 per cent. Ontario was at only 11 per cent. Environics, May 25-28, 1997. The same finding emerged in the NDP's polling of its priority ridings.

[25] This was the first time in the entire history of the CCF-NDP the vote was over 100,000 for Nova Scotia. See Whitehorn, *Canadian Socialism*, pp. 262-264.

[26] Most notably former NDP MLA, now Liberal MP, Elijah Harper was defeated by a New Democrat.

[27] She was elected president of the Socialist International Women (SIW).

[28] See *Political Activists* p. 92. More women (64) in general were elected than the previous best of 53 in 1993.

[29] Interview with Peter Julian, Assistant Federal Secretary, July 1997.

[30] See A. Whitehorn, "A Parliament in Bits and Pieces", *Vancouver Sun*, July 10, 1997.

[31] See Whitehorn, *Canadian Socialism*, #9; Archer & Whitehorn, *Political Activists #14*; J. Laxer, *In Search of a New Left: Canadian Politics After the Neo-Conservative Assault* (Toronto, Viking, 1996).

Six

Reform at the Crossroads

by Faron Ellis and Keith Archer

The 1997 federal election results were greeted with mixed emotions by Reformers. On the one hand, the party had achieved its goal of displacing the Bloc Québécois as Canada's official opposition.[1] As a party that was first created in 1987, and one with strong western regional roots, this is no mean feat. On the other hand, Reform fell well short of its goals of winning a majority government, or of making a breakthrough in Ontario. Despite its success in setting the agenda throughout much of the campaign, Reform fared only marginally better in 1997 than in 1993. The 1997 election campaign was successful in enabling Reform to recapture its western base of support, solidifying gains made in 1993 and bringing "back to the fold" many of the supporters who had drifted away during the intervening years between the 1993 and 1997 elections. However, the campaign did not produce any significant inroads into Ontario, the country's electoral linchpin. If anything, Reform emerged from the 1997 election as a party with even more of a Western regional character than it had at the outset. The paradox for the Reform Party is that its position on a single issue — the Quebec question and national unity — contributed both to its strength in the West and its weakness in Ontario. In order to solidify its western base, it seemingly sacrificed its expansionary agenda. Its reward has been to capture the consolation prize of Official Opposition. The cost of doing so, however, is that the first prize of Canadian elections — government status — may have become even more elusive and difficult to achieve in the future. Such are the tradeoffs in Canada's increasingly fragmented and regionalized party system.

Into the 35th parliament

Many of the challenges facing the party at the outset of the campaign can be attributed to its performance during the 35th Parliament. The party was beset by internal disagreement within its first parliamentary caucus, and these had a negative impact on its popular support — in early 1997, Reform had only 11 per cent support in national public opinion polls.[2] Reform's 52 new MPs entered the 35th Parliament declaring that they would act differently than MPs from the traditional parties. Caucus solidarity would be less important than faithful representation of their constituents. At the same time, Reform was determined to expand its electoral base in an effort at becoming a truly national party. Reform leader Preston Manning had the difficult task of brokering between the conflicting agendas the party had set for itself. Manning was often pilloried in the press for the positions expressed by some of his MPs, despite their protestations that they were simply representing what they believed to be majority opinion in their constituencies. When he took action to stem the tide of media criticism, he was often openly criticized by the Reform rank-and-file for appearing to ignore advice from the grassroots membership of his own party. Foreseeing some of the problems that were on the horizon, Reform MP Art Hanger commented that "[Manning's] got a real job on his hands... some of us are rather on the outspoken side."[3]

The tensions between members of the Reform caucus and the party's leadership surfaced early in 1994 when Stephen Harper revealed that Manning was receiving a $31,000 expense allowance from the party after having turned down a government car and other parliamentary perks. When eight other MPs publicly criticized the stipend, Manning was faced with the first test of his ability to lead a parliamentary caucus. The incident proved a catharsis, according to Reform Deputy Leader Deborah Grey, and after a lengthy meeting prior to the opening of the spring Commons session, the party emerged with a more unified public profile. This unity enabled it to become much more effective in Parliament in opposing the government's fiscal policies.

The expense allowance incident was the harbinger of a pattern that would characterize Reform's inter-election performance. The party's MPs would often make public statements from which Manning felt he had to distance himself. Caucus would then meet to sort out their differences and emerge with a greater sense of unity, temporarily performing better in Parliament until another incident arose. By mid-1994 Reformers both in and outside of the caucus were becoming critical of the perceived ineffectiveness of Reform's parliamentary performance due, among other things, to the "cluster" groupings of parliamentary critics rather than specific critic appointments.[4] The discontent prompted a July caucus meeting that saw critic responsibilities reallocated on a more traditional, individual basis.

The caucus and party leadership also encountered resistance from the rank-and-file members to its "national agenda" and particularly to its move into Quebec. The Quebec expansion plans served as another example of the inherent contradictions within Reform's agenda. At the same time as the party established a twelve-member Quebec organizing committee and opened a regional office in Montréal, the party's language critic was introducing amendments to the Official Languages Act that critics perceived to be anti-French. The Quebec expansion was only one part of an ambitious demographic, geographical and ideological expansion strategy that often confused and sometimes angered many of the party's core supporters. For example, the party seemingly broke with its anti-affirmative action policies by establishing committees to plan expansion strategies for youth, women and visible minorities. "I'm a bit worried about this expansion mentality," stated former policy advisor Tom Flanagan. "They've got to make sure they stick to promoting the party's agenda rather than watering it down to pull in more people."[5]

Back to the grassroots: Assembly '94

At Reform's first major policy convention after the 1993 election, Manning faced the first significant challenge to his leadership style. The 1994 Assembly would be characterized by two significant outcomes. Delegates positioned the party's policy platform more solidly to the right, and Manning rallied the delegates around his leadership. The Assembly opened with public opinion polls placing Reform at only 10 per cent nationally, and down to only 15 per cent in its Alberta heartland. Many party members began to openly suggest that Reform's leadership had lost its direction since its 1993 breakthrough. In an effort at damage control, Manning allowed the delegates to promote their agenda and debate proceeded with little interference from the leadership. Unlike the 1991 Assembly, where Manning chaired policy debate and intervened often, he did not participate in the policy debate at the Ottawa gathering. He left it up to several MPs to intervene at critical junctures when they believed debate was moving too close to what some saw as the extreme right.

> Although [MPs] did have the effect of moderating some of
> the party's policy stands, the positions eventually adopted
> still reflect a party that is far more radically conservative

than any other political grouping in Canada... Even if some of their MPs might appear susceptible, the delegates were determined to show they were not in danger of catching the Ottawa disease.[6]

The result was a policy agenda that appealed to Reform's core supporters,[7] but again left many in the national media speculating about a fringe party bent on appealing to extreme elements within Canada. Nevertheless, Manning backed the delegates' agenda by stating: "I don't see anything there to apologize or back off from."[8]

In a campaign-style keynote address to the Assembly, Manning demonstrated what would become evident during the 1997 election campaign, that he performs better in front of a live audience than he does in front of the television cameras during Question Period. His speech demonstrated both a determination to represent Reform's core values and his commitment to challenging what the party regards as the Ottawa establishment. He acknowledged Reform's lackluster performance over the previous year and assured delegates that the situation would change as Reform attempted to challenge Quebec separatists and supplant the Conservative Party as the voice of conservative Canadians.

> Some of you may feel that we need [to represent the core constituency] with more energy and effectiveness — and we accept that advice... But still more is required to advance our vision of a new and better Canada. The battle for the future of Canada will not be won or lost in the daily routine of the House of Commons, but out in the constituencies — the real political world where the people are. And while our valiant band of 52 is doing battle with the separatists and the status quo federalists in Ottawa, I want you to be doing the things that Reformers do best — out where the people are... I want our great army of Reform volunteers to be going from community to community, town to town, house to house, farm to farm, communicating our vision of a new and better national home for Canadians.[9]

Manning closed his speech by dedicating Reform to achieving three objectives: 1) to engage Quebec separatists in a fight for the future of Canada; 2) to challenge the "status quo federalists"; and 3) to offer Canadians a constructive alternative to the traditional parties and the status quo. Manning's Assembly performance helped him achieve a 92 per cent vote of support when delegates responded to the mandatory leadership review on the final day of the Assembly.

The return to Parliament

Reform improved its parliamentary performance during 1995 in the lead up to the Quebec referendum. The caucus returned to its conservative economic strategy and continued to challenge the government's fiscal plans.[10] Manning began to forge what he termed a 'working relationship' with Ontario's newly-elected Progressive Conservative Premier Mike Harris, and the party made Atlantic Canada the main focus of its fall recruitment drive. In a more controversial move, Manning disbanded the "posse", a band of Reform MPs whose job it was to expose government waste and corruption. Many felt the "posse" was largely responsible for the party's improved parliamentary performance, but the caucus decided to concentrate less on parliament and spend more time campaigning in the constituencies. This decision angered some supporters when it appeared that the party was again changing strategies just when it was beginning to shine in parliament. The move also did little to endear Reform to the Ottawa press corps. As one observer commented, "the Posse was good media relations... If the press knows there's the posse on the trail of every scrap and morsel of government error, it's a big asset."[11] The move can best be explained as a shift in emphasis, on Manning's part, away from fiscal matters and onto the national unity question, a similar strategy as would be implemented during the 1997 campaign.

Parliament resumed with Manning on the attack over national unity. He upstaged both the Prime Minister and the Leader of the Opposition when he demanded that the government recognize the legitimacy of a 50 per cent plus-one-vote in the referendum. So effective was Manning's performance that the Prime Minister summoned him to a lengthy meeting to discuss their differences and Manning's planned role in the referendum. With Manning and Harper again working well together on the national unity issue, the rest of the caucus was left to run with other issues. While Manning, Harper and a selection of other MPs would participate in the Quebec referendum debate, Reform was not a major player. In the post-referendum parliamentary debate, Reform stumbled briefly when it appeared that Harper and Manning were abandoning the party's "equality of provinces" position by supporting the government's plan to endorse constitutional proposals only if they were supported by five regions.

However, the party continued to oppose "distinct society" and began working on its own proposals for dealing with Quebec secession. The resulting 20/20 document would form the basis of Reform's national unity plank in the 1997 election.[12]

Buoyed by its performance in several by-elections,[13] and with the Quebec question on the back-burner after the 1995 referendum, Reform returned to an attack on the government's fiscal policies. The Reform caucus had the government reeling over the GST when Justice Minister Allan Rock introduced the sexual orientation amendments to the Canadian Human Rights Act. In its worst public performance of the 35th Parliament, the Reform caucus imploded over the gay rights issue. A hint of things to come occurred in the fall of 1995 when Calgary Southeast MP Jan Brown quit the party's family caucus because she claimed it was taking a legal stand on moral issues that required a survey of constituent opinion. At that time, Calgary Center MP Jim Silye and Brown both mused about not running for re-election unless the party moderated its stance on controversial social issues. When Reform whip Bob Ringma and Athabasca MP Dave Chatters waded into the gay rights issue by stating that businesses should have the right to "move homosexuals to the back of the shop" if they were disturbing customers, Brown publicly pronounced the Reform caucus to be rife with extremist elements and again threatened to abandon her caucus colleagues.[14] Manning was noticeably absent from parliament when the gay rights controversy erupted. Upon his return to Ottawa he suspended all three MPs from caucus; Ringma and Chatters for their perceived intolerance and Brown for portraying the Reform caucus as being rife with extremism.

Manning's handling of the situation drew fire from all quarters. He was criticized by the party's right-wing and populist elements for punishing Ringma and Chatters.[15] At the same time, many in the media chastised him for driving out the 'moderate' Brown.[16] Reform again appeared to be caught in its own trap of trying to mesh representation of its core constituency with its expansion strategy aimed at appealing to a broader cross-section of Canadian society. In the face of growing criticisms, Reform MPs rallied around Manning while Brown severed all ties with her former caucus colleagues and sat as an independent.[17]

Preparing the ground: Assembly '96

On the heels of the gay-rights fiasco, Reformers met in Vancouver for the last time before the 1997 election. The anticipated public showdown between the leadership and the party's right-wing did not materialize.

Manning laid down the gauntlet early in a closed-door meeting with constituency association presidents where he announced that he would remain leader and the campaign team that had already been assembled, would stay in place. He repeated the message to a similar meeting of MPs. Both the constituency presidents and the MPs fell in line, unwilling to fight a divisive leadership battle so close to an election. At the same time, delegates debated and passed 38 policy resolutions that were, in most respects, vintage Reform.[18] Delegates and MPs also gave the press little controversy to report, and with the policy debate out of the way, Manning and his campaign team took center stage.

Campaign Chairman Cliff Fryers and Campaign Director Rick Anderson unveiled Reform's 'go for broke' election strategy. The campaign team told delegates to 'do whatever it takes to win 153 seats.'[19] They made it clear that Ontario would be the focus and that Reform would target seats in the suburbs around Toronto. Manning used his keynote speech to outline the campaign theme and lecture delegates on the need to exercise 'self-discipline'.

> Tonight I want to close, not by talking about the Liberals' lack of integrity, but about the integrity of the Reform Party. How committed are we to sticking to our principles and commitments? To sticking to the big issues of priority to most Canadians, and not allowing ourselves to get side-tracked by the pursuit of secondary agendas? Are we prepared to face up to the fact that while more and more Canadians agree with the core policies of the Reform Party, many will be reluctant to vote for us until the perceptions of narrowness and extremism — however unfair those may be — are laid to rest?
>
> Are we prepared, not just to get the right policies and platform for the next election but to strive for a new level of competence — in the party, from the leader, in the caucus, among the candidates — so that Canadians will have confidence in our willingness and ability to deliver on what we promise?
>
> Are we prepared to make the effort and to exercise the self-discipline needed to make the transition from an opposition party to a governing party?[20]

Manning finished his speech by outlining three 'hard truths' that he felt Reformers and Canadian voters must recognize if Reform was to succeed in the 1997 election.

1) The key to growth and opportunities — to more and better jobs and lower taxes — lies in smaller governments, spending and borrowing less.
2) The national unity issue must be driven to resolution, not just managed indefinitely. That requires a major restructuring of the federation and a contingency plan for dealing with secession, and both are required now.
3) For a new party to become a governing party we must first master the government of ourselves.[21]

He urged delegates to present Canadians with a party that would stick to the big issues and maintain its focus, rather than be distracted by side issues. Manning's closing line demonstrated the twin meaning of Reform's Fresh Start campaign. He offered Canadians "a party committed to governing both itself and the nation with integrity... a party able to give Canadians a fresh start, because it was capable of making a fresh start itself."[22] The following morning, delegates provided Manning with an 86 per cent approval rating, his lowest yet but still large enough to put any leadership question to rest until at least after the 1997 election.

The fresh start

Signifying the importance of Ontario to Reform's national campaign, Manning introduced the *Fresh Start for Canadians* in London, Ontario in mid-October of 1996. The speech outlined the major components of what would become Reform's 24 page campaign promotional booklet. The *Fresh Start* consisted of "a six-point plan to build a brighter future together." Designed as a communications document rather than a formal statement of policy, it included Reform's intention to reduce the size of government as the primary vehicle for job creation, its tax reduction proposals, provisions to make families a priority, justice reform, plans to repair the social safety net, and, most importantly, Reform's plans to end the uncertainty caused by the national unity crisis.[23]

Based on the 20/20 proposals for a new confederation, the *Fresh Start for Unity* emphasized Reform's commitment to decentralize federal government powers and make federal institutions more democratically accountable. While not as detailed or specific as the 20/20 document, the *Fresh Start* document outlined how any secession negotiations would focus on the interests of Canada, potential partition of Quebec, debt sharing, revoking passports and citizenship of secessionists, transportation rights across an independent Quebec, and approval of the secession agreement by all Canadians through a national referendum. Given that all the parties would be offering some form of tax relief by the mid-point in the campaign, national unity would offer Reform its best issue to distinguish itself from the other parties.

The final sections of the *Fresh Start* booklet returned to Reform's populist message. It offered Canadians a guarantee of democratic accountability, including freer voting in the House of Commons, a Triple-E Senate, referendum on important matters, recall and initiative. The release of *Fresh Start* signified that Reform would campaign on a thoroughly right-of-centre platform, and was warmly received by important Reform supporters who had previously questioned the party's ideological grounding.[24]

Candidate recruitment

Reform's candidate recruitment process formally commenced June 15, 1996 and took a form similar to that which the party employed in 1993.[25] Constituency associations were in control of the process with the National Office acting in only an advisory capacity. The one qualification to this rule was the provision contained in the *Elections Act* which requires party leaders to provide written confirmation of the candidates' acceptability to carry the party banner in the election. Constituency associations established Nomination and Selection Committees to screen and assess the qualifications of all interested candidates and to conduct background checks. Candidates were asked to provide a detailed list of personal information and attitudinal data as part of the screening process. The nomination committees conducted interviews and recommended to the nomination meetings those candidates whom they felt should be considered by the general membership. Candidates could contest the nomination without the support of the nomination committee but their prospects for success would not be high.

Nomination meetings for ridings without a sitting MP could be held as early as October 1, while constituency associations with sitting Reform MPs would not start holding their nomination meetings until December 15, 1996. MPs not seeking reelection were asked to make their intentions clear by October 1, 1996. A number of prominent Reform MPs decided against seeking reelection, including Stephen Harper, Jan Brown, Bob Ringma, Herb Grubel, Jim Silye, House Leader Ray Speaker, and Reform's only Ontario MP Ed Harper. The candidate recruitment process was not as highly contested as it was in the lead-up to the 1993 election when the process was largely responsible for swelling Reform's membership to almost 140,000.[26] The 1997 process also witnessed the party hierarchy openly encouraging constituency associations to seek out and recruit young and ethnic candidates. The candidate recruitment process produced mixed results. The party succeeded in nominating a significant number of qualified ethnic and youth candidates and a full slate of candidates in the West. However, its success in recruiting candidates was modest in Atlantic Canada (23 of 32 ridings) and poor in Quebec (11 of 75 ridings).[27]

Financing the campaign

Reform has traditionally relied for its financing on contributions from individual party members and from membership subscriptions that are shared by the national party and the constituency associations. During the pre-writ period, contributions collected by constituency associations are split 80/20, with the local organization keeping the lion's share. Likewise, the national office keeps 80 per cent of the contributions sent to it and refunds the remaining 20 per cent to the constituency association from which the contribution originated. During the campaign period, however, the national campaign kept 100 per cent of the funds it raised through its phone-a-thons and letter campaigns with the local campaigns keeping all funds raised through local efforts.

Unlike in 1993 when the war-chest was minimal at the campaign's outset, Reform began 1997 with $1.5 million in cash reserves and secure in the knowledge that it could raise sufficient funds to host a full leader's tour and a national advertising campaign. During the first four months of 1997 the national party raised approximately $3.2 million. By the end of the election, it had raised an additional $3.3 million, allowing it to spend almost $8 million on its national campaign without borrowing any funds, and finish the campaign with a surplus. Party officials report that $1.5 million was contributed to the national campaign by the constituency associations. Another one-half million dollars were raised through membership subscriptions. A further $1.5 million was collected from businesses, Reform's most successful efforts to date, with another $3 million raised by way of individual contributions from members and supporters. Party officials estimate that the constituency associations and individual candidates raised another $5–$7 million, the vast majority of this coming from individuals and small businesses.[28]

Campaign organization and platform promotion[29]

Reform's 1997 campaign was similar to its 1993 campaign in that most of the key players remained. It differed from 1993 in that it was organized around a professional communications strategy that more fully integrated the national campaign's media efforts with the local campaigns. The campaign organization consisted of four primary groups: 1) the war room and national office organization; 2) the leader's tour; 3) the research office in Ottawa; and 4) the local campaigns.[30] The Calgary war room was commanded by Campaign Chairman Cliff Fryers and served as the center of the national campaign's activities. Fryers was assisted by communications expert Bryan Thomas and pollster Andre Turcotte, the two most significant additions to the 1997 team.[31] Campaign Director Rick Anderson advised Manning on the leader's tour. Together, these individuals constituted the core of the national campaign team with responsibilities for coordinating the national communications strategy.

Reform's communication strategy was built on three pillars: The *Fresh Start* literature distribution; television advertising; and news coverage of the leader's tour. Brian Thomas unveiled the communications strategy to candidates at their pre-election training seminars held in Toronto the same weekend that the Prime Minister called the election. The national campaign would focus solely on television advertising, leaving print and radio for the individual campaigns. The national television budget was set at $1.3 million and was broken down by region with some ads running nationally but others running only in selected provinces or regional markets. The strategy attempted to lump the Liberals and Tories together in an effort at distinguishing Reform from its major, traditional-party competitors. The overriding campaign theme stated that with Reform, "now you have a real alternative." All ads were thoroughly tested through focus groups held across the country. While the party continued to use focus group testing throughout the campaign, it did not conduct any campaign tracking polls of its own. The communications plan was based on a one time, 2,500 respondent, public opinion poll conducted by Turcotte. Results indicated that establishing a clear issue focus would be a particular challenge in the campaign, since no single issue was emerging at the outset as a dominant theme. For example, health care (8.7 per cent), jobs (8.7 per cent), political accountability (8.6 per cent) and safe streets (8.5 per cent) topped the list of issues that most concerned Canadians. But the gap between these issues and a host of "secondary" issues was slight. "Equality of all Canadians" placed seventh on the list (8.2 per cent), while national unity placed thirteenth (7.4 per cent). When analyzing the top three or four issues in every province, and region of province, the "equality of all Canadians" issue surfaced only in the Vancouver area and in rural Manitoba. However, further probing indicated that the potential likelihood of voting Reform improved by a net of 30 per cent when voters were asked about Reform's promise to ensure the equality of all Canadians. Forty-three per cent of voters stated that they would be more likely to vote Reform if it would ensure equality while only 13 per cent stated that they would be less likely to cast a ballot for Reform given its unity position. This compared with a net 16 per cent drop in respondents' likelihood of voting Conservative if that party recognized Quebec as a distinct society (21 per cent more likely to vote PC as compared to 37 per cent less likely). Turcotte estimated the potential impact of the national unity issue on the Reform vote to be positive in every region except the Ottawa area. The positive impact varied from a low of only 12 per cent in Winnipeg, to a high of 56 per cent in rural Manitoba, 50 per cent in rural Saskatchewan and 45 per cent in the BC lower mainland and Edmonton.[32] Interestingly, the results predicted the potential impact of the national unity issue to be a net gain for Reform of 44 per cent in Southwestern Ontario and 31 per cent in the Greater Toronto Area. The polling results also indicated that Reform would gain support if it could convince Canadians that political accountability was a major issue and that Reform was the solution. However, results indicated that both Reform and the Conservatives would gain support based on their tax cut promises with Reform gaining slightly more (25 per cent net gain) than the Tories (14 per cent net gain). In view of the estimated potential net impact of these issues, it is not surprising that Reform strategists decided to emphasize national unity and accountability over tax reduction.

For communications purposes, the campaign was broken down into three phases. Phase One covered the early campaign period (days 36 through 27)[33] and focused on the *Fresh Start* content. The strategy intended to maximize the impact of a full week of TV advertising beginning around the 30th day and lasting until the 23rd day. Television commercials focused on the platform and asked voters to watch for a copy of the *Fresh Start* book in their mailboxes.[34] The local campaigns' ability to effectively distribute the printed material was central to the strategy. Strategists were convinced that the power of the TV campaign, in conjunction with the book drop campaign, would inoculate voters against the image of Reform as a regional party rife with extremist elements. Phase Two, the longest and most important stage of the campaign, covered days 26 through 8 and employed a "compare and contrast" theme. No specific literature pieces were developed to complement the TV campaign during this phase. Reform would again lump the Liberals and Tories together in what Thomas promised to be 12 "very hard hitting" commercials, including one "surprise" ad. Some commercials would run nationally while other content would again vary by region. Phase Three asked voters to make a decision during the last week of the campaign. "Attack" TV ads would provide a "harder compare and contrast message."

This phase was intended to be Reform's most aggressive and included the highest penetration of TV ads complemented by a second and final national literature drop, again to be delivered or mailed by the local campaigns. The printed piece would again dove-tail with the TV ads, focusing on contrasting the Liberal/Tory record with Reform's proposals. The last literature piece would be printed locally to allow for last minute fine-tuning, a quick turnaround, and also to allow candidates to customize the piece with their own personal information. Six TV commercials were developed for this final phase. Local campaigns were also asked to consider regional or local collaboration to "top up" TV advertising in selected markets where the national campaign believed its buy to be too thin.[35] Other key personnel such as Campaign Finance and Fundraising Director Glenn McMurray and Fundraising Manager Brendan Robinson worked to ensure that the national campaign raised sufficient funds to mount its advertising campaign, and helped coordinate the extra TV buys with local campaigns. For the most part, the 1997 campaign dynamics allowed Reform to stick to its three-phase agenda. Candidates were instructed to base their local campaigns on the three phases and to not deviate from the plan. Reform made extensive use of traditional campaign media techniques under the direction of Larry Welsh, who acted as Campaign Press secretary with assistance from Ron Wood and Line Maheaux. The national campaign communicated with local campaigns by daily e-mailing or faxing two newsletters that emphasized Reform's media events and other campaign activities. The war room established telephone hotlines for candidate support, opposition information and the leader's tour. The party also supplied a candidate support e-mail line, several fax lines and a direct line to the research department. Paul Wilson acted as Campaign Research Director in Ottawa providing research support to Reform's national and the local campaigns.

Although local campaigns maintained their traditional independence, in order to help implement the communications strategy the national campaign attempted to group them as regional teams. Red Deer MP Bob Mills served as the Western Campaign Team Chair, Marnee Stern acted as Ontario Chair, Gilles St. Laurent was the Quebec Chair while Manning's former Chief of Staff, Steve Greene, acted as Atlantic Campaign Team

Chair. Reform also established several Action Teams that were given various special responsibilities during the campaign. Medicine Hat MP Monte Solberg headed up the Taxation Team with assistance from former Canadian Taxpayers Federation president and Calgary Southeast candidate Jason Kenny. Reform caucus chairman Chuck Straul and Port Moody–Coquitlam MP Sharon Hayes co-chaired the Family Action Team while Fraser Valley West MP Randy White headed up the Justice Campaign. Each action team was responsible for formulating and articulating various "issue-specific" mini-campaigns within their areas of expertise. The Action Teams distributed "issue-specific" briefs articulating Reform's position on these issues as campaign dynamics permitted, or necessitated.

The campaign and leader's tour

The campaign opened with Manning on the attack, but battling the press rather than the other political parties. Reform's chief BC organizer, George Rigaux, had made comments that were deemed by the national press to be derogatory towards the Sikh community in Vancouver. Rigaux had told a Vancouver Sun reporter that a Sikh organization was attempting to take over the nomination process of every political party in the riding of Surrey Central. Rigaux resigned on the heels of what the national media reported as his "racial slurs against the Sikh community".[36] Manning went on the attack when a Conservative organizer seemingly backed-up Rigaux's assertions by commenting that the Tories were seeking a 'white' candidate to counter the Sikh organizers in the riding, and the national media gave the story only limited coverage.

Manning accused the media of using a double standard by playing up Reform's mistakes but not those of the other parties. In a campaign speech directed as much at Reform candidates as at the media, Manning accused the media of conducting witch-hunts.[37] The incident, and Manning's response, served to remind Reform candidates of the Brown-Ringma-Chatters affair and the need to avoid making any comments that could garner national media attention and damage the party, as well as their own electoral prospects. It also allowed the party to further emphasize its strategy of ensuring that local candidates did not deviate from the national campaign plan in any significant way. For the most part, Reform candidates adhered to the strategy.

During the advertising black-out period early in the campaign, the media focused primarily on the leaders' tours. Unlike in 1993, Reform could finance a leader's tour that resembled those of the Liberals and Conservatives. Reform chartered its own campaign plane that crisscrossed the country, often making 3 or 4 stops in one day. For example, during the first week of the campaign the tour began in southern Ontario, traveled to Quebec and the Maritimes before moving west to BC, and returning to Ontario after making stops in Alberta and Manitoba. Manning demonstrated his campaigning talents by running at a hectic pace and setting the national campaign agenda during the first week. Manning also unveiled the Liberals' campaign platform two days before its scheduled release and received considerable news play by publicizing an obscure *Elections Act* clause that would have allowed the Chief Electoral Officer to postpone the vote in southern Manitoba due to the flooding in the area. He also launched Reform's national unity campaign while in BC, the province Reform believed to be most receptive to its unity message.

Week two saw Manning step up his attacks on the Liberal and Tory leaders by conjuring up memories of past prime ministers, attempting to link Chrétien with the Trudeau record and Charest with Mulroney. While the Reform campaign usually did not distinguish between the Liberals and Conservatives, the early focus was clearly on the Prime Minister. Manning revisited a theme from the 1993 campaign in portraying Chrétien as tired and worn out, barely muddling his way through the campaign.[38] Like the other parties, Reform also began its television advertising campaign during the second week. As per their stated intentions, Reform aired television commercials that focused on its *Fresh Start* platform in every region except in BC, where it ran its first "hard hitting" national unity commercial attacking distinct society.

Given Reform's early momentum, the Liberals and Conservatives stepped up their attacks. The Liberals charged that Reform's policies were excessively right-wing while the Tories accused Reform of not being a truly national party. Manning largely ignored the Liberal charges, believing it to be in Reform's interests to be portrayed as right-wing. He did however respond to the "regional party" attacks by evoking a western alienation theme aimed at solidifying Reform's base in BC and Alberta. "It's considered perfectly possible to be a national party with your roots [in central Canada], but you can't have your roots in western Canada and be considered a national party... We think it's possible to be a national party and have your roots in Western Canada... We're out to prove that."[39] Interestingly, Manning defended Reform's western roots from Toronto. This strategy was employed to demonstrate that he would not shirk from representing western interests in other parts of the country, but also to reinforce his attacks on Charest who refused to use the term distinct society when making his first campaign stops in Alberta.

Manning headed into the leaders' debates with considerable momentum. A Southam/CTV/Angus Reid poll measured Reform challenging the Conservatives for second place nationally, but more importantly, running atop the polls in both BC and Alberta, and ahead of the Tories in Manitoba and Saskatchewan.[40] With Charest continuing to sound conciliatory to Quebec, and former Quebec premier Jacques Parizeau having firmly placed national unity on the agenda, Manning was determined to use the debates to promote Reform's unity position and further distinguish it from all of the traditional parties.

Manning performed credibly during the English language debate, but often allowed Charest to out flank him on issues where Reform had built up momentum during the first two weeks of the campaign. Manning's style of posing questions to the other leaders often left him silenced while he allowed them to answer. At times, his approach simply turned the podium over to one of the other leaders in a debate format where each of the five leaders struggled to get their message heard. Manning's best performances occurred when he challenged the Prime Minister over distinct society and Chrétien's lack of preparation for the 1995 Quebec referendum. Manning also scored blows when he revisited Charest's record in the Mulroney government. Although early analysis suggested that no leader was a clear winner or loser during the English language debate, media attention soon focused on Charest's performance and his passionate response to the unity issue.[41]

Charest's post-debate momentum forced Manning to shift more of his attention to the Tory leader. Manning continued with his criticism of the Mulroney record and GST. But Reform believed Charest to be most vulnerable on the national unity issue. When the French language debate stalled due to the illness of its moderator, Manning was presented with the opportunity to continue to distinguish himself from Charest on that issue. As one election observer commented, "it's the one big issue that the Liberals and Conservatives do not want to talk about. And it is the one thing that distinguishes Reform from every other party."[42] Manning used the CBC TV Town Hall on unity and a trip to Quebec to reiterate his opposition to distinct society status and Reform's hard line against the separatists. With respect to distinct society, he told Quebeckers that "it is not going to happen" because of opposition in other provinces and that if Quebeckers vote for sovereignty they will "find themselves in a room with a steely-eyed, hard-nosed lawyer from Toronto or Calgary, and he's going to say to you, 'we want money, we want territory, and we want the date nailed down for the revoking of passports.'"[43]

With Charest continuing to gain momentum in Quebec after the French language debate, Manning went for broke and challenged Chrétien and Charest to a special debate on the unity issue. Manning further intensified his attacks against Charest prior to the Tory leader returning to Alberta. Charest countered by having popular Alberta Premier Ralph Klein introduce him to a Calgary audience. However, Charest took up the challenge that Manning had issued earlier in the campaign and spoke about distinct society while in Alberta, a move that sealed the Tories' fate in that province.

Manning's unity message began to show results, both in the polls and in the level of hostility it generated from the other leaders. With the other leaders accusing Manning of using 'hot button politics', Reform dropped its bomb by airing its 'secret ad' on national unity. The ad suggested the two federalist-party leaders from Quebec could not be trusted with the future of Canada. It continued by asking Canadians to reject distinct society status for Quebec in favour of Reform's proposal to treat all provinces and citizens equally. Visually, the ad showed grainy black-and-white photographs of Chrétien and Charest with the message "last time, these men almost lost our country." It went on to show similar pictures of Quebec Premier Lucien Bouchard and Bloc leader Gilles Duceppe and stated that the federalist leaders "will do it again with distinct society when these men hold the next referendum." The ad caused considerable controversy because, in the view of many, it equated the leaders of Canada's major federalist parties, the Liberals and Conservatives, with the leaders of Quebec nationalist parties, the PQ and BQ. This image was reinforced when the ad called for "a voice for all Canadians, not just Quebec politicians" and the on-screen image placed a large red circle with a slash through it across all four leaders. The ad concluded with the suggestion that it was time for a prime minister from outside Quebec, a sentiment shared by many Reformers but not often publicly stated by any national party.

The ad appears to have had several effects. It further reinforced the prominence of national unity as a key campaign issue. It also appears to have halted Reform's growth in support in Ontario and the Atlantic region, while bolstering the party's support in the West.[44] Response from the major federalist party leaders was swift and strong. The Prime Minister accused Manning of running the most divisive campaign in Canadian history. Charest claimed that Reform's campaign had reached a new low. However, as some journalists commented, "the raging controversy underlined just how much Reform, which started a decade ago with a few dozen Albertans who supported Mr. Manning's ideas, has dominated the election campaign for the first four weeks."[45]

Reform's national unity ad and the controversy it generated continued to dominate the campaign for the final week. However, Reform moved away from the unity issue in the last week, opting instead to close the campaign with its accountability theme. While Reform advisors are still divided over whether this was the best strategy, the move illustrated several features of its 1997 campaign. Reform had set the agenda throughout much of the campaign and forced the national unity message to the top of the agenda, despite the other federalist parties' desires to downplay the issue. Given that the campaign dynamics did not force Reform to significantly alter its original campaign strategy, Reform strategists may have been justified in believing that they could continue to set the agenda during the final week. However, the accountability message did little to help Reform make its much hoped for breakthrough into Ontario, a fate which likely was sealed in any event through the party's positioning on national unity. Accountability is often used as a code word in Western Canada to encapsulate many issues related to 'western alienation' and a mistrust of Ottawa. Although this message has appeal in BC and Alberta, it is less relevant in Ontario. Given that Westerners had "bought" this message from Reform in 1993, it is somewhat curious that Reform would return to this theme at the end of a campaign where it was assured of maintaining its western base, but needed to make significant inroads into Ontario.

Conclusion

The 1997 federal election campaign began with many pundits predicting a Liberal landslide while dismissing Reform as a one-election phenomenon. After conducting a campaign that was largely successful in setting the election agenda for all parties, Reform achieved some of its goals, but also likely defined the limits of its future success. The party achieved a major goal by becoming Official Opposition, with 60 seats. The party also succeeded in solidifying its western base, making significant inroads into Saskatchewan and to a lesser extent Manitoba. But in doing so, it appears to have sacrificed much of the effort that had gone into its expansion drive in Ontario and the Atlantic region for the preceding 6 years. The 1997 Ontario results were particularly disappointing for Reform. After spending millions of dollars and thousands of volunteer hours organizing in Canada's most populous province, the party lost its only seat in Ontario and finished second in fewer ridings than it did in 1993.

Reform appears to be stuck on the horns of a dilemma that confronts all regional parties that have national aspirations. The electoral system in Canada rewards parties with regionally concentrated support, and thus a regional base is almost a prerequisite for party development. Yet, to have any realistic chance of forming a national government, the party must shed its regional character and expand its base of support to at least one other major region. The problem for Reform is that some of the issues with which it is associated (western alienation, and simultaneously, effective regional representation in Ottawa; or taking a relatively hard-line on the national question regarding Quebec) play very differently in the West, its core region of support, than in Ontario and the Atlantic region, its two areas of potential growth. The other major issues with which Reform is associated (fiscal conservatism, and support for 'law and order') transcend regional differences, and hold some promise for potential growth in support. In the 1997 election, however, Reform championed the national unity issue, solidifying its western base, but weakening its support in Ontario and the Atlantic regions. Canadians' partisan affiliations are sufficiently flexible, and issue positions sufficiently malleable, that the party may be able to recover the momentum to expand into Ontario and Atlantic Canada. That, however, is for another day. In the short-term, Reform's solid position as representative of the West is the main product of the 1997 election.

Notes

[1] The authors would like to thank the many Reform staff and volunteers who consented to interviews and provided documentation. We would especially like to thank Brendan Robinson and Glen McMurray of the national office, Brian Thomas of TC&P, Andre Turcotte of ATRS, and Lethbridge campaign archivist Marion Jardine, for supplying useful information and documentation. The Reform web site was also an important source of information and can be located at www.reform.ca.

[2] The Angus Reid Group, "Federal Political Parties' Popular Support Levels: October 1993 to Late May 1997," www.angusreid.com.

[3] Steve Chase, "Stepping out of Preston's shadow: Reform's new, outspoken MPs are making a mark for themselves," *Alberta Report*, February 21, 1994, 10.

[4] For a list of other Reform 'breaks with parliamentary tradition' during the first sessions of the 35th parliament, see Tom Flanagan, *Waiting for the Wave: The Reform Party and Preston Manning*, (Toronto: Stoddart Publishing Co. Ltd., 1995), 170-73.

[5] As quoted by Robert Owen, "Pancakes with the enemy: Reform's

breakfast for the BQ is part of Manning's grand design," *Alberta Report*, January 24, 1994, 8.

[6] Hugh Winsor, "Reform's ideological purity diluted: The party's parliamentary wing argued for policies that would be more salable in mainstream politics," *The Globe and Mail*, Monday, October 17, 1994, A4.

[7] Reform Party of Canada, "Assembly 1994 Successful Policy Resolutions and Amendments to the Party Constitution," October, 1994. For a demographic and attitudinal profile of Reform Activists see, Keith Archer and Faron Ellis, "Opinion Structure of Party Activists: The Reform Party of Canada," *Canadian Journal of Political Science*, XXVII:2, June, 1994, 277-308.

[8] Tu Thanh Ha, "Manning spoiling for a fight on unity: Reform Leader foresees crisis," *The Globe and Mail*, Monday, October 17, 1994, A1–2. See also Flanagan, *Waiting for the Wave*, 196-200.

[9] Preston Manning, "A New and Better Home for Canadians," keynote address to the Reform Party Assembly, Ottawa, October 15, 1994.

[10] Reform Party of Canada, *The Taxpayers' Budget: The Reform Party's Plan to Balance the Federal Budget and Provide Social and Economic Security for the 21st Century*, February 21, 1995.

[11] University of Calgary political scientist Barry Cooper as quoted by Michael Jenkinson, "Reform's new fall session: The Posse is disbanded, but the Manning-Harris alliance is sure to be a hit," *Alberta Report*, September 11, 1995, 6-7.

[12] Reform Party of Canada, *20 Proposals for a New Confederation, 20 Realities About Secession: A Vision For The Future Of Canada*, January, 1996. See also Preston Manning, "Awakening the Sleeping Giant," speech to the Canadian Club, London, Ontario, November 2, 1995.

[13] Despite not winning either of the two seats it seriously contested, Reformers were encouraged by their showing and the Tories' dismal performance. In Labrador, Reform won over 30 per cent of the vote and in Etobicoke North, Reform support nearly doubled from 20.8 per cent in 1993 to 36.1 per cent. The Tories, in contrast, garnered only about 10 per cent of the vote in each riding.

[14] Jan Brown, "'I've drawn my line in the sand'," excerpts from a letter to members of her Calgary Southeast constituency, *Calgary Herald*, Saturday, May 18, 1996, A11.

[15] Miro Cernetig, "Grassroots angry over spat: Mood swinging; Manning's leadership being questioned," *The Globe and Mail*, Saturday, May 11, 1996, A2.

[16] Susan Delacourt, "Focus is on Manning's role as Brown leaves Reform: MP's departure raises questions of leadership, caucus tolerance," *The Globe

and Mail, Saturday, May 11, 1996, A1–2.

[17] Brown ran unsuccessfully as the Tory candidate against Manning in Calgary Southwest during the 1997 election. She finished a distant third with 18 per cent support as compared to Manning's 58 per cent. Bob Ringma did not run again in the 1997 election while David Chatters was re-elected in the Alberta riding of Athabasca with 55 per cent of the popular vote.

[18] The bulk of the 38 policy resolutions that were adopted dealt with justice (10), federalism, citizenship and equality (11), and taxes and economic issues (9). Delegates passed resolutions calling for binding national referenda on capital punishment (89 per cent support) and abortion (58 per cent support). They also formally adopted the party's 20/20 proposals as official policy.

[19] To meet its goal of 153 seats, the campaign team predicted that Reform must win 35 per cent of the popular vote and have it translate into 29 seats in B.C. and the North, 43 in the Prairie provinces, 66 in Ontario, 6 in Quebec, and 9 in the Atlantic provinces.

[20] Preston Manning, "A Fresh Start: Keynote Address to Assembly '96," Vancouver, June 8, 1996.

[21] Ibid.

[22] Ibid.

[23] Reform Party of Canada, *A Fresh Start for Canadians: A 6 Point Plan to Build a Brighter Future Together*, 1996.

[24] Ted Byfield, "Three cheers for Manning—the Reformers are back on the path that leads to victory," *Alberta Report*, October 28, 1996, 44. The Liberals also reacted by claiming that the *Fresh Start* demonstrated that Reform was a right-wing extremist party, a position that produced its own backlash. See B'Nai Brith Canada News Release, "B'Nai Brith Criticizes Liberal Misuse of Language," October 30, 1996.

[25] See Faron Ellis and Keith Archer, "Reform: Electoral Breakthrough," in Alan Frizzell, Jon H. Pammett and Anthony Westell, eds, *The Canadian General Election of 1993*, 59–78.

[26] Reform membership peaked in 1992 at 138,000 members. It began dropping after the 1993 election to a low of 69,000 in September of 1994. Reform began 1997 with approximately 72,000 members, a level it considers to be its core membership. The 1997 candidate recruitment process and election added about 20,000 members, leaving the party with a total membership of 91,500 at the end of May, 1997.

[27] Reform fielded a total of 227 candidates in the 1997 federal election. Reform candidates ran in all western and northern ridings, 102 ran in Ontario, 11 in Quebec, 2 in P.E.I., 9 in Nova Scotia, 8 in New Brunswick

and 4 in Newfoundland.

[28] At the time of writing the Party's national office had not finished compiling the final financial statistics. However, Fundraising Manager Brendan Robinson was able to provide the unofficial totals presented here.

[29] See Reform Party of Canada, "National Organizational Structure," May, 1995; and Reform Party of Canada, "Victory Team '97," April 16, 1997.

[30] The party also established what it called a Youth Swat Team, led by Kory Tenyke, that traveled throughout Southern Ontario during the campaign.

[31] Thomas is senior partner with the advertising firm TC&P in London, Ontario and produced television advertising for Ontario Premier Mike Harris' successful 1995 campaign. Turcotte is head of the public opinion research firm ATRS in Toronto.

[32] Turcotte based his report on a 14 category breakdown of selected markets. These included; Vancouver, BC Lower Mainland, BC Interior, Edmonton, Calgary, Rural Saskatchewan, Saskatoon, Rural Manitoba, Winnipeg, Southwestern Ontario, Suburban GTA, Ottawa, Atlantic Canada and all of Canada. Andre Turcotte, "The Issues of the Election '97," April 26, 1997.

[33] Election strategists typically count 'election days' backwards from the day the writ is dropped (day 36 in 1997) to voting day (day 1).

[34] Candidates were given the back page to personalize with their own message, picture and campaign office address. This strategy, and the book's design, ensured a consistency of message in that the entire Reform platform would accompany, and dominate, the literature delivered by volunteers working on individual candidates' campaigns.

[35] The national campaign believed it needed 50 per cent more ad time in Calgary, 13 per cent in Vancouver, and a further 10 per cent in the Toronto/Hamilton region.

[36] Rigaux maintains that his comments were directed at one particular Sikh temple, not the general Sikh community. See Sheldon Alberts and Kin Lunman, "Reform organizer quits over Sikh slur," Calgary Herald, April 23, 1997, A4.

[37] The Fraser Institute's National Media Archive Studies from the 1997 election supported Manning's assertions about media bias. See The National Media Archive News Release, "Election Campaign News Heavily Favours Tories," and "Study Finds Reform Treated Unfairly on Race Issues," May 30, 1997.

[38] See Stephen Clarkson, "Yesterday's Man and His Blue Grits: Backward Into the Future," in Frizzell et al, The Canadian General Election of 1993, 27-42.

[39] Manning as quoted by Norm Ovenden, "Manning defends national

standing," *Calgary Herald*, Wednesday, May 7, 1997, A12.

[40] The Southam/CTV/Angus Reid poll placed the Liberals at 42 per cent, the Conservatives at 19 per cent, Reform at 18 per cent, the NDP at 11 per cent and the BQ at 9 per cent. Reform led in B.C. and Alberta with 41 per cent and it stood at 25 per cent in Manitoba and Saskatchewan. See Lisa Dempster, "Campaign survey says we're heading for Reform Opposition - Liberal Government," *Calgary Herald*, May 10, 1997, A1.

[41] See Chapter 11 of this volume.

[42] Barry Cooper as quoted by Michael Jenkinson, "Distinct society strikes again: Though a bane to the Grits, Reform may yet force the issue forward," *Alberta Report*, May 12, 1997, 8; and Reform Party News Release, "Manning Extends Unity Challenge," May 14, 1997.

[43] Manning as quoted by Jeff Sallot, "Reform uses Quebec podium: Manning's visit a bid to woo voters outside province," *The Globe and Mail*, Thursday, May 15, A7.

[44] Susan Delacourt and Rheal Seguin, "BQ, Reform gain in own territories: Poll showing movement in Quebec and West suggest more of same after June 2," *The Globe and Mail*, Thursday, May 29, 1997 A8; Jeff Sallot, Murray Campbell and Anne McIlroy, "Manning attacked over unity views: His Quebec message and new Reform ad draw angry words from Liberal, NDP and Tory leaders," *The Globe and Mail*, Saturday, May 24, 1997, A 7.

[45] Sallot et. al., "Manning attacked," *The Globe and Mail*, Saturday, May 24, 1997, A7.

Seven
The Bloc Québécois
by André Bernard

Taking into consideration its breakthrough in the 1993 Canadian federal election, the Bloc Québécois (BQ) has experienced an indisputable set-back in the 1997 election. Seen proportionally to the number of seats or votes, the support it gathered in 1997 is 25 per cent lower than in 1993. In 1993, the BQ had won 49.5 per cent of the votes cast in Quebec and 54 of the 75 Quebec seats in the Canadian House of Commons; with its 54 seats (two more than the Reform Party), it became the Official Opposition. In the 1997 election, the BQ obtained the support of 37.4 per cent of Quebec voters who registered valid ballots and it only got 44 of its 75 candidates elected, losing to the Reform Party the status of Official Opposition.

Whatever explanation of their set-back is offered, the Bloc Québécois members cannot but worry about the future.

The pre-election period

Some members of the Bloc Québécois caucus began to fear for their party when, in the fall of 1996, dependable surveys showed that their main opponents were picking up strength in Quebec. One of these members, Réal Ménard, even started asking for changes. He was quoted, on November 30, 1996, in a Canadian Press feature, saying that, "in the interest of the party", the new leader, Michel Gauthier, "had to think about the decision he was to take."[1]

On December 2, 1996, Michel Gauthier resigned as leader of the Bloc Québécois.[2] Less than ten months earlier, he had been chosen by the party authorities as successor to the BQ founder, Lucien Bouchard, who, in January 1996, had taken over from Jacques Parizeau as leader of the Parti Québécois and prime minister of Quebec. According to Gauthier, the selection of a new leader could heal the wounds inflicted on his party by the October 1995 Quebec referendum and by the subsequent events.

Analyzing the resignation of Michel Gauthier, political commentators underlined the fact that "recent surveys had shown the Bloc slipping down to the benefit of the Liberal Party" and that "the BQ leader had not yet been able to get known to the Quebec voters."[3] Contrary to his predecessor, Lucien Bouchard, little-known Michel Gauthier was not the "popular" leader needed to give the Bloc Québécois a new version of its 1993 success. Having been chosen by a group of less than 160 persons, acting as a "conclave" electing a new pope, Gauthier was lacking the kind of legitimacy provided by democratic ways of selecting leaders. Moreover, the unprepossessing style of Gauthier could explain why hitherto undecided voters were now leaning to the Liberal Party.

As a consequence of the growing strength of the Liberal Party of Canada in Quebec, and taking into account the specific circumstances of each district, it was clear that several persons, in the caucus chaired by Michel Gauthier, could be defeated in the forthcoming election. Gilles Duceppe, one of the contenders in the leadership campaign, even stated, on December 18, 1996, that the Bloc Québécois could have as few as 38 of its candidates elected in a new federal election,[4] that is 16 fewer than in 1993.

According to surveys based on large samples, between the 1993 election and the summer of 1996, the support for the Bloc Québécois had been relatively stable, but for a short period early in 1995. From the referendum campaign of 1995 up to the summer of 1996, surveys had shown the Bloc Québécois well ahead of the Liberals in declared vote intentions.[5] The results of a Quebec survey, by the Centre de recherche sur l'opinion publique (CROP), produced in March 1996, awarded as much as 53 per cent of the declared vote intentions to the BQ, and 35 per cent to the Liberal Party of Canada.[6] Again, the same polling organization, in June 1996, credited the BQ with 51 per cent of vote intentions, and the Liberal Party of Canada with 35 per cent.[7] However, in the fall of 1996, the gap between the BQ and its major opponent had decreased to a mere 10 per cent.

In January 1997, the renewed interest in the Bloc Québécois, spurred by its leadership campaign, gave new hope to the sovereigntists. According to a Quebec survey, between January 17 and January 22, 1997, the BQ was still favoured by 49 per cent of the 803 decided respondents, while the Liberal Party of Canada had the support of 36 per cent.[8] Michel Gauthier went as far as to predict the election of "between 55 and 60" of the 75 BQ candidates in the new Parliament.[9]

If the revival of the party was the reason for the leadership campaign, then the type of selection process and the type of leadership campaign were inadequate. The contest was to be resolved by polling all the registered members of the party, by mail ballots. The campaign itself was to be punctuated by a series of "confrontations" between the candidates who, on stage, were likely to stick to what was already known as the programme of the party. Indeed, when one of the six candidates, Yves Duhaime, spoke of "renewal", the other five replied by saying that the caucus members had done a marvellous job in the House of Commons and deserved the praise of their party.

The leadership campaign was met with considerable apathy, as the pretenders to the leadership did not succeed in giving their party the "puff of fresh air" that it apparently needed. In spite of their desire to stick with the party programme, they were unable to paper over the cleavages exacerbated by the size of the public debt, separating those who oppose cuts in public spending from those who approve of these cuts. None of the candidates showed the level of popularity or notoriety of a charismatic leader. Moreover, the two front runners could not hide their dislike of each other.

In spite of all the solicitation to which they were exposed, 55 per cent of the 113 000 Bloc Québécois members did not return the mail ballots which they had received. At the end of the process, the winner, Gilles Duceppe, was the first choice of a mere 48 per cent of the members of the BQ who had filled valid ballots, and he was the second choice of another 5 per cent. Together 47 per cent of the ballots gave preference to either Yves Duhaime (33.9 per cent) or Rodrigue Biron (13.3 per cent).

The count of the votes received by mail was presented during the convention of the Bloc Québécois which had been scheduled for March 15, 1997. From the standpoint of the television viewer, that convention looked like a disaster. The hall in which it was held seemed, at best, half full. The mood of the convention was very dull, and the whole thing appeared amateurish. One of the speakers (Yves Duhaime) was even interrupted by a bigot bearing a Quebec flag where each fleur-de-lis had been replaced by a swastika (this person had not only been able to get into the convention hall, he had been able to come near to the platform and to jump behind Yves Duhaime!).

The March convention provided an occasion for expressing grievances. Michel Gauthier talked publicly of his disappointment. One of his friends,

André Néron, said that the worst thing that could happen would be the victory of Gilles Duceppe. Nic Leblanc, a member of the BQ caucus since 1990, repeated that he would sit as an "independent" if Gilles Duceppe was chosen leader. The runner-up, Yves Duhaime, loosing with 33.9 per cent of the votes, was unable to conceal his displeasure. All in all, the convention showed a spectacle of dissension.

Many observers blamed the failure to revive the party on the electoral process used by the Bloc Québécois to select its new leader. By giving the vote to any person who had paid a membership fee, the BQ authorities had made it possible for one candidate or the other to "buy" a majority and, as a consequence, mistrust had been high. (In fact, only 17 000 new members were added to the 96 000 who were already on the party lists). Moreover, for want of "personalized" ballots, the BQ authorities made it possible for anyone to fill in and mail ballots obtained from friends; that also had fed mistrust. But, above all, the BQ authorities had chosen a selection process which does not culminate into a climax of the kind achieved by the "old parties". There was not much glamour in an election conducted by mail. The kind of leadership convention favoured by the "old parties" is likely to have a more positive impact on the voters' interest than the would-be "democratic" exercise applied by the Bloc Québécois.[10]

A few weeks after the end of the leadership campaign, a new survey registered a decline in the support level of the Bloc Québécois. In April 1997, for the first time since 1993, this survey put the BQ behind the Liberal Party of Canada in expressed vote intentions in Quebec. Based on 918 interviews completed in Quebec between April 17 and April 22, 1997, that survey, conducted for the two networks of the Canadian Broadcasting Corporation (CBC) and for La Presse,[11] put the BQ (with the support of 35 per cent of the respondents) behind the Liberal Party (37 per cent). The results of that survey reflected the order in which the questions had been asked (the question on vote intentions followed some 15 questions meant to put the respondents into the context of an election campaign). These results astonished the BQ members who were still hopeful. These results contrasted with those of two other Quebec surveys,[12] also conducted in late April 1997. These two other surveys, conceived in the classical manner (without a warm-up series of questions), still gave the lead to the Bloc Québécois, but by a narrow margin of 5 or 6 points. The CBC survey of late April proved to be an harbinger. Two weeks later, early in May 1997, the pollsters were giving an unanimous verdict: in Quebec, the Bloc Québécois and the Liberal Party of Canada were neck to neck.[13]

The Bloc Québécois in the May 1997 race

Well before the official announcement of the date of the election, the Bloc Québécois strategists had planned a nomination meeting in the mid-town Montréal electoral district of Laurier-Sainte-Marie, where Gilles Duceppe was to bear the colours of his party. Held on April 28, 1997, that meeting, attended by Quebec prime minister Lucien Bouchard, was meant to "launch" the Bloc Québécois electoral campaign, showing the perfect unity between the Parti Québécois leader (Lucien Bouchard) and the Bloc Québécois leader (Gilles Duceppe). However, the mood of those present (about 400 persons) was saddened by the broadcast the same evening of the results of the CBC survey which had been conducted a few days earlier.

Although dismissed as "being off track", the CBC survey results broadcast on April 28, 1997, reflected the support obtained the same day by the sovereigntist forces in two Quebec provincial by-elections. The Parti Québécois share of the votes in each district had declined considerably compared to the proportion registered in the 1994 provincial general election. The decline in the support obtained by the Parti Québécois in the two by-elections could have been a consequence of the policies of its leader, Quebec prime minister Lucien Bouchard, who had decided to restrict public spending as much as necessary in order to balance the Quebec provincial government budget by the year 2000. That type of policy was hurting a lot of people in the sovereigntist half of the French-speaking electorate in Quebec.

According to the sovereigntist leaders, notably Gilles Duceppe, the unpopular decisions made by Lucien Bouchard had been taken in the context of the federal government policy of cutting social expenditures and subsidies to the provincial governments. The day after the by-elections, Duceppe went as far as to say that the difficulties facing prime minister Bouchard were caused, in many cases, by the federal government shovelling its problems into the province's backyard. That argument has been used repeatedly since the birth of the Quebec sovereigntist movement, because it is usually effective, but, in the context of the 1997 electoral campaign, it did not bring new votes to the sovereigntist parties. Indeed, the CBC survey of late April, 1997, had shown that only a minority of the Quebec respondents blamed the federal government for the cuts in the most sensitive sector, that of health.[14]

By making the federal government responsible for the decrease in the support obtained by the Parti Québécois, Gilles Duceppe implicitly linked that decrease to the budget of the Quebec government. However, it could also be linked to a decrease in the proportion of sovereigntists among Quebec voters.[15] In the CBC survey of late April 1997, 35 per cent of Quebec respondents were in favour of granting Quebec the status of a sovereign state, down from 45 per cent according to another CBC survey conducted in March 1996 and from the 49.6 per cent registered in the October 1995 referendum. Conversely, an additional 42 per cent of the Quebec respondents stated their preference for a devolution of powers to the benefit of the government of Quebec, an increase of 5 points by comparison to the CBC survey of March 1996.

The decrease in the proportion of sovereigntists among Quebec voters was noted by other surveys conducted in May 1997. According to a survey conducted between May 16 and May 21 for the Montréal daily La Presse,[16] only 37 per cent of those interviewed would have answered YES to the question of the 1995 referendum, and 51 would have answered NO. Among those who revealed their vote intentions 31 per cent said they would vote for the Bloc Québécois candidates, 31 per cent for the Liberal Party of Canada candidates and 30 per cent for the Progressive Conservative Party candidates.

During the first three weeks of the election campaign the support for sovereignty had been falling but the support for the Bloc Québécois had fallen even more rapidly. The reasons for this abrupt decrease, registered in less than one month (the first survey pointing to this decrease had been conducted in the second half of April 1997), could have been the consequence of the Quebec government policies but it could also have reflected reactions to the statements of Jean Chrétien and to those of Jean Charest, the leaders of the two political parties which fight the Bloc Québécois in Quebec. The Bloc faced a situation where its two main opponents were waging a well-organized and well-presented electoral campaign against them. The problems experienced by the Bloc Québécois probably had much to do with the decrease in support for Quebec sovereignty but can also be linked to the Parti Québécois government policies.

The BQ leader, Gilles Duceppe, was clearly outdistanced by the popular Jean Charest in the perception of many voters, and, for the Bloc Québécois, the first weeks of the campaign looked like a long martyrdom. During the first weeks of the campaign, the Bloc Québécois organization fell into many pitfalls. For instance, on April 29, while visiting a cheese factory in Sorel, the BQ leader had to put on a hair-net type of headgear that, seen from the eye of a camera, looked laughable or ludicrous (during the whole campaign, caricaturists and opponents made fun of this hair-net). The same day, he was heard saying that Quebec was getting an inadequate share of the federal government subsidies to farmers:

opponents were quick to contrast his criticism of the federal government policy and the sorry plight of all those Manitoba farmers who were, at the very same time, hit by a terrible flood. Again on April 29, in Saint-Hyacinthe, Duceppe made a visit to a higher-education school that was deserted. On May 2, the bus carrying journalists arrived one hour late to the Cascades paper-mill in Kingsey-Falls where Duceppe was to meet potential supporters. The bad landings that were occurring every day led eventually to the resignation of the Bloc Québécois campaign director Michel Daviault, who was replaced by the more experienced Bob Dufour.

Dufour was not yet in his office when Gilles Duceppe, on May 7, had to face another crisis: Jacques Parizeau, the former Parti Québécois leader and former prime minister of Quebec, had written a few controversial sentences in a book, *Pour un Québec souverain*, that was to appear in the bookstores by May 12. According to these pre-publication reports the Quebec government could have proclaimed Quebec sovereignty immediately after getting a majority in answer to the question put to the referendum of October 1995. Gilles Duceppe (and other sovereigntist leaders) were quick to repudiate these sentences, because the question put to the Quebec voters in 1995 stated clearly that the declaration of sovereignty had to come after an formal offer of partnership had been presented to the rest of Canada. Finally, after a few days, put in their context, these sentences were shown to refer to one simple hypothesis which had been discarded. But the harm had been done.[17]

The crisis raised by Parizeau's controversial sentences was still raging when, on May 9, the largest workers' union of Quebec (with 480 000 members), the Fédération des travailleurs et travailleuses du Québec (FTQ) known also as the Quebec Labour Federation, withdrew its help from the Bloc Québécois. The reasons: the policies of the Quebec government, which was formed by the political allies of the Bloc Québécois. Bad news followed more bad news and, in mid campaign, the electoral campaign of the Bloc Québécois looked to have gone from bad to worse.

The Bloc Québécois electoral platform

The Bloc Québécois strategists had produced an electoral platform which could, in their view, gain the votes of their fellow-citizens who were unhappy with the federal government's policies. In its full text, that platform covered 122 pages. For general distribution, the platform was synthesized into a 35-page booklet, which related solely to the federal government policies.

The Bloc Québécois, of course, is universally known to pursue one main objective: to make Quebec a sovereign country within a Canada-Quebec union. This central purpose of the Bloc Québécois was conveyed in the slogan appearing on its election campaign posters: "Parole de Québécois". That slogan was completed by an explanation: "Le Bloc est là pour vous". That slogan was meant to show that the Bloc Québécois "is the voice of Quebec", by contrast to its opponents. By comparison, in French, the catch-phrase of the Liberal Party of Canada ("Agir ensemble") was meant to underline the main objectives of the chief opponents to the Bloc Québécois: to set things going in order to keep Quebec and the rest of Canada together. The English version, "Together we move forward", does not suggest the same idea.

It has been said that the leaders of the Liberal Party of Canada have planned to keep Quebec a province of Canada "like the others", by using whatever means necessary. There is also talk of a secret "Plan B" to be applied if a majority in Quebec voted to make Quebec an independent country. ("Plan A" would seek to accomplish this by persuading the population of Quebec that it is desirable to keep Canada united.) According to the sovereigntists, that secret "Plan B" is (or was) a denial of the "right" of the majority in Quebec to decide its constitutional future by raising constitutional and legal objections. In the 122-page electoral platform of the Bloc Québécois, the very first page condemns that secret "plan B". In that first page of the platform, one section is titled: "NON au Plan B, OUI au Québec, OUI au partenariat."

The platform goes on to state: "Nous pouvons comprendre que les Canadiens ne veuillent pas transformer leur pays pour reconnaître au Québec les pouvoirs et moyens qu'il estime nécessaire... nous n'avons pas d'autre choix que de travailler à hâter le moment où le Québec, ayant décidé de devenir souverain, offrira au Canada de négocier le partenariat, contribuant ainsi à régler la perpétuelle crise constitutionnelle canadienne".

After the first 6 pages of the full platform have dealt with the main objective of the Bloc Québécois, the accession of Quebec to sovereignty, the other 116 pages are devoted to the party's proposals in the field of current federal jurisdiction. These are the pages which were synthesized in the 35-page booklet, *Plate-forme électorale. Document synthèse. Bloc Québécois.*

Reading the full text of the Bloc Québécois platform, one has to conclude that the writers, in the years preceding Quebec sovereignty, favour three main objectives: (a) policies meant to put people to work and to sustain continuous improvement in the quality of life, (b) policies aimed at a more equal distribution of individual disposable income, (c) policies that enhance and increase the powers of the provincial governments. The first of these objectives is common to all parties, but each party has his own way of aiming at it. The proposals of the Bloc Québécois are somewhat akin to those of the New Democratic Party, as are its proposals related to the second objective (more equality). The Bloc Québécois stands alone from the viewpoint of its third objective dealing with the federal government policies (more powers to the provincial governments), as it stands alone in its desire to make Quebec a sovereign country.

In the view of experienced campaigners, the Bloc Québécois can get a high level of support only if its message stresses its "difference" from other parties. If the Bloc Québécois does not focus on its main objective (the sovereignty of Quebec), many sovereigntists may desert it, opting for not taking part in elections or giving their votes to the party which best suits their interests in areas other than the "national question". This line of reasoning is not held by every member of the Bloc Québécois; here and there exists a person who proposes to keep silent on the main objective of the party, believing that such a tactic can bring new votes. Apparently, such a person has had the last word in the writing of the 35-page booklet, *Plate-forme électorale. Document synthèse*, because it only refers once to the main objective of the Bloc Québécois and it does so in the following words: "En attendant le jour proche où les Québécoises et les Québécois se donneront un pays, le Bloc s'engage à défendre leurs intérêts et à prendre la parole pour le Québec". For his part, the new campaign director, Bob Dufour, said that, for the remainder of the campaign, the Bloc Québécois had to focus on the project making Quebec a sovereign country.[18]

If voters simply chose the party whose platform is the closest to their own preferences, then the Bloc Québécois should have received the votes of those who ask for a devolution of federal powers to the benefit of the Quebec government and who, at the same time, favour "equalitarian" policies. But things are not that simple. Only a proportion of the voters know much about the party platforms, and those who do make a choice on this basis are known to take several other criteria into account. One of these other criteria is the past performance of each party.

The Bloc Québécois record as an opposition party

Between the election of 1993 and April 1997, the relatively stable level of support given the Bloc Québécois, as measured by surveys, shows that the performance of the sovereigntists in the House of Commons was considered satisfactory by those who side with the sovereigntists.

According to a survey conducted during the first week of May 1997, the proportion of Quebec respondents satisfied with the Bloc Québécois caucus in Ottawa's Parliament was almost equal to the proportion of respondents giving their vote to that party.[19] Precisely, 39 per cent of the Quebec respondents were satisfied with the BQ caucus, 44 per cent were not, and 17 per cent felt unable or unwilling to say whether they were or were not. The same survey showed that the proportion of Quebec respondents satisfied with the government of Canada (41 per cent) was in the vicinity of the proportion of respondents giving their vote to the Liberal Party of Canada.

The same early May 1997 survey showed the Bloc Québécois' new leader, Gilles Duceppe, was trusted by a proportion of the respondents more or less equivalent to the proportion favouring his party.[20] 39 per cent of the respondents said that Gilles Duceppe was "trustworthy", while 41 per cent felt the same about Jean Chrétien, and 59 per cent about Jean Charest. However, according to another survey, conducted between May 6 and May 10, only 9 per cent of the Quebec respondents felt that Gilles Duceppe was the leader who had done the best campaigning.[21] According to 31 per cent of the respondents, Jean Charest had been, so far, the best campaigner; a similar proportion of the respondents felt that he was the leader likely to best represent the interest of Quebec in Ottawa. While being ranked third from the viewpoint of campaigning, Gilles Duceppe was seen by 26 per cent of the respondents as the leader best able to represent Quebec interests in Ottawa.

The last two weeks of the election campaign

Charest's ratings were helped by his performance in the television debates. The day after the second part of the French-language television debate (held on May 18), in which Gilles Duceppe was unable to overcome his opponents, the Bloc Québécois activists looked panic-stricken. A number of former high-profile figures of the Parti Québecois, such as television artist and producer Lise Payette, got into the campaign in the hope of reversing the down-hill slide of the Bloc Québécois.

And then came the unexpected: a controversial television clip produced by the Reform Party made many French-speaking Quebecers feel that they were not wanted in Canada. In a few sentences, on May 23, the leader of the Liberal Party of Canada, Jean Chrétien, showed his indignation. But, the day after, Gilles Duceppe was quick to say that it was the attitude of Jean Chrétien himself and that of Jean Charest towards the majority of French-speaking Quebecers that was fuelling the Quebec bashing outside Quebec.   On May 26, 1997, in a televised interview, Jean

Chrétien repeated that he would not "recognize" the verdict of a referendum on Quebec sovereignty if only a "majority of 50 per cent plus one" had sided with the sovereigntists.[22] That statement was regarded as undemocratic by a great many Quebecers.[23] It was hastily condemned by Jean Charest and, vehemently, by the sovereigntist leaders.

For the Bloc Québécois, the events of the last days of the election campaign were a gift. The results of the last surveys of the campaign, published 72 hours before election day, put the Bloc Québécois ahead of the Liberal Party of Canada in the vote intentions of Quebecers. For the Bloc Québécois, the worst had been avoided.

Results and outlook

The disappointing results for the BQ likely resulted from several sources. First, many people who voted "Yes" in the 1995 referendum did not vote in the election, or supported other parties. Second, the Progressive Conservative Party led by Jean Charest has lured, in 1997, many voters who, in 1993 or 1995, sided with the sovereigntists. Moreover, the CBC survey of late April 1997 showed that among the Quebec respondents leaning in favour of the Progressive Conservative Party, 23 per cent were "sovereigntists."[24]

The revival of the Progressive Conservative Party in 1997 has made a difference in almost every district where a member of the 1993 Bloc Québécois caucus was beaten. In 1997 the four new Quebec seats gained by the Progressive Conservative Party were seats taken by the Bloc Québécois in 1993. Moreover, looking at the detailed results of the election, we find that the gains of the Liberal Party of Canada in most of the new Quebec districts coincided with the revival of the Progressive Conservative Party. This is the case in Ahuntsic, Saint-Lambert, Compton-Stanstead, Brossard-Laprairie, and Bellechasse-Etchemin-Montmagny-L'Islet, these five districts being represented by the Bloc Québécois when the election was called.

The decrease in the support given to the Bloc Québécois, in the election of 1997, cannot be explained by a single factor. It cannot be explained simply by the "frankness" and "stiffness" of its new leader, Gilles Duceppe, and by the easy-going manner of Jean Charest. It cannot be explained simply by the election campaign. In the first days of the election campaign, the Bloc Québécois and the Liberal Party of Canada were neck and neck in the vote intentions registered by the pollsters. The pollsters then noted a decrease in the level of support for the Bloc Québécois and saw a link between this decrease and the blunders made by the BQ organization during the first weeks of the campaign. Then, the results of the election make one believe that by focusing on its main objective, Quebec sovereignty, the Bloc Québécois was able, in the last days of the campaign, to recover a little. All in all, the election has produced what was already shown in the surveys of the first days of the campaign.

We should seriously consider the impact of the Quebec government's policies on the support granted to the sovereigntists and to sovereignty in 1997. The decrease in that support coincides with the unpopular measures taken by the Quebec government in the few months preceding the 1997 election. The new Quebec government policy of restrictions on its actions is a factor which started to play in the year 1996-1997 and especially in the first months of 1997. In contrast, the attitudes of Jean Chrétien or of Jean Charest have not changed since 1993 and they cannot explain much because the decline suffered by the Bloc Québécois is clearly traceable to April-May 1997.

Once in a while, commentators question the utility, for sovereigntists, of the Bloc Québécois being well represented in the Canadian House of Commons. On May 22, 1997, the chairman of the Fédération des travailleurs et travailleuses du Québec, Clément Godbout, has said publicly that the relevance of the Bloc Québécois was debatable.[25] When the question was asked to a sample of voters, 42 per cent of the respondents said that the Bloc Québécois was "still useful" in Ottawa,[26] an opinion held by 88 per cent of those who were planning to vote for the Bloc Québécois. To most sovereigntists, the Bloc Québécois presence in the Canadian House of Commons is a "must": it is required in order to help the Parti Québécois in its endeavours. The Bloc Québécois members certainly recognize that their future is linked to the future of their provincial ally, the Parti Québécois. The election campaign of 1997 has shown, once again, after the 1992 referendum, the 1993 Canadian election, the 1994 Quebec provincial election and the 1995 Quebec referendum, that the two parties are very close friends indeed.

Notes

[1] See Jules Richer, "La dissension éclate au grand jour - Le député Réal Ménard demande à son chef, Michel Gauthier, de "réfléchir" à son avenir", Le Devoir, November 30, 1996, pages A12.

[2] Michel Gauthier was chosen leader of the Bloc Québécois on February 17, 1996. He had been prefered to Francine Lalonde, who was the other candidate to the leadership.

[3] See, for instance, Gilles Gauthier, "Gauthier démissionne", La Presse,

December 3, 1996, page A1, or Michel Venne, "De l'air frais au Bloc", *Le Devoir*, December 3, 1996, page A8.

[4] Pierre O'Neill, "Duceppe fixe la barre à 38 élus", *Le Devoir*, December 19, 1996, page A4.

[5] See Édouard Cloutier et Yann Strutynski, "L'opinion publique québécoise", pages 107-117 in *L'année politique au Québec 1995-1996*, sous la direction de Robert Boily, Montréal, Éditions Fides, 1997.

[6] This survey of 1 050 Quebec voters was conducted for the Canadian Broadcasting Corporation and Société Radio-Canada, by the Centre de recherche sur l'opinion publique (*CROP*) and *Environics*. The results of this survey were published in various newspapers on March 26, 1996.

[7] Mario Fontaine, "Les souverainistes ont la cote", *La Presse*, June 1, 1996, page B10 (the survey data quoted by Mario Fontaine reflected the answers produced in 1 009 interviews).

[8] The results of this survey were published by *La Presse*, on January 25, 1997.

[9] Lia Lévesque, "Gauthier promet la "surprise de sa vie" à Chrétien", *Le Devoir*, January 25, 1997, page A4.

[10] For one elaborate criticism of the process used by the Bloc Québécois to select its leader, based on this type of argument, see Lysiane Gagnon, "Un mode de scrutin déficient", *La Presse*, March 15, 1997, page B3.

[11] This survey had been conducted in Quebec by the Centre de recherche sur l'opinion publique (*CROP*) in conjunction with *Environics*, a Toronto firm which made a similar investigation elsewhere. The results were broadcast by CBC and Société Radio-Canada on April 28, 1997, and were published in *La Presse*, on April 29, 1997. The survey dealt with several topics related to Canadian politics and not only with vote intentions.

[12] A Quebec survey conducted by a firm led by Jean-Marc Léger (*Léger et Léger*), between April 16 and April 22, 1997, awarded 43 per cent of the vote intentions to the Bloc Québécois, and 37 per cent to the Liberal Party of Canada. Another Quebec survey conducted at the same time by another polling organization (*SOM*) gave 40 per cent of the vote intentions to the Bloc Québécois and 35 per cent to the Liberal Party of Canada.

[13] According to the weekly Quebec surveys conducted by *Léger et Léger* during the election campaign, the vote intentions favouring the Bloc Québécois fluctuated between 33 and 37 per cent, and those favouring the Liberal Party of Canada fluctuated between 33 and 39 per cent. The results of these surveys were published, every Saturday of the campaign, by *Le Journal de Montréal*. Other weekly Quebec survey results, obtained from *SOM*, were published in *La Presse*: according to the *SOM* surveys, the

support in favour of the Bloc Québécois, in May 1997, fluctuated between 31 and 39 per cent of the vote intentions, and the support in favour of the Liberal Party of Canada ranged from 33 to 39 per cent of the vote intentions.

[14] Michèle Ouimet, "L'optimisme renaît", *La Presse*, April 30, 1997, page B1.

[15] Michèle Ouimet, "La souveraineté perd des plumes", *La Presse*, April 30, 1997, page B1.

[16] André Pratte, "L'appui à la souveraineté fond avec la popularité du Bloc", *La Presse*, May 23, 1997, page B1.

[17] For example, *La Presse* carried the story in four of its pages in its edition of May 8. Its leader writer, Alain Dubuc, said that Jacques Parizeau, in 1995, "had chosen to lie to the Quebec voters" but, cautious, he said also that "one can wonder if the idea was anything but a fancy without substance" (my translation). See, Alain Dubuc, "Jacques Parizeau, l'arnaqueur", *La Presse*, May 8, 1997, page B2.

[18] Denis Lessard, "Le Bloc québécois recentre son discours sur la souveraineté", *La Presse*, May 6, 1997, pages B5.

[19] André Pratte, "Les Québécois sont insatisfaits du gouvernement et... du Bloc", *La Presse*, May 13, 1997, page B1.

[20] André Pratte, "Le Bloc et les libéraux se retrouvent à égalité", *La Presse*, May 8, 1997, page B1.

[21] André Pratte, "Charest gagne les coeurs, mais pas les votes", *La Presse*, May 13, 1997, page B1.

[22] Chantal Hébert, "Une majorité simple ne suffirait pas. Chrétien ne reconnaîtrait pas un OUI obtenu avec une majorité de 50% plus un", *La Presse*, May 26, 1997, page A1.

[23] According to a survey conducted for *La Presse*, 45 per cent of the 1002 Quebec respondents feel that the federal government should accept the verdict of a Quebec referendum on sovereignty, whatever the question put, and an additional 39 per cent feel that it should accept that verdict only if the question had obtained its agreement. On this, see André Pratte, "Ottawa devrait avoir son mot à dire sur la question", *La Presse*, May 24, 1997, page B1.

[24] André Pratte, "Les néo-bleus sont des bloquistes mous", *La Presse*, April 30, 1997, pages A1 and A2.

[25] Louis-Gilles Francouer, "Le président de la FTQ s'interroge sur la pertinence du Bloc", *Le Devoir*, May 23, 1997, page A1.

[26] André Pratte, "Les Québécois partagés sur l'utilité du Bloc", *La Presse*, May 30, 1997, page B1.

Eight

The Television Coverage: A History of the Election in 65 Seconds

by Christopher Dornan

Media coverage of the 1997 federal election left few lasting televisual impressions. Even the moderator's sudden collapse during the French language debate occurred just off camera. There was no equivalent of Brian Mulroney's "You had an option, sir" hectoring of John Turner during the 1984 campaign, or Turner's assault on Mulroney's patriotism over Free Trade during the 1988 debates, or Kim Campbell's impolitic remark at the onset of the 1993 campaign that Canadians could look forward to an upturn in employment "at the turn of the century." If there was a signature image that captured the dynamic of the 1997 election, it was not an encounter between politicians, between a politician and the public, or between a politician and the news media. It was a television advertisement: the Reform Party's "unity" ad.

The previous election had featured an even more infamous ad, the Tory spot that focused on Jean Chrétien's disfigurement. In some respects at least, the two ads resemble one another. Both aired only briefly and late in the campaign — one of the last things voters saw before going to the polling stations. They were both "attack ads". Each was volatile enough that the ad itself became a campaign story for the news media. Both, surely, were crafted by party professionals who had to wonder whether they might not be taking a step too far.

There the similarity ends. The Conservative ad of 1993 was widely interpreted as a sign of desperation on the part of a failing campaign. It backfired badly. It made no difference to the party's fall from government, but it may have made the difference between the Tories winning or losing official party status. Whatever the motivation for the Reform ad, it was not desperation. Far from failing, the Reform campaign was attempting to hold and build momentum. The ad was controversial, but it did not obviously backfire. It may have made a difference in Reform winning the status of Official Opposition. It may also have made a difference in the Liberals winning a majority government. Which is to say, it stiffened resolve in both camps. The Reform ad flashed up black-and-white photos of Jean Chrétien, Jean Charest, Gilles Duceppe and Lucien Bouchard, before stamping their images with a red, slashed circle — the international symbol for "verboten." A narrator intoned: "Not just Quebec politicians."

The ad itself did not ignite the unity issue. Jacques Parizeau did that, even before the first leaders' debate. Just as his memoirs were about to be published in the midst of a federal election, word leaked out that Parizeau confessed in his book to planning an immediate declaration of Quebec independence had the referendum yielded a majority "Oui" vote. In both Quebec and anglophone Canada, this was a newsworthy development. For someone presumably about to launch a book tour, Parizeau's behaviour was odd. He was not available to comment. Then, when he did appear before the cameras, he pointed to a contusion on his forehead by way of explanation. At first, both Bouchard and Duceppe distanced themselves from the story. Two days later, both the PQ and the Bloc were defending the former premier as a statesman of the cause.

The incident provided an opportunity for Reform. It was evidence of the duplicity of the separatist element. More than that, it revealed how hesitant the other major federal parties had become; neither the Liberals nor the Conservatives pounced to exploit this embarrassment to the separatists, seemingly too nervous about upsetting needed voters in Quebec. Preston Manning and his party had found the issue that spoke to their constituency. Manning pressed the unity issue from the first debate to the final days of the campaign. The advertisement was simply a logical endpoint of a specific campaign strategy. It crystallized the division between Reform and the other federalist parties in that its import shifted according to one's perspective, like a gestalt figure drawing that appears to be either a vase or two faces in profile, but not both at once. To sovereigntists, the ad was yet another sign of English Canadian antagonism toward Quebec. "Old school" federalists greeted it in similar terms, horrified by what they saw as the ad's message of intolerance. This was the Reform Party's unvarnished contribution to the question of national "unity"? An ugly, self-serving appeal to division?

But from the Reform perspective, the reaction the ad provoked within the political and media establishment only demonstrated what the advertisement was arguing: that the dialogue of governance in Canada had become a closed conversation in which even the separatists and the established federal parties shared the same hostile reaction to the regions' complaints of alienation. As Manning said repeatedly during the English language leaders' debates: "You're not listening." The fact that he said it while another leader was attempting to speak only revealed that he was not listening either.

That, in the end, was the campaign dynamic of the 1997 election. The defining media moment came, not from the coverage rendered by journalists, but from a campaign propaganda message. This is not to say that the television coverage of the election was without consequence, but it was unintrusive in the sense that the dynamic was established by the political actors, not by the media who were shadowing them. The legacy of the networks in the 1997 election was not so much the substantive content of their coverage as the way in which that coverage was organized behind the scenes — that is, how the networks agreed they would present the campaign to the public. Ironically, procedures of coverage designed to let the politicians speak to the people in as unmediated a manner as the media could manage were criticized by the public as something approaching a dereliction of journalistic duty.

If an election is begrudged by the electorate, perhaps it is inevitable that its coverage will be too. Certainly, in the early summer of 1997, the country was hardly flush with enthusiasm for a contest over how it should be governed. From start to finish, the election was a dutifully tolerated annoyance. The public was sceptical to begin with, irritated at being summoned to the polls for no apparent good reason. The campaign was grating. The outcome was unsurprising and uninspiring. After the fact, the national mood seemed to be that matters were no further ahead than when the writ had been dropped — the country had resolved nothing.

This was not the fault of the media, although the media provided the stage on which it all played out. If the public was dissatisfied with Election '97, blame attached primarily to the political classes, but in some regard the media were implicated. There is nothing new in blaming the media for skewed, superficial or shoddy campaign coverage. Politicians do it almost by reflex. Defeated Maritime Liberal MP Roger Simmons did it before television cameras immediately after the election, attributing the loss of his seat to how the media conferred or denied publicity. Nor is it unusual for the public to disparage media coverage, for any number of reasons. However, one of the noteworthy aspects of Election '97 was the way in which the public found the media wanting.

From the point of view of party machines, elections are exercises in mass persuasion; they are about convincing as many people as possible to act in a way helpful to one's cause. The media, especially television, are society's agencies of public address; they provide the means to speak to as many people as possible. The independence yet interdependence of these two social actors — the political classes and the fourth estate — is one of the central tensions of liberal democracy. It is a power relation in which neither side can be seen to exercise purely discretionary authority. The government, or those who would form a government, cannot be allowed to control the content of the news media. The political classes must surrender their public representation to paid witnesses, none of them on the payroll of the competing parties.

By the same token, the media cannot act capriciously. Columnists and editorial boards may throw their weight behind parties or candidates according to their best judgement, as long as these are different parties and different candidates. Whether by diktat from corporate headquarters or a general closing of ranks, the news media as a whole cannot be permitted to favour one party over others. In short, democracy is founded on the promise that the state is prohibited from policing what can and cannot be said in public. The media, for their part, are expected to array the various options for the benefit of the electorate, and to do so without prejudice. But if democracy relies on an independent fourth estate, what if this independence is compromised or unreliable?

The usual complaint about the news media is that they fail to properly discharge their duties because their coverage intervenes in the course of events, unfairly playing to one side or another. That is, the media arrogate to themselves an authority to which they are not entitled: the way in which they chronicle the election becomes a factor in its outcome. On both sides of the political spectrum, the complaint is typically that the media "frame" the issues — i.e. set the conditions of coverage — so as to ignore or denigrate alternatives. The left insists that a corporatist mindset on the part of the media has eroded the democratic process. The right is equally convinced that rational governance has become all but impossible, given how automatically obstinate the media have become.

From the point of view of the professionals in the news media, therefore, the task is not to intrude but to let the campaign unfold of its own accord. Commentary, analysis, judicious observation, editorial tub thumping — these are all permitted. A general election campaign, after all, is a nationwide argumentative conversation about how people wish to be governed. But the media's bedrock responsibility is to let the candidates have their say before the public as the candidates see fit. This is the tacit contract between the state and the fourth estate in a liberal democracy: neither player is allowed to highjack the proceedings. Curious, then, that the common complaint about the journalism of Election '97 was that the media failed to muscle in on the course of events, as though reportage alone was insufficient.

The exemplar of straight reportage is the Cable Public Affairs Channel, CPAC. For unsullied coverage of campaign minutiae, this was the television channel of record in 1997. Its cameras followed candidates on doorbell-to-doorbell treks through their constituencies, not merely for a minute or so but for hours, just to give viewers an idea of what a campaign is like for local candidates or party workers. On the evening of the election, before the polls closed, while the other networks were gearing up to cover the returns, CPAC aired behind-the-scenes interviews with senior editors at The Globe and Mail, The Montréal Gazette, CTV News and so on, covering the preparations to cover the returns.

Two days after the election, a CPAC camera crew boarded a VIA Rail train heading from Halifax to Montréal. The team moved down the train from car to car, stopping to ask passengers about their reactions to the vote. One young woman, asked whether she thought Canadians were well informed going into the election, answered that "You really had to go out and look for it." That is, the information she wanted to hear was not readily available. The media, she suggested, constrained the election agenda, limiting attention to a narrow range of campaign issues set by the politicians. "We heard a lot about national unity," she said, "which I suppose is a good thing." But she argued that various other issues which should have been discussed were somehow absent. This sentiment was echoed in different ways by other passengers aboard the train, and it was likely the general reaction. People spoke about the lack of attention paid to issues such as health care, education, social security, and especially jobs. Even though, strictly speaking, health care and education are provincial responsibilities, the federal government does play a role in both health care and education through transfer payments to the provinces and other mechanisms, and the voters wished to hear their concerns addressed by those who sought federal office.

What voters wanted, it seemed, was a debate between the parties about the state of the nation, its social and economic well-being. For the most part, they felt they were denied it. Instead, for the first two weeks or so, they were treated to a lacklustre exercise. In the final weeks, the campaign became a fractious, divisive, posturing and frankly exasperating exchange. It was a debate about the state of the nation, yes, but it was framed in terms of national unity — which is to say, it was about the Quebec question. Worse, it was a debate that many judged did more harm than good, merely entrenching hardline positions and raising the ambient temperature while accomplishing nothing. If the electorate was not engaged — and the lowest voter turnout in 50 years suggests it was not — it was because of a dislocation between the concerns of the voters and the contours of the campaign. The terms in which the politicians spoke were not those the public would have chosen. It was as though the politicians managed to sidestep the issues, and the media let them get away with it. When the campaign dynamic turned to name calling over Quebec, again the media failed to call things to heel.

In the eyes of the public, the sin of the networks and newspapers in this campaign was not that they highjacked the proceedings, but that they should have. By not doing so, by hewing to the politicians' agenda, they became blameworthy. If the election debate did not unfold in terms the public would have preferred, according to whose terms did it unfold? Presumably someone else's — the political classes and their handservants, a far-too-compliant press corps. The two mutually suspicious social actors were tarred by the same brush.

This complaint was not limited to the public; it was voiced by journalists themselves. *Ottawa Citizen* media writer Chris Cobb, writing in the Canadian Association of Journalists' *Media* magazine, argued that reporters "failed to distinguish themselves in an election campaign in which jobs should have been the main focus." The media, Cobb maintained, gave short shrift to the NDP, the sole party attempting to campaign on the issue of jobs. This "sent the unfortunate signal to the other federal parties that the news media were about as committed to making jobs the number one campaign issue as they, the politicians, were."[1]

Though genuinely felt, this is an altogether vague complaint. In what regard would media intervention in the campaign have been justified? How and on what occasion could the fourth estate have taken control of the agenda? Even if it had been possible, even if it were desirable, by what right could the media have superseded the politicians to impose their own campaign dynamic? And what precedent would this have established? Nor is it clear that the NDP were somehow muzzled by a press corps indifferent to the party's message and dismissive of its electoral prospects. It is simply not true that the New Democrats were ignored by the media; their campaign was covered as a matter of course. If the NDP campaign message failed to ignite, this may have had as much to do with the message as anything else. It is one thing to recognize a public anxiety over jobs and job security; it is another to persuade the public that one's platform offers the solution. Though the public may well have been concerned about the issue of jobs, in a climate in which people increasingly accept that government alone can do little to create employment, the NDP platform may have fallen on unreceptive ears. Even the surprising showing of the NDP in the Maritime provinces — surprising because few in the press corps, the punditry, the political classes, or indeed the electorate, anticipated it — may have had as much to do with the brute arithmetic of how the vote split in Atlantic Canada as with the resonance of the NDP message with Maritime voters.

Nor were the media in lockstep in their coverage of the election. The news media are not a monolithic entity, and the coverage and commentary they provide ranges from the network newscasts' nightly digests to the op-ed analysis carried by daily newspapers; from the unmediated coverage of CPAC to the panel discussions of CBC Newsworld; from the forum of open-line talk shows to the unabashedly partisan coverage of publications such as *Alberta Report*. One may have had "to go out and look for it," but there was a range of coverage available if one did.

Likely, relatively few voters made the effort. On CBC's Sunday Report the night before the election, reporter Susan Bonner offered an assessment of the public mood on the eve of the vote. Her report contained a series of person-in-the-street interviews in which voter after voter confessed to minimal interest in the election. Pollsters testified that the public was not simply apathetic but alienated from the campaign. Given the dislocation between the campaign and the electorate, it seemed this was an election most voters watched out of the corner of one eye. And when one is not fully attentive to the details of an election, one is ever more reliant on the nightly digests of the network reporters. Television, or at least the television newscast, is the preferred medium of the quick snapshot and the brief update.

To be fair, the public had good reason not to be fully engaged by the election. Quite apart from the apparent absence of a pressing reason to go to the polls, other events competed for attention, especially in the first weeks: the Manitoba flood, the unravelling of the Bre-X fiasco, the Stanley Cup playoffs. In the early days of the campaign, even the networks seemed otherwise preoccupied; often the election was not the lead item on the evening newscasts.

As a result, network television coverage provided a register of the moments and mood of the campaign, but otherwise exercised little direct influence on the course of events. By its nature, television has always been better at capturing images than communicating substantive detail. Or, rather, image is its substance. The strength of the medium is affect, not content; emotion rather than information. In an election short on clearly articulated policy differences but in which the tempo of rhetoric picked up toward the finish, television coverage was an oscilloscope that charted the campaign's telltale rhythms.

The parties are well aware of the character of the medium and therefore they design campaign events with the needs of the cameras and the requirements of the newscasts in mind. Thornton Wilder once described literature as "the orchestration of platitudes." He never witnessed a modern media campaign. If, as Jurgen Habermas argues, democracy has been reduced to a series of periodic plebiscites on one set of administrative managers over others, the further flaw is that not even this contest is decided through informed public discussion of different administrative options. Instead, it is waged on the basis of symbolic gestures that are somehow supposed to speak the parties' various positions. What the parties look for in their campaign events — and hope for in their representation on the networks — is the succinct performance that will play as scripted and resonate with viewers.

That is why the leaders' debates are invariably disappointing. As regular and expected as they have become, the debates are really campaign innovations of the television age, and in every election they are negotiated anew between the parties and the broadcasters. What will be the venue? How will time be apportioned? Who will be the interlocutors? What will be the responsibilities of the moderator? How will the set be dressed? How will things look?

Though the debates are television's attempt to throw the leaders together in an unscripted format, allowing enough time for genuine differences of policy and ability to emerge, they rarely live up to the ideal. As an exercise in shedding the theatrics of the modern media campaign, they are self-defeating. Because they are rare opportunities to see the party leaders interact with one another directly, supposedly without the benefit of handlers and without the intrusion of the press corps, the debates are a moment of attentiveness in any campaign, and therefore a spike on the media oscilloscope. That makes them grist for the machinery of the instant verdict and the abbreviated account after-the-fact. The debate itself may last an hour, 90 minutes, two hours — it hardly matters. What will matter in the end is the media's snap characterization, complete with defining utterance or exchange, replayed again and again on news outlets across the country. Knowing that, the politicians play to the videotape. A televised debate is little more than a struggle for soundbite supremacy. In the heat of the moment, whatever the barb, the well-briefed leader will always have a rehearsed response at the ready. The debates are by now little more than "advertorials" in which the worst prospect for any leader is to be caught sputtering, failed by one's prepared script and bested by another's.

By the same token, because the news media know that the parties work to cloak themselves in self-serving imagery, the media are on the lookout for telling images of their own. Some of these may puncture the best-laid political plans. They may be incidents the parties would prefer passed unnoticed; they might be campaign tactics represented in a way to which the tacticians take exception; they might even be unplanned occurrences serendipitously favourable to one campaign or another. There is nothing worrisome about this stance on the part of the fourth estate. Correctly, political journalists see their job as telling attentive voters what they need to know about the election as it unfolds. If their running account differs from the politicians' version, that is only to be expected. On balance, it is probably to be applauded.

More revealing than any content analysis, CBC Television produced its own digest of the televisual moments of Election '97, distilling the entire five-week campaign down to 22 images packaged in 65 seconds — almost exactly three seconds per image. This aide memoire aired on Sunday Report the night before the election, one final briefing note for the benefit of the electorate. Other networks aired their own versions, but the CBC summation was as representative as any.

Here is an annotated shot list of the CBC's compendium of the media moments of the 1997 election:

1. The Prime Minister standing outside the Governor General's residence, addressing the media and announcing that "A general election will be held on June the second."

    Here, the CBC might have included Mr. Chrétien's fumbling response to the question of why the election had been called, but chose not to.

2. Newfoundland protesters rocking a Liberal campaign bus containing members of the press.

    The bus was heading to what had been planned as a triumphant Liberal campaign event, the opening of the Hibernia oil platform. Visually arresting and an expression of passionate dissatisfaction with the government's record, this departure from the party's script is the type of incident beloved by the media. It did not hurt, either, that members of the media were themselves cast as actors in the story.

3. Reform MP Deborah Grey and leader Preston Manning, both

wearing Edmonton Oilers hockey shirts, smiling astride a motorcycle on an airport tarmac, Grey declaring "Riding to victory!" before the bike guns away from party supporters and media cameras.

This is a textbook example of a campaign appearance staged for the cameras: the spectacle is just unusual enough to warrant inclusion in the nightly newscasts, while the theatrics have been designed to suggest that the party is heading into the election in a spirit of confidence, enthusiasm and fun. But what, exactly, makes it unusual? Is it the picture of Preston Manning, a leader with the charisma of a take-charge school principal, saddled aboard the emblem of devil-may-care rebellion, the motorcycle? Is it that Grey has the handlebars while Manning sits astern? Or is it that neither of them are wearing helmets? And why are they not wearing helmets, as required by law? Is this symbolic of their Western Canadian refusal to submit to federal law when it infringes on individual liberties? Is it somehow evocative of Western frustration with the Liberal governments' gun control initiatives? Or is it simply that protective headgear defeats the image of being astride a motorcycle, and that therefore, for the benefit of the cameras, it is better to break the law than look goofy? (See Gilles Duceppe, below.)

4. Preston Manning on the boardwalk in Québec City, unveiling a leaked copy of the Liberal Party platform, Red Book II. "Goodbye Red Book," he says. "Hello chequebook."

5. Manning pitching copies of Red Book II onto the floor from behind a podium, demonstrating that the document will not fly.

In these two shots, the embarrassment to the government of Reform upstaging the release of the Liberals' own platform has been packaged in the form of succinct slogans and televisual gestures.

6. Jean Charest grilling and flipping a copy of Red Book II at an outdoor barbecue. "A few onions on the Red Book?" he laughs.

This was the Tory attempt to belittle the Liberal manifesto, but as a campaign gesture it was not nearly as successful as Reform's. In some quarters it was seen as needlessly disrespectful and too reminiscent of book burning.

7. Alexa McDonough on the streets of Halifax with an NDP party official speaking on her behalf. "Alexa has lost her voice," he explains.

While true — McDonough was suffering from laryngitis — the

image seemed to symbolize the seeming voicelessness of the NDP in the campaign.

8. The Bloc Québécois bus driver, clearly hopelessly lost.

9. Gilles Duceppe bounding up a flight of stairs at a dairy factory, wearing a plastic hair net.

Neither of these incidents was of any real consequence in what is supposed to be a debate over policy differences, but the media seized on them nonetheless. They were taken to be symbolic of a directionless, disorganized campaign. The plastic hair net, or the "condom hat" as it came to be known, was especially egregious in an age when party campaigns are built on the projection of image. It supposedly made Duceppe look foolish. His failing, and the failing of his campaign, therefore, was an inability to anticipate how he would be perceived. If politicians cannot manage image, how can voters trust them to manage substance? No matter that such headgear is required by law in food processing plants and worn every day by the people who work in them, the hair net was a symbolic stigma in the eyes of the media. This begs the question of what the media would have had Duceppe do. Forego the hair net, break the law, and pollute the company's products by shedding into yogurt vats? Or are such factory workplaces now off-limits to politicians, on the grounds that anywhere one has to wear a blue-collar uniform is not image-friendly?

10. Gilles Duceppe telling the media: "That won't happen again, count on me."

Duceppe fired the bus driver (who promptly complained he was being scapegoated) and never again handed the media an image that could be so easily used to make sport of him.

11. The leaders filing in for the first debate.

12. Jean Charest speaking during the first debate, promising that "If there's one commitment to my children, it's that I'm going to pass on to them the country I received from my parents. I'm determined to make that happen."

This became the network highlight from the first debate, if only because it was the sole moment at which the audience in the debate chamber broke into spontaneous applause. Coming hard on the heels of the advance revelations from Jacques Parizeau's memoir, Charest's declaration, the applause that greeted it, and the play of the clip on the network newscasts, all sealed the fact that national unity would be a campaign issue to contend with. At least three of the parties stood to gain.

For the Bloc, at the very least the unity issue would provide an occasion to speak to Quebeckers about the need for sovereignty; doubtless it would also provide evidence (supplied by Reform) that could be used to show how the rest of Canada stood opposed to Quebec's interests. The Tories and Reform, meanwhile, could remind voters of how the Liberals — running on apparently nothing more than their record as managers — very nearly had lost the referendum through mismanagement. Jean Charest could capitalize on his well-received performance during the referendum, contrasting it with the Prime Minister's, while Reform could further distinguish itself from the other federalist parties by insisting that the old ideas are clearly bankrupt.

Only the Liberals and the NDP would have preferred that the unity issue remain muted. As the governing party, and a party that assumed it would retain power, the Liberals could ill afford to be forced to spell out how they proposed to handle Lucien Bouchard. For the NDP, excessive attention to unity could only detract from what it hoped would be the chief issue of the campaign: the Liberal record on the social fabric; the triumph of technocrats over compassion.

13. The highlight from the second debate: Radio-Canada's Jean-Francoise Lepine, in the midst of posing a singularly pointed question to the Prime Minister, looks flummoxed and glances off camera at the stricken figure of the debate moderator, Claire Lamarche, who had fainted.

   Her collapse would have been dramatic by itself. That it occurred just as the Prime Minister was being called upon to answer whether he would respect a simple majority in the event of a separatist victory in any upcoming Quebec referendum made the entire evening bizarre. What was called for was an unequivocal answer to the unity issue's most volatile question. The question hung in the air over the entire country.

14. Claire Lamarche being carried out of the building on a gurney by ambulance attendants as a figure in the foreground attempts to shield her from the cameras, pleading "S'il vous plait ... "

   The distress of this public figure at such a public moment suddenly became a private matter. To their credit, most Canadians concurred. Though Ms. Lamarche had been on television screens across the country only moments before, television had no business shoving cameras in her face simply because she had been taken ill. Note that when she collapsed, the staff in the TV control room during the debate chose not to swing their cameras toward her.

15. Preston Manning at a campaign stop, declaring "This is the unity blocker."

    He was not referring to himself, but the fact that Reform was about to pursue the unity issue to the fullest.

16. A snippet from the Reform "unity" ad, with the red slash across the images of Chrétien, Charest, Duceppe and Bouchard, and the slogan "Not just Quebec politicians."

    Note that the slogan was not "No more Quebec politicians," although the other parties reacted as though it were. One could argue that the ad was merely a plea for inclusion, not a call for exclusion. On the other hand, the red slash could well be taken to signify a contention that the problem with Canada is that it is run by Quebeckers.

17. Alexa McDonough at a morning press conference, warning that "Where Preston Manning's policies would lead us in this country is straight into a civil war."

    This remark was widely criticized as being as intemperate as any of Manning's — fighting rhetorical fire with rhetorical fire merely further inflames matters. But it was certainly newsworthy that a federal political leader had suggested that the unity dispute, handled improperly, might end in civil war. Had Alexa McDonough been a serious contender to form a government or an opposition, for the words "civil war" to have passed her lips would have made her the object of the most intense media scrutiny. When that happens, the politician has all but ceded control over her own image from her handlers to the media. One false step in that sort of spotlight and a campaign can be ruined overnight. As it was, the remark was one of the few occasions when the media gave hot, rather than dutiful, attention to McDonough.

18. Manning at a campaign stop being accosted by a young man speaking to him insistently in French, while Manning, with a forced but unwavering smile, attempts to disengage, repeating "Merci."

    This was a confrontation calculated for the cameras. The young man was clearly a federalist, intent on making the point that Manning did not know what he was talking about because he cannot speak the language of those he was talking about. As an incident embarrassing to Manning — who, unlike McDonough, was most definitely in the media spotlight — it was seen as apropos, and given prominent play.

19. Jean Charest on a television interview program, stating: "Let me be clear that Mr. Manning's a bigot."

By this time, the lines of rhetorical conflict had been vividly drawn. Manning's position had attracted the charge of racism. His supporters might protest that he was merely pointing out that the federal discourse on Quebec's place within confederation has been dominated by figures from Quebec, to the exclusion of precious few from elsewhere in the union. His detractors pointed out that Manning's objections to the federal discourse were drawn along the lines of geography, culture and language.

20. Jean Chrétien saying "I never get dirty."

Just in case anyone was wondering why the Prime Minister was staying out of a dispute in which his opponents were sniping at one another.

21. Alexa McDonough at a podium, plaintively asking "Hellooo?"

This brief image, included in the CBC digest of election images before the vote, puts paid to the notion that the media systematically ignored the NDP. It stands as a concise reminder that the NDP had been trying to wage a campaign according to issues very different from those that came to hold sway, and that the networks acknowledged this. McDonough's query asked whether anyone had been listening to what the NDP believed was truly at stake. By selecting it as one of only 22 campaign images, the CBC at least asked the same thing.

22. Chrétien at a podium, his wife Aline by his side, a row of Canadian flags in the background. His arm raised in salute, he proclaims "Vive le Canada! Merci beaucoup," as supporters in the foreground erupt into cheers.

These were the Prime Minister's final words at the end of the campaign before a rally in his home riding. As a staged moment for the cameras, it was indistinguishable from what a victorious leader might have said in conclusion to the party faithful 24 hours later, once the election had been won.

One might quibble with particular selections in this sampler of campaign images. (Where, for example, was Parizeau? Where was the image of Jean Chrétien visiting the Winnipeg flood site just before the election call, being handed a sandbag and asking: "What do you want me to do with it?") But abbreviated and highly edited though it may have been, on the whole this quick TV reprise was a fair account of how the 1997 election unfolded.

A simple tabulation of the shot list reveals that the 22 images were disproportionately distributed among the five leaders and their parties. One of those images is a stock shot of the leaders filing into the first debate. Two others are devoted to Ms. Lamarche's collapse. Of the remaining 19, the Prime Minister is shown only three times: once to declare the election, once to conclude the election, and once to say that he is not getting involved in the election. Similarly, Alexa McDonough is shown only three times: once to explain why she cannot say anything, once to make a heated remark to which everyone paid attention, and once to complain that few have been listening to her. Gilles Duceppe and the Bloc are also accorded only three shots: the lost bus driver, the condom hat, and Duceppe's disavowal of both. Jean Charest features in three shots as well: barbecuing the Red Book, pleading his passion for the country on behalf of his children, and calling Preston Manning a bigot.

Manning, by comparison, shows up in five separate selections. The clip of the Reform ad surely counts as a sixth, while two more are clips in which McDonough and Charest react heatedly to Manning by name. In sum, Manning dominated the CBC's overview of the 1997 election. This does not mean that the network favoured Manning to win or wished him to do so. Many of these images are not especially favourable to his cause. Still, the network spotted Manning and Reform taking the reins of the election in such a way that the other parties were forced to respond, with the prominent exception of the Liberals, who stayed as distant from the fracas as they could.

If this was what the public saw of the election on television, how much was the result of the way in which the networks set out to cover the campaign? The apparatus of storytelling can be crucial to the stories that are told, and the networks changed their customary practices significantly in this election in two ways. First, the parties were offered 15 minutes of free air time on CBC Newsworld each morning, Monday to Friday: five minutes to speak uninterrupted and 10 minutes to field questions from the media. Politicians constantly complain that the media get in the way of what they want to say directly to the people. Fair enough. The idea here was to provide the parties with a morning soapbox from which to address the electorate and react to campaign developments. The initial hope was that this would be a daily forum for the party leaders. As it turned out, different parties made different use of the opportunity. Jean Chrétien appeared at none of these news conferences, despatching other Liberal candidates instead.. Preston Manning made good use of them, going so far as to dress the set behind him and to change the backdrop from appearance to appearance.

Second, the networks agreed to pool their resources in covering the leaders aboard their respective campaign planes and buses. In the past, each network had placed its own camera crew (a reporter, producer, editor, camera operator and sound technician) on each of the leaders' planes. But in the past, there were only three major parties and the networks had more money to spend. In this election, there were five leaders to cover and not a lot of money to spare. As a result, the networks agreed to cut costs by sharing resources. Each plane would carry a pool of five individuals (a pool producer, editor, sound technician and two camera operators) who would feed daily coverage to the five major networks (CBC, CTV, CanWest Global, Radio-Canada and TVA) who agreed to participate. This meant that each network was committing a basic corps of five people to covering the leaders' planes, a considerable saving over what it would have cost under the previous arrangement, given that a seat on one of the leaders' planes cost on average $15,000. The networks still placed their own reporters on the aircraft, but they often hopped on and off.

The 1997 practice was a major departure from how federal election campaigns had been covered in the past, when a network crew would be assigned to a leader's campaign and stay with it, criss-crossing the country from start to finish. Under this new regime, senior political correspondents would be assigned to geographical regions of the country. They would stay put, and the leaders would come to them. Both innovations were the handiwork of the CBC, and specifically Chris Waddell, the Parliamentary bureau chief, along with Alvin Cator, his second-in-command. Waddell convinced all five major parties to accept the morning news conference format and five major networks to contribute to the pooling arrangement.

Not everything went according to plan. The morning news conferences never established themselves as a preferred platform for party announcements or election electricity The only major development to break at one of these in-studio performances was Alexa McDonough's remark about Manning's policies leading "straight into civil war." As well, print reporters grumbled about being used as props for network coverage, and some vowed not to ask their best questions while the cameras were rolling, a puzzling position, given that print reporters think nothing of asking their most pointed questions during Parliamentary scrums, in the midst of a forest of microphones and cameras.

The pooling arrangement also had its critics. Those who were on the planes saw coverage assembled by correspondents on the ground using raw pool footage. Oftentimes, they complained that network HQ failed to capture the true mood or nuance of what was actually going on aboard the aircraft. As well, when the plane set down, each network would expect its own reporter to record what is called a "stand-up": a segment in a correspondent's report, usually at the beginning or the end, or possibly both, in which the reporter addresses the camera directly. Given that there were five networks on the ground and only one pool crew per plane — also responsible for filing three network feeds per day of between five and 10 minutes each — the demands on the pool crew were harrowing. Finally, with five campaigns to cover and only a finite amount of airtime on the nightly newscasts, the networks often resorted to what were dubbed "melt-downs." Rather than devote five separate news stories to the day's events of each leader's campaign, often the pool footage from different campaigns was rolled into one news story narrated via voice-over by an in-studio anchor. This had the effect of reducing the airtime allotted to politicians' soundbites.

Nevertheless, the innovations in campaign coverage worked well enough that they are likely to be features of election journalism henceforth. The parties cannot decline the invitation to participate in the morning news conferences without also surrendering their complaint that the media will not allow them to speak directly to the voters. If the morning conferences were not a prominent feature of the 1997 election, this may have been simply because the parties were cautious on being confronted with this new opportunity. Nor are the networks about to discard the basic model of the pooling arrangement. There is too much money at stake. They may fine-tune the model. They may place reporters of their own aboard selected leaders' planes to shape the footage supplied by the pool, but the days are likely past when each network maintained its own full crew on every leader's plane.

In the election of 1997, these structural adjustments in how the campaign was covered were relatively neutral with regard to how the election played out. That is, the flow of the election took its shape from the cut and thrust of the politicians themselves — in particular, from the way the Reform Party went on the offensive — and not from any overt intervention on the part of the media. Though many voters may have been dissatisfied with the contents of the campaign, attaching blame to the messenger in this case may well have been misplaced. The media merely provided a showcase for the politicians to address the electorate, and this is how it should be. It is not for reporters on the campaign trail, the public's paid witnesses, to pass judgement on the worth of a party's platform or performance. That is for the voters to decide. If the public found the election wanting in 1997, this was likely the result of circumstances in which it appeared that only one party had a chance of forming a majority government, and of the parties themselves: the Liberals, who said little in hopes of coasting to a second consecutive victory; Reform, who irritated the raw nerve of the unity issue in hopes of pressing it to their advantage; the NDP, who could not wrest control of the election agenda; the Bloc, who remained steadfastly parochial; and the Progressive Conservatives, who failed to present themselves as a distinct or altogether credible alternative.

Nonetheless, in a future election called under different circumstances, the structure of television coverage of the campaign could well be a factor. In the 1993 election, although the same five major parties took the field, the media at first concentrated their attention on the three traditional parties, the Conservatives, Liberals and NDP, and were caught off-guard by the strength of Reform in the West and the Bloc in Quebec. In 1997, the media accorded all five parties dutiful coverage. Now both the networks and the parties have the experience of at least one election in which five different options are presented to the electorate, and have experimented with new ways of appealing through television to the voters. It is possible that in the next election the parties will craft their campaign strategies in light of the lessons of 1997. In a crowded field, and with limited airtime on the newscasts, the media spotlight can shift to the party that acts boldly, thereby crowding out the others, or at least forcing them to react. The morning news conferences could provide a forum from which to seize the campaign agenda. Knowing that, the media may have to adjust their coverage so as to compensate, so that they remain agents of the electorate and not simply of the party most adept at turning the mechanisms of coverage to its advantage.

Notes

[1] Cobb, Chris. "Jobless Journalism," *Media*. Summer 1997, p. 28

Nine
Electoral Reform in the Charter Era
by Louis Massicotte

The 1997 general election was held 15 years after the proclamation of the Canadian Charter of Human Rights and Freedoms. In the interval, issues involving electoral reform have been thoroughly debated in Parliament, in the courts, among election officials, in academia, and in various official reports, including that of a Royal Commission. Sometimes, they were acted upon as well. The purpose of this chapter is to summarize those developments, especially those that took place during the 1990s.

One way to understand better the impulse for reform in Canadian electoral rules is to examine its sources. At least seven sources can be identified. Not all were equally important or lasting, or pushed in the same direction. Yet all raised worthwhile issues, contributed to the debate and sometimes resulted in action. They may be summarized as follows:

1. The Charter. The adoption of the Constitution Act, 1982, is now acknowledged, if not universally hailed, as a landmark development in the evolution of the Canadian polity. The Charter of Rights and Freedoms included few provisions dealing with democratic rights. Section 3 guaranteed every Canadian citizen the right to vote and to be a candidate at both levels of government. Another section prohibited extending the duration of a Parliament or of provincial legislatures beyond their standard five-year term, in time of real or apprehended war, invasion or insurrection, against the will of one-third of Members. The Charter also required at least one legislative sitting every twelve months. Those were the only democratic rights specifically protected by the Charter, and they did not appear initially to mean very much, insofar as

Canada was already acknowledged on the world scene as a parliamentary democracy where suffrage was universal and well established. The protection against the Crown shutting out Parliament for a year predated Confederation by a long time, while the clause regulating the extension of the term of the existing House had been in force federally since 1949.[1] Yet the Charter jeopardized *prima facie* the existing disqualifications against prison inmates, judges and mentally disabled people. Opponents of those disqualifications were now offered an additional forum, the courts, for challenging the provisions of the *Canada Elections Act* which excluded them from the electorate. Either they could win at that level, where some deeply-seated popular prejudices could not prevail as easily, or Parliament might be frightened enough to remove those disqualifications in advance so as to spare itself the costs of facing a legal challenge, and the embarrassment of potentially losing it.

2. Chief Electoral Officers' statutory reports. The duties of the Chief Electoral Officer of Canada are chiefly administrative, and as a rule occupants of the office have carefully avoided being drawn into what they rightly saw as basically political issues. Nevertheless, it is the duty of the Chief Electoral Officer, in the absence in Ottawa of any political structure empowered to deal specifically with those issues, to suggest ways to improve the electoral process and to point out to Parliament the complaints made by election officers and by the public against existing provisions of the Act. This Chief Electoral Officer Hamel did in his various statutory reports between 1983 and 1989. The 1983 report was an important document, because in addition to suggesting improvements of the minutiae of the electoral machinery, it pointed out various aspects of the election process that were open to challenge on Charter grounds. While Parliament acted in 1983 in relation to third-party spending, it failed to act throughout the 1980s on most of the issues raised by those reports. The reports of the Standing Committee on Privileges and Elections in 1984, and of a caucus committee of Conservative backbenchers in 1986, ultimately evolved into a government White Paper on Electoral Reform in 1986 and a substantial electoral reform bill (C-79) tabled the following year. This bill included several innovative provisions, like granting the right to vote to Canadians abroad, removing existing disqualifications against judges and mentally disabled people, and making polling stations more accessible to handicapped electors. However, it was objected to on various grounds by opposition parties, and died on the order paper. By then, it was fairly obvious that the political parties were unable to agree among themselves, which opened the way to other actors and reform processes.

Hamel's successor, Jean-Pierre Kingsley, also issued in 1996 a set of recommendations pertaining to the electoral system.[2] Taking the torch from the Royal Commission on Electoral Reform, he reiterated proposals for staggered voting hours and greater transparency in the political process, including disclosure of the finances of local associations of political parties and of leadership campaigns, trust funds, contributions to Members of Parliament, transfers between a party and its candidates, campaign surpluses, and surplus funds of independent and non-affiliated candidates.

3. The 1988 free-trade election. The subsequent acceptance by the Liberal Party of the inevitability and positive side of free trade has led many Canadians to forget how bitter and divisive was the electoral campaign which resulted in the victory of the pro-free trade Tories in 1988. Among nationalists opposed to it, free trade was denounced as a betrayal of the nation's soul and its supporters were hinted to be traitors to the nation ("You sold us to the United States!"). A \$4.7 million last-minute media blitz financed by business groups, thanks to a loophole in the *Elections Act* created by the courts, was indicted by opponents of free trade as the decisive factor which caused their defeat. Others pointed out that the Tories had got only 43 per cent of the vote and won a majority thanks to the division of the anti-free trade vote among two parties.[3] Some called for a reconsideration of the first-past-the-post electoral system, and loud cries were heard among the Left for the limitation or prohibition of third-party spending.

4. Concern over business political contributions. Meanwhile, the ruling Tories came to be widely denounced as corrupt following scandals which resulted in numerous ministerial resignations throughout Prime Minister Brian Mulroney's first term. Quebec members were fingered by the English media as being especially unethical or even corruption-prone. Conservative MP François Gérin counter-attacked by pressing for a reform of the election legislation that would prohibit business and labour contributions to federal political parties, so that parties could receive contributions only from registered electors, subject to a \$5000-ceiling. This would have established in Ottawa the rules imposed in Quebec ten years earlier by the Parti Québécois, a party Gérin was close to, as his subsequent career decisions would confirm. His proposal was endorsed by the Quebec Tory caucus, and by Mulroney himself during the 1988 campaign, though many Tories outside Quebec were adamantly opposed to it.

5. The rise of identity politics. The drive for electoral reform was fueled by the spread, from the late 1980s onwards, of identity politics. This stream of opinion, very strong among academics, political activists and the Left, pinpointed the under-representation in Parliament of various segments of society like women, aboriginals and multicultural Canadians, and pushed for reforms that would ensure fair representation of those groups among political elites.

6. **The drive for direct democracy.** The years 1985–1995 have been labelled by Peter Newman the years of "the Canadian Revolution". Canadians lost confidence in their political institutions (except the judiciary), in political parties and in politicians. In Newman's words, deference gave way to defiance.[4] This sentiment was fueled by the unwillingness of most of the federal and provincial elites of English Canada to reflect the growing hostility among their constituents, and indeed the blind rage among some of them, against the Meech Lake Accord. Though the procedure followed for the ratification of Meech was impeccably constitutional, the hitherto unchallenged assumptions underlying representative democracy were widely questioned. The referendum tradition in the country, almost dormant since the 1930s (with the outstanding exceptions of conscription in 1942, Newfoundland in 1948 and Quebec sovereignty in 1980), was re-awakened with a call for the introduction of direct democracy devices like the referendum, the popular initiative, and even the recall of elected officials.

7. **The cost-cutting drive of the early 1990s.** "Democracy has no price". What a provincial Cabinet minister could say during the late 1970s without looking unconnected with reality, a responsible politician could hardly say today, when people are reminded daily that in education and health care costs do matter. Though the costs of Canada's electoral system and political institutions appear minimal in relation to the national finances, the general trend to cut government spending found some expression in that area as well. There was pressure for introducing new systems and technologies that would reduce the reliance on paid officials, notably in the field of elector registration.[5]

The Royal Commission on Electoral Reform

In response to the political impasse on Bill C-79, and to several of the sources of reform described above, the Mulroney government appointed in the Fall of 1989 a Royal Commission on Electoral Reform and Party Financing. Chaired by Montréal businessman Pierre Lortie, the Commission included representatives from each major federal party. Former Chief Electoral Officer Hamel served as an advisor to the chairman, while an ambitious research program, carried out under the direction of political scientist Peter Aucoin, ensured that the knowledge of the academic community would be a meaningful input. In addition, public hearings were conducted throughout the country involving high- and middle-rank election officials as well as the general public. The Commission thus benefitted from a wide range of expertise and public input, which it digested with minimal prejudice, though it was clear right from the start that some reform options opposed by the chairman, especially the banning of corporate contributions, were not in the cards.

The Commission reported in early 1992. Together, its four-volume report[6] and 23 volumes of research studies represent the most impressive examination ever conducted of electoral reform issues in this country, and one of the best contributions of that kind in the world. While it re-edited or reformulated some recommendations already made, it also aired scores of fresh ideas. For example, the Commission recommended the creation of aboriginal electoral districts, a new formula for reapportioning seats among provinces, and mechanisms for encouraging women candidacies. It suggested the creation and registration of publicly-subsidized think-tanks known as "party foundations", empowered to develop and promote public policy options, to educate party members on matters of public policy and to provide parties with research and advice on policy. Hardly any detail of Canadian electoral arrangements escaped close scrutiny by the Commission.

Legislative developments

a. The Representation Act, 1985

The first major initiative of the Tory government in the field of electoral reform was prompted by the redistribution process following the 1981 census. When Mulroney took over, the process established by the *Electoral Boundaries Readjustment Act* had been carried almost to its conclusion, though it had been delayed by Members, who wanted to preserve the existing boundaries at least for the 1984 election. A caucus committee of the ruling party took a fresh look at the issue, and concluded that the 1974 redistribution formula would result in too many ridings and Members. Following that suggestion, the government tabled in June 1985 a White Paper which called for a new, much simpler, redistribution formula as well as minor reforms of the redistribution process itself. Subject to a few amendments, this was passed in early 1986 as the *Representation Act, 1985*.[7]

The redistribution of 1987 was carried out under the new rules, and resulted in a 295-seat House of Commons where the faster-growing provinces (Ontario, British Columbia and Alberta) were slightly under-represented thanks to the subtle "electoral equalization" effect embedded in the new rules.[8] The boundary commissions took little advantage of the new provision which allowed them to establish ridings with populations deviating from the provincial quotient by more than 25 per cent, as only five such districts were created. At the same time, the loophole in the 1964 Act which allowed Members to postpone indefinitely the redistribution was eliminated. Little action in other areas followed until 1992, partly because the appointment of the Royal Commission was used as a justification for postponing reform.

b. *The Referendum Act, 1992.*

Concern over the very existence of the country, more than thoughtful reflexion, led in 1992 to the quick passage of the first federal statute providing for the future holding of referendums on the Constitution of Canada.[9] Such a statute was promised in the Speech from the Throne of May 1991, but opposition from the Quebec Tory caucus postponed its adoption by one year. This legislation provided for "Triple-IF" referendums. Those would be called *if* the Prime Minister and both Houses of Parliament ordered so; they would be held country-wide only *if* the Cabinet so decided; and finally, the results of the referendum would be complied with only *if* Parliament so decided, as such referendums were advisory rather than binding.

The chief issue throughout the debate on the Bill was the regulation of the referendum campaign itself. Umbrella committees on the Quebec model were advocated but rejected, ostensibly on the ground that they would be challenged and might well be held *ultra vires* by the courts. Rather, Parliament opted for a ceiling on the expenditures each registered referendum committee[10] could make, without imposing any limit to the number of referendum committees that could be created for each option, a decision which in practice meant no ceiling at all.[11] During the 1992 referendum on the Charlottetown Accord, the YES side outspent the NO side by a ratio of 13 to one — and lost! This referendum established a very strong precedent that in the future a constitutional amendment of some importance would have to be put to a referendum, even if nothing in the Constitution or in the referendum legislation so directs.

In contrast to the enthusiasm displayed in some Western provinces for direct democracy devices,[12] no other measure in that direction has been adopted in Ottawa. A procedure for recalling elected Members was advocated in early 1994, when 30,000 electors petitioned for the resignation of a freshly-elected Member who had allegedly faked his resume, but the only output, apart from the resignation of that Member from the ruling party caucus, was a report of the Procedure and House Affairs Committee rejecting that measure.[13]

c. Bill C-114, 1993

The release of the Royal Commission's report in early 1992 sent the electoral reform issue back to politicians again, as there was no longer any justification for postponing reform. The Commons instructed a special committee on electoral reform, chaired by MP Jim Hawkes, to examine the report, but its deliberations were stalled shortly after, in view of the necessity for adopting referendum legislation. When they resumed, Members decided to divide reform issues into three "stages"[14] to be dealt with in succession, with Lortie's boldest and most original recommendations being bumped into the third (less urgent) category, which Members did not have the time to deal with.

The only concrete and immediate result of the Royal Commission's report was therefore Bill C-114, which received support from all three parties and was given Royal assent in May 1993, just in time to apply at the election held in the Fall.[15] In view of the expectations that had been aroused by the Royal Commission, Bill C-114 came as a disappointment to many observers. Yet, the package it enacted included many useful reforms advocated by Chief Electoral Officers Hamel and Kingsley, as reviewed by the Royal Commission.

In addition to formally enfranchising judges and people with mental disabilities (albeit five years after the courts had so decided), Bill C-114 granted the right to vote to provincial civil servants posted outside Canada, to Canadians abroad employed by international organizations and to other Canadians abroad (this time, only if they had been out of the country for less than five years), as well as to inmates serving prison terms of less than two years, on the rationale that only the worst offenders should have their voting rights suspended.

The new measure also facilitated electoral registration in a number of ways. Enumeration and revision were standardized for urban and rural polling divisions. Two enumerators (they now could be 16- or 17-year olds) would be appointed everywhere, not just in urban areas, and after having visited each residence unsuccessfully at least twice, would leave a Mail-In Registration Card that electors could fill in and return to the returning officer in order to get registered. Revising agents were empowered to conduct a second enumeration in areas where the information obtained for the preliminary list was not satisfactory. The list was to be "closed" at the end of the fifth day (instead of the 16th day in urban areas) preceding polling day. Further, polling day registration, already allowed in rural areas, was extended to urban areas, subject to the presentation of a satisfactory proof of identity. This cocktail of measures aimed at reducing the phenomenon of "administrative disfranchisement" which had been a major complaint of many ordinary Canadians as the standard techniques of door-to-door enumeration increasingly failed to register numerous electors in the context of modern times. Measures were also taken to facilitate the registration of homeless people. As a cost-cutting measure, the new legislation followed the Referendum Act of 1992 by empowering election officials to use the lists of electors used at an election or referendum held within the previous 12 months, instead of conducting another new enumeration. This allowed the lists of electors used at the 1992 referendum to serve as preliminary lists at the 1993 election, subject of course to a revision during the campaign.[16]

The new Act consolidated various measures which had proliferated in a somewhat disorderly fashion over the years in order to accommodate specific categories of voters. Proxy voting, voting under the Special Voting Rules and advance polling in the office of the returning officer were replaced by a new "special ballot" (a mail-in ballot) to be used by electors serving in the Canadian Forces, Canadians abroad, inmates serving sentences of less than two years, and all electors residing in Canada who were unable to vote in their polling division at the advance polls or on polling day.

In contrast, the rules for becoming a candidate were tightened. The number of signatures needed for a nomination paper to be accepted was increased from 25 to 100 (in a few Northern districts: 50). Moreover, the $200-deposit was increased to $1000, and was made refundable on the following conditions: half of it was to be reimbursed to candidates getting 15 per cent of the vote in their district (the whole $200 was previously refundable on that condition), while the other half was reimbursed only to candidates who submitted their election expenses return in time. This reflected concern over the multiplication of frivolous candidacies, but also over the administrative costs associated with them.[17]

At least two of the changes introduced by the Act proved controversial and led later to court challenges. The publication of the results of opinion polls was banned on polling day and during the two preceding days. The other measure had to do with the touchy issue of regulation of third-party spending. In a report which otherwise was offering little to those concerned with the influence of big money on the political process, and in line with its determination to reaffirm the primacy of parties in electoral campaigns, the Royal Commission had proposed that third-party spending be limited to $1000 per organization, and that collusion among those organizations to mount a common spending drive exceeding $1000 be prohibited. This recommendation was watered down in two steps. First, the Hawkes Committee proposed that only advertising expenses be so regulated. Then, in C-114's final version, only advertising expenses incurred for the purpose of promoting or opposing directly a party or a candidate were subject to the $1000 ceiling. A media blitz like the one which outraged many in 1988 would not have been prohibited by that provision, since it focused on the free trade issue and did not directly promote the Conservatives. Even this last pathetic attempt by politicians proved too much for the National Citizens Coalition, which immediately mounted a successful court challenge against it. The only other major contribution of the Bill in the field of party financing was a prohibition on contributions from non-Canadian sources.

d. The redistribution of the 1990s

The "electoral earthquake" of 1993 offered reasonable hope for a fresh perspective on electoral reform issues. No less than two-thirds of the Members were newcomers, and two new parties were prominently represented. Yet, some would dismiss the first initiative of the new House in relation to electoral reform as "politics as usual" at its worst.

The interest of the new House was immediately captivated by the next redistribution. The existing rules called for the process to be started in 1992. The new census figures predicted a House of 301 Members, with 4 additional seats for Ontario, 2 for British Columbia, and the status quo everywhere else. As the Royal Commission's report had just made sweeping recommendations covering all dimensions of the process, Parliament saw it fit to postpone the operation by one year,[18] until June 18, 1993. Nothing having been done meanwhile, boundary commissions were appointed under the *Electoral Boundaries Readjustment Act* in September 1993, and their proposals were made public in early 1994. They immediately ignited a furor among Liberal and Bloc Québécois Members, who complained about the magnitude of the changes. The Chrétien government gave way and in mid-March, introduced Bill C-18, which provided for the immediate dissolution of boundary commissions and for the suspension of the redistribution process for the next two years. While the measure was supported by an unholy alliance of Liberal and Bloc Québécois Members, it was criticized by the Reform Party and the media, which accused the government of trying to ensure that the redistribution could not be carried in time for the next general election. Such criticism found an echo in the Senate, still dominated by the Conservatives, which obliged the government to retreat on two points. First, the boundaries commissions were allowed to complete their public hearings and to table their final reports. Second, the duration of the suspension was shortened by a year, to June 22, 1995.[19] Meanwhile, a committee of the House was instructed to conduct a review of the whole redistribution process, including the redistribution formula, the selection of members of the boundaries commissions, the rules governing their work and "the nature of the involvement of the public and of the House of Commons" in the process. The stage was set for the most direct attack ever on the non-partisan redistribution process established thirty years ago.

The report of the Committee, tabled in late November of the year,[20] indicated the understandable preference of Members for as little change as possible in existing boundaries. It rejected Reform-inspired proposals for reducing the size of the House (a measure that several provinces adopted throughout the 1990s), and advocated no change to the existing constitutional rules for distributing seats among provinces. However, the reports of the boundaries commissions appointed in 1993, which had cost about $5 million, were to be set aside. Provision was made for MPs to object to the appointment of future members of boundaries commissions other than the chairman, and commissions were instructed to prepare three redistribution plans instead of one. While the population of electoral districts was still not supposed to deviate from the provincial quotient by more than 25 per cent, the report proposed the creation of a new category of privileged ridings, which were exempted from the 25 per cent criterion. The list of those "statutory" ridings was unspecified, being left at the discretion of Parliament, and there was no limit to the number of ridings which could be made "statutory". Proposals of the commissions were no longer to be published in newspapers, thus reducing opportunities for public involvement. In the hope of minimizing decennial changes, the report also included a provision (inspired by the report of the Royal Commission) for readjusting boundaries on the basis of the population figures of the quinquennial censuses, but only if 10 per cent of the ridings in a given province (excluding statutory ridings) exceeded the 25 per cent tolerance limit. On the other hand, no commission was to be appointed following a decennial census if the number of seats for the province was the same and if no seat exceeded the 25 per cent tolerance limit.

The likely result of this proposal would have been a process more closely controlled by politicians and less open to the public, which de-emphasized the primacy of the population factor and reduced the likelihood for electoral boundaries to be altered. *The Electoral Boundaries Readjustment Bill (C-69)*, introduced by the government a few months later, was similar to the bill drafted by the committee, except that the provision for statutory ridings had been replaced by a provision allowing commissions to exceed the 25 per cent tolerance rule under "extraordinary circumstances". However, the Tory Senators substantially amended the Bill by reducing the tolerance level from 25 per cent to 15 per cent, by deleting the clause which exempted a province from redistribution in the absence of a change in its representation or of ridings exceeding the 25 per cent tolerance level, and the possibility for MPs to object to the appointment of members of boundaries commissions. In addition, they provided for a new definition of "community of interests", and required that members of commissions be residents of the province for which they were appointed. The House responded by accepting only the latter amendment, while rejecting all the others. No further response was heard from the Senate, and so Bill C-69 remained stalled until prorogation the next year, when it passed away, unsung and unmourned by most, with the understandable exception of those Members who had wasted a full year debating the issue.[21]

The failure of Parliament to pass Bill C-69 by the June 22, 1995 deadline cleared the way for the completion of the process. The reports of boundary commissions were duly enacted through a representation order in January 1996, and established the boundaries that were in force at the 1997 election. Paradoxically, even though it occasioned an unprecedented bold attack by MPs against the basics of the existing process, the redistribution of 1996 became the first since the 1960s to be carried out, if belatedly, on the basis of the reports of the commissions initially appointed. As in previous redistributions, commissioners proved quite responsive to complaints from the public and Members. Two-thirds of the ridings initially proposed were altered following public hearings. Of the 81 objections filed thereafter by Members as to the name or shape of districts, 27 were partially or entirely accepted, resulting in alterations to 47 districts.[22]

This episode highlighted the gulf between the progressive approach taken by the Royal Commission, and the deeply-held conviction of most MPs that redistribution should not be taken out of their hands. It also revealed how fragile was the so-called tradition of all-party consensus on electoral matters, which had been invoked in order to postpone reform in the late 1980s. Both Bill C-18 and Bill C-69 were carried against the wishes of one major party, with closure being invoked in relation to each. The Reform Party was disappointed the opportunity had been missed to reduce the size of the House, while the Bloc supported C-69 only before the rejection by all other parties of its amendment calling for a guarantee that Quebec would be entitled to 25 per cent of the seats in perpetuity.

Only 31 of the former 295 (now 301) electoral districts were spared any change. The new delimitation was fairer than the previous one, as 80 per cent of districts had populations within 12.5 per cent of the provincial quotient.[23] The New Brunswick and Quebec commissions tended to take greater advantage than others of the full tolerance level allowed. The emphasis on Rep. by Pop. was underlined by the fact that the "extraordinary circumstances" provision of the Act was invoked in relation to only two districts (Manicouagan in Northern Quebec, and Labrador in Newfoundland) whose populations differed from the applicable provincial quotient by respectively 40.2 per cent and 62.6 per cent. Yet riding populations still ranged from 21,242 in Nunavut to 117,418 in Calgary Centre. The time-honoured tradition of naming a district so as to include every portion thereof was dutifully carried on, and one can have only sympathy for the Speaker who will have to identify correctly "the Honourable Member for Kamouraska-Rivière-du-Loup-Témiscouata-Les Basques",[24] or distinguishing the Member for Perth-Middlesex from those representing "Elgin-Middlesex-London" or "Lambton-Kent-Middlesex."

While the position of the ruling Liberals was slightly improved, the new delimitation did not alter significantly the political make-up of the country: the transposition of the 1993 results into the new boundaries, conducted by Elections Canada, gave the Liberals 184 seats instead of 177, partly because of the addition of four new seats in Grit Ontario. The Bloc got 55, one more than under the old boundaries, Reform also got one more (53). The Tories stayed with two seats, while the NDP emerged as the great loser of the operation, with 6 seats instead of 9. Independent Member Gilles Bernier would have been returned under the new boundaries as well.

e. A new register of electors, 1996.

For decades, complaints about the waste of time and money in enumerating electors, and the length of exhausting election campaigns, became standard post-election grievances. Knowledgeable observers could nevertheless point out that enumeration at least produced lists of electors that were quite inclusive and accurate, especially in comparison with those of Canada's main neighbour.[25] The tide started to turn in 1995 when Quebec, in anticipation of its referendum on secession, introduced permanent lists of electors to be used for provincial, municipal and school board elections. The Liberal government introduced a bill in October 1996, which provided for a permanent register of electors. Two months later, this was the law of the land.[26]

The Royal Commission on Electoral Reform had taken the view that provincial electoral registers or recent lists of electors should be used in the future as preliminary lists of electors for each federal election, subject to a federally-organized revision. This implied in practice that Ottawa would lose control over the register used for federal elections. In contrast, the approach taken by Bill C-63 was for Elections Canada to hold in April 1997 a last door-to-door enumeration countrywide (except in Alberta and PEI, where the availability of recent provincial lists of electors eliminated the need for a federal enumeration), and to update thereafter on a continuous basis the computerized lists so prepared. Sources for updating the list include information from electors themselves and from existing federal, provincial and territorial data sources, like Revenue Canada and provincial and territorial drivers' licence files (for Canadians who moved or turned 18), Citizenship and Immigration Canada (for new citizens) and provincial and territorial vital statistics files (for deleting the people who died). The Chief Electoral Officer is expected to contact new 18-year-olds to confirm their eligibility to vote and their agreement to be on the register. The revision of preliminary lists will be done in the future by returning officers. Precautions have been taken in order to protect the confidentiality of personal information in the register. The Chief Electoral Officer is empowered to conclude agreements to share the register with provincial, territorial, municipal and school-board jurisdictions, provided that the information is to be used only for electoral purposes.

The two main arguments for this innovation are the reduction of the length of electoral campaigns from 47 to 36 days, and the reduction of costs. Building the register was expected to necessitate a $41-million investment at the time of the 1997 election, to be offset by estimated savings of $30 million at each of the next two elections, and between $36 and $47 million at the subsequent three elections.[27] Those considerations were not enough to convince the two main opposition parties to support the measure.

Bill C-63 also included a provision which purported to meet an old grievance in the West against "central Canadian domination". The existence of uniform voting hours (9 AM to 8 PM) across the country created the feeling among some Western voters that the outcome of the election was decided before they had themselves finished voting. Voting hours were therefore staggered as follows : 8:30 AM to 8:30 PM in the Newfoundland, Atlantic and Central time zones, 9:30 AM to 9:30 PM in the Eastern time zone, 7:30 AM to 7:30 PM in the Mountain time zone, and 7:00 AM to 7:00 PM in the Pacific time zone. This also meant that polling stations would be opened one more hour than before. The only inconvenience for central Canadian electors was that election night started later. For Western voters, polls closed earlier than they were accustomed.[28] All Canadians were offered a shorter election night.

At the same occasion, much to the delight of the business community, the number of consecutive hours an employee is entitled to for voting on election day was reduced from four to three. A private Member's bill also passed during the Fall of 1996 instituted a revised threshold for reimbursing election expenses of political parties. The threshold is now 2 per cent of valid votes in the country, or 5 per cent of the valid votes cast in the districts where that party had a candidate. Previously, only parties having spent at least 10 per cent of the maximum amount allowed, irrespective of the vote they had polled, were reimbursed.[29]

Administrative developments

Election officials typically receive little attention in the literature dealing with electoral systems. This is to be regretted, as many decisions they make have to do with more than day-to-day administration. In 1988, in view of the failure of Parliament to act in relation to Bill C-79, Chief Electoral Officer Hamel took upon himself the issuing of guidelines which enacted the provisions of that Bill dealing with the handicapped, so that the offices of returning officers, central polling places and advance polling stations be accessible. This included a strong encouragement to seek locations with level access for isolated polling stations. As a result, some 92 per cent of polling stations at the 1988 election were accessible. In 1992, Parliament passed a Bill formally enacting those provisions.[30]

In 1990, Jean-Pierre Kingsley was appointed Chief Electoral Officer by the House of Commons, with the concurrence of all parties. He contributed to electoral reform by appearing before the Royal Commission and assigning some of his staff to provide advice on various reform issues. Lortie's proposal for putting the Chief Electoral Officer under a newly-created "Elections Commission" was quickly (some would add: deservedly) forgotten, and Elections Canada provided advice to the government and Parliament on the Referendum Bill and all subsequent election measures. Both Bills C-78 and C-114 included specific provisions confirming the duty of Elections Canada to inform electors about the electoral system. Starting with the 1992 referendum, all lists of electors were computerized. The reports of Elections Canada following each referendum or election were expanded so as to become a source of specialized information on the electoral process.[31] Meanwhile, Elections Canada continued its involvement on the international scene by sending experts abroad to advise new democracies on electoral arrangements or observing elections.

Judicial developments

Enfranchisement.

Throughout the 1988 campaign, Elections Canada had to keep ready to provide for the registration and voting of groups that might be enfranchised by the courts on short notice. Shortly before that election, applications were made to the Federal Court for eliminating the disqualifications against the mentally handicapped and judges. Neither was opposed by the Crown, and both were successful.[32]

The issue of inmates serving sentences in federal penitentiaries or provincial correctional institutions proved to be much more complex. Members of Parliament, especially the Conservatives, were generally opposed to their enfranchisement. Therefore, the attempts by inmates to get the right to vote were opposed by the Crown in the courts, which had to determine whether such disqualification was a "reasonable limit" to the right to vote. Various courts were not unanimous on the issue, as indicated by dozens of contradictory judicial pronouncements on the relevant provisions of the *Canada Elections Act* and of provincial election statutes. On this author's count, inmates so far have lost nine times and won fifteen times. Throughout the 1980s, inmates lost in British Columbia and Ontario courts, and failed narrowly to be enfranchised by the Federal Court and by Manitoba courts.[33] The tide started to turn in 1991, when Justice Strayer of the Federal Court found the existing disqualification of all inmates, regardless of the nature of their crime, to be excessive and unconstitutional. In 1992, this decision was confirmed by the Federal Court of Appeal, while the High Court of Ontario, in *Sauvé*, overturned a 1988 decision of a lower court denying inmates the right to vote.[34] In May 1993, all three decisions were confirmed by the Supreme Court of Canada.[35]

Strayer's ruling may have inspired the Royal Commission, which recommended that only those serving sentences of 10 years or more be deprived of their right to vote. Bill C-114 established two years as the benchmark, which meant that only persons serving sentences in provincial institutions (some 22,000) would be enfranchised. At the 1993 election, only 7500 (one-third) of them registered, and 6956 voted. This, coupled with the requirement that their vote be counted in their former district of residence rather than in the district where the prison was located, meant that the political impact of voting by inmates was mostly symbolic. Only inmates serving sentences of two years or more remained disfranchised, but even this was declared unconstitutional in January 1996 by the Federal Court of Canada, which argued that this hindered the rehabilitation of offenders and their successful reintegration into the community.[36]

Third-party spending.

By far the most important impact of the Charter has been on the spending provisions of the *Canada Elections Act*. The framers of the 1974 *Election Expenses Act* had reasoned that for the spending limits on parties and candidates to be meaningful, the right of "third parties" to incur election expenses had to be restricted. In November 1983, Parliament clarified the law so that such spending would be explicitly prohibited. This move, supported as it was by the three main parties, met with unexpected and determined opposition from the right-wing National Citizens' Coalition, which immediately mounted a challenge in the Court of Queen's Bench of Alberta. In June 1984, the Court struck down the prohibition of third-party spending as a breach of freedom of expression that could not be justified in a free and democratic society, and the federal government decided not to appeal from that decision which, the Chief Electoral Officer understood, was then applicable to the whole country.[37] While third parties did not intervene at the ensuing election, they did so, on a grand scale, in 1988 in order to ensure the passage of the Free Trade Agreement.

As noted above Parliament, in the wake of the Royal Commission's report, attempted to restore some control over third-party spending in Bill C-114, but the weak provision of the new Act was immediately attacked in the courts. In the *Somerville* case (June 1993), the Alberta Court of Queen's Bench struck it down, a decision which was upheld three years later by the Alberta Court of Appeal in a unanimous and more strongly motivated decision.[38] The Minister of Justice then decided not to appeal from that decision, which again is applicable everywhere in the country.

Both judgements, especially the latter, are important and revealing. In determining whether an infringement of freedom of expression was reasonable, in conformity with the mechanics of the Charter, the onus of the proof was put on the shoulders of the government. The expert who had inspired the Royal Commission's recommendation was unable to convince the judges that in 1988 third-party spending had significantly altered the results of the election, since it was found on cross-examination that academics were far from unanimous on that point. But even if they had been, Justice Conrad said in a revealing *obiter*, this would likely not have changed the court's verdict, since "there can be no pressing and substantial need to suppress [the input provided by third-party spending] merely because it might have an impact".[39]

A significant difference between the rationale of both courts in *Somerville* and the 1984 decision in *National Citizens' Coalition* is that in the former the restriction on third-party spending was held to breach not only freedom of expression, but also the right to vote itself. In an interesting contrast with the strict and literal reading of the "right to vote" taken by other courts,[40] though in line with many other court judgements, both courts in *Somerville* accepted the argument that the right to vote implied some "right to an informed vote" and was therefore impaired by spending limits applied to third parties. The practical consequence of that fine exercise in judicial creativity was to eliminate any chance that Parliament may override those decisions under section 33 of the Charter, since that provision cannot be resorted to in relation to section 3 which guarantees the right to vote. Such a possibility was always remote anyway, in view of the reverence for the Charter that prevails among federal politicians and the population, but should there be a change of heart in the future among federal political elites on the wisdom of the *Somerville* decision, Parliament will remain powerless.[41]

Merely suggesting that the Charter is not the ultimate embodiment of human wisdom is held by many to be politically incorrect today, at least outside Quebec.[42] Yet, the *Somerville* decisions help us to understand why the adoption of the Charter was so bitterly opposed in 1980 by politicians as different in ideological outlook as Sterling Lyon, Allan Blakeney and René Lévesque. Legislatures (not the people, because for all the rhetoric on "The People's Charter", there was no referendum on the issue) were then invited to entrench some values in a Charter because those commanded wide support and were not seriously challenged by anybody. Yet the process of judicial reasoning leans towards the extension *ad infinitum* of the meaning of these concepts well beyond their original or common understanding, in order to arrive at conclusions which may not reflect any popular consensus at all, and indeed do not even command majority support. In this case, the courts' decisions struck down a policy approach endorsed by an almost unanimous House of Commons, and whose principle was supported by a strong majority of Canadians.[43]

Some courts are less inclined than others to take the view that freedom of expression should override any other consideration. In 1992 and 1995, two Quebec courts in succession found Quebec's highly restrictive referendum umbrella committees to be a reasonable limit on freedom of expression.[44] One can therefore wonder what the final outcome would have been if those or similarly-minded courts had had to make the decision in *Somerville*. By refusing to appeal from the latter decision to the Supreme Court of Canada, the federal government ensured that court decisions from more conservative parts of the country would apply to the whole. Ironically, in October 1997, the Supreme Court of Canada, in the *Libman* case, hinted that, if asked, it would probably have taken a more favourable view of Bill C-114 than the Alberta courts!

Publication of opinion polls.

An application for a declaration that the black-out on the publication of opinion polls within three days before an election was unconstitutional was rejected both at trial and by the Ontario Court of Appeal.[45] The Supreme Court of Canada granted leave to appeal from that decision but, in the midst of the 1997 election campaign, refused to suspend the application of the blackout provision until the appeal be heard.

Broadcasting issues.

The broadcasting provisions of the Act were challenged by the Reform Party on Charter grounds, as they provide for the distribution of free broadcasting time between parties on the basis of the results of the previous election. The Alberta Court of Queen's Bench agreed that the formula for allocating broadcasting time between parties violated the freedom of smaller and emerging parties, but this was overturned by the Alberta Court of Appeal, if by a narrow margin (3 to 2). However, the latter court took the view that prohibiting parties from purchasing additional broadcasting time within their spending limits (ss. 319c and

320 of the Act) was unconstitutional, a decision which was not appealed.[46] Two Alberta courts as well as the Federal Court rejected attempts by party leaders to obtain a constitutionally guaranteed right to participate in televised leaders' debates.[47]

Those who were involved in some of these court cases can testify that they are intellectual exercises of high quality, where careful reasoning predominates over emotions and prejudices, even widely held ones. Yet, the logic underlying various decisions is not always compelling. The courts have taken a generous view of the right to vote, to the point of expanding its meaning well beyond what strict construction would have suggested, but failed to protect the very right to vote of individuals at referendums. Our right to an informed vote includes the "right" to be subjected to media blitzes from interest groups, but not the right to be informed of the results of the latest polls. The courts placed a high premium on the ideal of equality when it comes to the franchise and to electoral boundaries, yet failed to see that unrestricted spending has at least the potential of distorting the popular will for the benefit of the most wealthy.

Conclusion

The bottom line of the 1980s and 1990s so far is that Members of Parliament have lost full control over the development of election law. Earlier reforms were actions of Parliament reacting to pressure either from the public or from within its own ranks, or to advice from the Chief Electoral Officer. The main advances made throughout the 1960s and 1970s, redistribution by commissions, disclosure of political contributions and control over election spending, were the work of legislators. Parliament might be wrong, but the only alternative open to those who thought so was electing other Members.

This is no longer the case. True, the House still acts, and can do so wisely, as evidenced by the *Representation Act 1985*, Bill C-114, or (hopefully) the electoral register. Yet a consequence of public disaffection for elected politicians is that the latter are now facing strong challengers when it comes to deciding on electoral reform issues, especially the hottest. The courts made decisions with regards to the franchise, redistribution and election spending. Senators killed the boundaries bill and arguably might have delayed the implementation of the electoral register in the absence of a provision on staggered polling hours. Much of the debate on electoral reform issues has been about determining not whether a measure was appropriate or fair, but whether it would stand up in the courts. Perhaps the most revealing aspect of those episodes is that neither the courts nor the Senate were subject to public vilification for overturning the decisions of elected representatives, and indeed were sometimes widely praised for doing so. We are thus facing a paradox: Canadians want their electoral system to produce a representative House, but at the same time they seem quite willing to allow unelected institutions to override their elected representatives, even in a field of major immediate interest for the latter.

Some may regret that development, but to some extent Members have only themselves to blame for it. While their record since 1982 includes many worthwhile reforms, it is also marred by a mix of procrastination and ill-considered actions. In this context, one can hardly blame those who were dissatisfied with the outcome to use any additional opportunity they could find, either to bring long-overdue reforms or to overturn decisions they disliked.

Canadians found enough to quarrel about throughout the election campaign not to fight in addition on the very rules of the game. The hottest controversy of the campaign in this field resulted from Prime Minister Chrétien's decision to call the election after the start in Manitoba of the worst flood witnessed during this century. Reform leader Preston Manning demanded the application of a little-known clause of the *Elections Act* providing for the postponement of the poll in ridings affected by a natural disaster. Chief Electoral Officer Kingsley visited the flooded areas and met with local returning officers, candidates and officials, and concluded there was no evidence that it would be impracticable to carry out the provisions of the Act in any of the nine or ten districts affected. As it happened, polling went smoothly in the areas affected. In view of the slim parliamentary majority the Liberals ultimately won, how six or ten Manitoba districts might have skewed the final results by voting three months later than other Canadians will remain forever a fascinating topic for speculation.

Finally, the results of the election are likely to re-ignite the old debate on the advisability for Canada to stick with the first-past-the-post electoral system. That the Liberals had been returned to office on a bare 37.8 per cent of the vote did not raise many objections. However, concern over national cohesion increased on election night when Canadians were confronted with a political landscape where regions were seemingly pitted against each other. Each of the five parties secured a majority of seats in at least one province, though consideration of the number of votes won by each provides the image of a far less polarized country. Canadians will have to weigh these obvious disadvantages of the existing system with those of a more proportional one. In view of the difficulty for Parliament to move on comparatively small issues, a wholesale change of the most basic electoral rule over the next few years would come as a surprise to many.

The author wishes to thank the following for their helpful comments on earlier drafts of this chapter: André Blais, Jean-Marc Hamel, Jean-Pierre Kingsley, Greg Tardi and, of course, the editors of this book. My thanks also to Alain Lachapelle and to Herschell Sax for computing or providing some figures on the redistribution of the 1990s.

Notes

[1] Constitutional Act 1791, s. 27; Union Act 1840, s. 31; B.N.A. Act 1867, ss. 20 and 86; B.N.A. (No. 2) Act, 1949.

[2] Jean-Pierre Kingsley, *Canada's Electoral System. Strengthening the Foundation. Annex to the Report of the Chief Electoral Officer of Canada on the 35th General Election*, Ottawa, 1996.

[3] On this campaign, see Alan Frizzell, Jon Pammett and Anthony Westell, *The Canadian General Election of 1988*, Ottawa, Carleton University Press, 1989.

[4] Peter C. Newman, *The Canadian Revolution 1985-1995. From Deference to Defiance*, Toronto, Viking, 1995. See also Neil Nevitte, *The Decline of Deference. Canadian value change in cross-national perspective*, Peterborough, Broadview Press, 1996; and Louis Massicotte, "Parliament: The Show goes on, but the public seems bored", in Alain-G. Gagnon and J. Bickerton (eds.), *Canadian Politics* (2nd edition), Peterborough, Broadview Press, 1994: p. 328-343.

[5] One might think of technological progress as another source of change, as it made conceivable the implementation of complex mechanisms like an electoral register, or of more direct links between the Chief Electoral Officer and returning officers.

[6] Royal Commission on Electoral Reform and Party Financing, *Reforming Electoral Democracy. Final Report*, Ottawa, Department of Supply and Services, 1991, 4 vols.

[7] S.C. 1985, c. 8.

[8] The "Robin Hood" effect of the formula can be best gauged from the figures of the 1991 census. The three faster-growing provinces then had 58.3 per cent of Canada's population, but got only 54.1 per cent of the seats.

[9] S.C. 1992, c. 30.

[10] Only committees intending to spend more than $5000 had to be registered under the Act.

[11] This author expressed his opinions elsewhere on the bill: see *Proceedings of the Standing Senate Committee on Legal and Constitutional Affairs*, Issue No. 25, June 15, 1992, pp. 25:30-48, and in "A Deal which leaves all Parties Unhappy. The Canadian Constitutional Referendum of 1992", *Zeitschrift für Kanada-Studien*, vol. 13 no 1, 1993, p. 125-140.

[12] Referendums held at the initiative of the people are now provided for in Saskatchewan and British Columbia, while in the latter province Members may be recalled subject to stringent procedures. In Alberta and British Columbia, referendums must be held before the Assembly ratifies a constitutional amendment.

[13] Standing Committee on Procedure and House Affairs, *Minutes of Proceedings and Evidence*, Issue No. 36, December 8, 1994, pp. 36:8 sq. The Royal Commission on Electoral Reform had reported unfavourably on the recall: see the *Report*, vol. 2, p. 242-47.

[14] Third report of the Committee, in *Minutes of Proceedings and Evidence of the Special Committee on Electoral Reform*, Issue No. 7, December 11, 1992.

[15] S.C. 1993, c. 19.

[16] Except in Quebec, where an enumeration had to be conducted in 1993, because no recent federal lists were available, as the 1992 referendum had been held under Quebec legislation.

[17] Actually, in comparison with the 1988 election, the number of candidates *increased* from 1575 to 2155 in 1993 even though the amount of the deposit had been increased by about 400 per cent.

[18] S.C. 1992, c. 25. The initial proposal was to postpone redistribution by *two* years.

[19] S.C. 1994, c. 19. For a summary of the debate in the House on Bill C-18, see Norman J. Ruff, "Representation Canadian style - or does anybody own a riding?", paper presented at a roundtable, annual meeting of the Canadian Political Science Association, Calgary, June 1994.

[20] House of Commons, Standing Committee on Procedure and House Affairs, *Minutes of Proceedings and Evidence*, Issue No. 33, November 25, 1994. For an analysis of the report, see Richard Jenkins, "Redistribution stories: Untangling the politics of electoral boundaries, 1993-1995", paper presented at the annual meeting of the Canadian Political Science Association, Brock University, June 1996.

[21] In a report to the House, dated December 8, 1995, the Committee on Procedure and House Affairs requested that a message be sent to the Senate protesting against the attitude taken by the Senate on Bill C-69. The House did not adopt that report, and there was no attempt to re-

introduce C-69 at the next session even after the Tories had lost their majority in the Senate. Incidentally, the misfortunes of Bill C-69 were not unprecedented, as the Senate had blocked two earlier redistribution bills in 1899-1900: see R.A. MacKay, *The Unreformed Senate of Canada*, Toronto, McClelland & Stewart, 1963, p. 97.

[22] The cumulative impact of the public hearings process and Members' objections was that the boundaries of 194 districts out of 300 (excluding Yukon) were altered.

[23] This was slightly less fair than the earlier proposals of the commissions, for which the comparable figure was 85 per cent. To put things in perspective, 57 districts out of 295 had electoral populations exceeding the 25 *per cent* tolerance level at the 1993 election.

[24] This particular name was one of the 22 which were selected by Members themselves through a private Member's bill (S.C. 1996, c. 36). Incidentally, as if to further drive the point that electoral matters were of interest to them, Senators amended three of these names. Among other challenging names reflecting a keen understanding of "the politics of inclusion" are "Hastings - Frontenac - Lennox and Addington", "Dufferin-Peel-Wellington-Grey" (not to be confused with either Waterloo-Wellington or Bruce-Grey), and "Bonaventure-Gaspé-Iles-de-la-Madeleine-Pabok".

[25] In 1996, four years after the introduction of the National Voter Registration Act (known as the "Motor Voter Bill"), still only 76 per cent of the voting age population in the United States were registered, compared with well over 90 per cent in Canada under the enumeration system. See *Elections Today. News from the International Foundation for Election Systems*, Vol. 6 No. 4, Winter 1997, p. 7.

[26] S.C. 1996, c. 35.

[27] Elections Canada, "Fact Sheet - Register of Electors: Estimated cost reductions compared to door-to-door enumeration", October 1996.

[28] The purpose of the legislation was frustrated by Saskatchewan's policy of having no daylight saving time legislation between April and October, unlike all other provinces. As a result, most of that province, while complying with the voting hours specified by the Act, actually voted later than anyone else in Canada, with its polling stations closing half an hour after those of British Columbia. Apparently none of Saskatchewan Senators or M.P.s had warned the government about that problem.

[29] S.C. 1996, c. 26.

[30] S.C. 1992, c. 21.

[31] See *The 1992 Federal Referendum. A Challenge Met* (Ottawa, 1994), and *Towards the 35th General Election. Report of the Chief Electoral Officer of Canada* (Ottawa, 1994).

[32] *Canadian Disabilities Rights Council v. Canada* (1988) 3 F.C. 622; *Muldoon v. Canada* (1988) 3 F.C. 628.

[33] *Re Jolivet and Barker and the Queen*, (1983) 1 D.L.R. (4th) 604 (Supreme Court of B.C.); *Sauvé v. Canada (A.G.)*, (1988) 53 D.L.R. (4th) 595 (Ontario High Court); *Gould v. A.G. Canada (T.D.)* (1984) 1 F.C. 1119, overturned by *A.G. Canada v. Gould (A.D.)* (1984) 1 F.C. 1133. The latter decision, which went against the inmates, was confirmed by the Supreme Court of Canada on September 4, 1984: see (1984) 2 R.C.S. 124. Also *Badger v. Canada (A.G.)*, Man. Court of Queen's Bench, November 4, 1988, overturned by the Manitoba Court of Appeal two weeks later: (1988) 55 D.L.R. (4th) 177.

[34] *Belczowski v. Canada (T.D.)* (1991) 3 F.C. 151; confirmed by the Federal Court of Appeal in (1992) 2 F.C. 440; *Sauvé v. Canada (A.G.)*, (1992) 89 D.L.R. (4th) 644.

[35] *Sauvé v. Canada (A.G.)*, (1993) 2 S.C.R. 438.

[36] *Sauvé v. Canada*, (1996) 1 F.C. 857. During the election campaign, the federal government requested a stay that would have prevented inmates from voting, but that request was denied on May 16, 1997, by the Federal Court. The government immediately appealed from that decision, in the midst of a campaign where Reform was hammering the crime issue, arguing inter alia that federal prisoners should be deprived of their right to vote. The Federal Court of Appeal confirmed the earlier decision on May 21. Accordingly, federal inmates voted at an advance poll on May 23. Even there, the federal government unsuccessfully asked the Supreme Court to order those votes not to be counted.

[37] *National Citizens' Coalition Inc. v. A.G. Canada*, (1984) 11 D.L.R. (4th) 481.

[38] *Somerville v. Canada (A.G.)*, (1996) 136 D.L.R. (4th) 205 (Alta C.A.). This decision also struck down the provision of the Act which prohibited advertising during the early weeks and the last days of the campaign.

[39] *Idem*, page 232. For a critical review of the decision, see Herman Bakvis and Jennifer Smith, "Third-Party Advertising and Electoral Democracy: The Political Theory of the Alberta Court of Appeal in *Somerville v. Canada (Attorney General)* [1996]", *Canadian Public Policy*, vol. 23, no. 2, 1997.

[40] In the *Haig* case, the Supreme Court held that section 3 of the Charter did not guarantee the right to vote in a referendum.

[41] In the 1997 election campaign, various groups intervened in the electoral process, though to a generally small extent. The Canadian Police Association engaged in negative advertising: the billboards, that were displayed near highways, included a picture of some M.P. "who voted for paroling those three killers" (the ad included pictures of Clifford Olson,

Paul Bernardo and Clinton Gayle). The revulsion sovereignists profess to feel against money spent outside the legal framework of elections did not prevent the *Partenaires pour la souveraineté* from running ads in newspapers against partition, or the *Société St-Jean Baptiste de Montréal* to print posters denouncing Liberal candidates, while the Quebec National Capital Commission, tearing a leaf from the Bronfman Foundation, broadcast radio spots reminding Quebeckers about hot episodes of their history like the battle of the Plains of Abraham. Only the Canadian Police Association tactics did raise controversy.

[42] Incidentally, skepticism about the Charter is in no way confined to Quebec or inspired solely by nationalistic opinions, as evidenced by the works of scholars like F.L. Morton and Michael Mandel.

[43] The Royal Commission on Electoral Reform (*Final Report*, vol. 1, p. 337) cited an attitudinal survey conducted in 1991, which concluded that 75 per cent of those interviewed supported spending limits for those who represented specific group interests.

[44] *Libman* v. *Quebec (Procureur général)*, (1992) R.J.Q. 2141 (Que. Superior Ct); confirmed by *Libman* v. *Quebec (Procureur général)*, (1995) R.J.Q. 2015 (Que. C.A.). While the Supreme Court of Canada overruled those decisions in October 1997, it lauded the objective of the legislation and suggested minor changes that would preserve the system of umbrella committees. Whether Quebec will comply with that decision (as most observers recommended) or derogate from the Charter still had to be decided by the Bouchard government at the time of writing.

[45] *Thomson Newspapers Co.* v. *Canada (A.G.)*, (1995) 24 O.R. (3d) 109; confirmed by (1996) 138 D.L.R. (4th) 1 (Ont. C.A.). The ban on polls attracted much criticism in the media at the end of the campaign. For a sample of negative editorial comments, see "Poll blackout offensive, unjust", *The Gazette* (Montréal) May 29, 1997, p. B2; Don Macpherson, "Campaign features absurd law on polls", *The Gazette* (Montréal) May 31, 1997, p. B5; "Censored by law", *The Globe and Mail* (Toronto), May 31, 1997, p. D6 (both newspapers had the elegance of pointing out in those comments they were party to the judicial proceedings against the ban).

[46] *Reform Party of Canada* v. *Canada (A.G.)*, (1993) 3 W.W.R. 139 (Alta Ct of Queen's Bench); (1995) 123 D.L.R. (4th) 366 (Alta C.A.).

[47] *Natural Law Party of Canada* v. *Canadian Broadcasting Corp. (T.D.)*, (1994) 1 F.C. 580.

Ten
The Regionalization of Canadian Electoral Politics[1]
by Michael Marzolini

To most of the players, the outcome of the 1997 federal election was never in doubt. The Canadian public, as well as the media, pundits, and the politicians themselves, anticipated a Liberal majority government. Preconditioning this expectation were four years of public opinion polls in the media showing the Liberals with the support of at least 43 per cent of decided voters, as well as anecdotal evidence of the popularity of the incumbent government, and much discussion on the fragmentation of the opposition parties. Only the size of the Liberal majority was disputed, as well as the question as to who would form the Official Opposition, and whether two of the parties would regain enough seats to attain official party status. A growing trend toward political regionalism however, would turn the campaign into a tight horse-race, with lasting effects on the nation.

Not until the last two weeks of the election did the media, reading the polls and speculating on the actions of the party leaders, start to suspect what all the political parties had known for more than two years, that a minority government was a strong possibility. The public were slow to grasp this concept, but the flurry of media polls released 72 hours before the vote, including a "rogue poll" on CTV showing the Liberals with only 36 per cent vs. the PC's 25 per cent, introduced the potential of minority government to the voters themselves.

This was not an easy conclusion to make based on the polling data reported in the media. National party standings were meaningless. The 1997 election was a "regional numbers game", and without a thoughtful reading of the regional variations in the media or private polls, it was only too easy to predict a majority government for any party attaining more than 35 per cent of national voter support. In reality, due to the extreme fluctuations of public opinion in all of the regions outside Ontario, a majority was technically possible with as little as 36 per cent nationally and a minority could be possible with as much as 41 per cent, the same level that had delivered a major sweep for the Liberals in 1993. To look only at the national polling numbers reported in the media was to be oblivious to the extraordinarily high amount of "wasted votes" present in this election campaign. Regionally concentrated levels of support for each party could either fall just short of translating into seats, or win some seats with huge pluralities. It was not one election — it was ten.

Regional Interests: The motivation of the electorate

The outcome of this election was a product of many factors which influenced voter behaviour. They are difficult to accurately quantify, as they all affect each other, but they can be roughly ordered as follows: 1. Regional interests; 2. Leadership (which impacts on regional interest, and for the Liberals on government record); 3. Government/Party Reputation (which impacts on leadership and regional interest); 4. Issues (where parties differentiate themselves from opponents, reflect regional interest, and demonstrate government record and/or leadership potential).

There were two "bedrock" attitudes that held up nationally in this election. The first was that Jean Chrétien would continue to be seen as the best choice for Prime Minister. This was never seriously challenged, even during the mid-campaign surge in Jean Charest's popularity. In Ontario, this was the Liberals' electoral cornerstone. The second unchanging view was that the Liberals would win the election. This attitude was both an electoral asset and a liability to the Liberals. As a Liberal asset, it prevented the PCs or Reform from picking up any bandwagon effect, but as a liability it also diluted the imperative to vote Liberal in order to elect a Liberal government. People believed the Liberals would be re-elected no matter how they voted individually.

In truth, more than half of Canadians wanted the Liberals to win, and most of them wanted a Liberal majority. Even many of those who didn't vote Liberal felt the Liberals deserved to win, and would do the best job. These attitudes held true even in Nova Scotia, where the Liberals would not win a seat. Why then were some people who thought the Liberals were best to lead the country, and who preferred Jean Chrétien as Prime Minister, reluctant to vote Liberal?

The answer can best be found in the answers to the question "Which party best represents your region's interests?" asked in our post-election

POLLARA survey. The results in each province closely mirror the actual voter support levels of each party, with some adjustment for the impact of leadership, party reputation and issues. Reform is seen as most regionally sensitive in all four western provinces, the Liberals in Ontario, the Bloc in Quebec, with a 3-way split between the PCs, Liberals and NDP in Atlantic Canada.

Figure 1
Best Party to Represent Your Region's Interests

	LIB	PC	NDP	REF	BQ	OTH	DON'T KNOW
Atlantic Canada	29%	24%	32%	5%	—	2%	9%
Quebec	35%	13%	2%	—	43%	—	7%
Ontario	58%	12%	8%	10%	—	1%	11%
Prairies	20%	9%	15%	48%	—	1%	7%
British Columbia	19%	3%	21%	47%	—	1%	8%

In each of the regions, there was a strong "native son or daughter" effect that the opposition campaigns encouraged. Westerners did not necessarily consider Preston Manning the best choice for Prime Minister, nor did Easterners endorse Alexa McDonough for this job, but voters expected both these leaders to stand up for their regions in the same way that Gilles Duceppe would stand up for Quebeckers. This tugging on regional heart-strings was far stronger than even Tory leaders Bob Stanfield or Joe Clark were ever able to command in the 1970's. Regional interests and regional leaders had a heavy impact in this election, both emotionally and organizationally, and this helped all the opposition parties.

Regionalism has been exacerbated, not just by leadership, but by issues as well. The past decade has seen a greater regional polarization based on concern for the two issues of employment and the deficit. Westerners tend to be deficit-focused, to the exclusion of much concern over jobs. Atlantic

Canadians are the opposite — seeing little value in deficit-cutting and focussing almost exclusively on employment issues. In the West during the election, the Liberals were perceived as weak on the deficit. In the East, they were viewed as weak on jobs. Only in Ontario did the Liberal positioning on these two issues mirror the views of the majority more effectively than did their opponents — and solely in Ontario were the Liberals seen as best representing regional interests.

In each of Canada's ten provinces however, it is the Liberals who are seen as best representing Canada's national interests. (Figure 2) Only in Ontario are regional interests and national interests perceived as interchangeable. In past elections, especially in the free trade-based election of 1988 and including the 1993 election, the interests of Canada as a whole were critically important to people's vote choice. It would appear though, that in 1997, voting based on national interest was no

Figure 2
Best party to represent national interests

	LIB	PC	NDP	REF	BQ	OTH	DON'T KNOW
Atlantic Canada	45%	19%	15%	6%	—	1%	14%
Quebec	53%	19%	5%	2%	10%	1%	10%
Ontario	56%	11%	5%	14%	—	2%	12%
Prairies	43%	10%	7%	27%	—	1%	12%
British Columbia	49%	6%	10%	23%	—	2%	10%

longer a high priority for Canadians. This poses one of Canada's greatest challenges for the future, because if Canadians are not going to return to voting based on the national interest, then national interests will be hard-pressed to survive.

Though regionality will endure as a problem, it was not the sole basis of voter decision-making in the 1997 federal election. Leadership, issues and party reputation together form a public opinion environment that influenced both regional views and electoral behaviour as a whole.

Overlaying these factors was a mood of suppressed economic frustration. The country was at a cross-roads, weary from the onslaught of economic problems that have characterized life in Canada since the 1990 recession.

The pre-election mood

After a brief two-year burst of economic optimism spurred by the Liberals' election in 1993, Canadians in good faith bought into both the problem and the challenge of the federal deficit in their approach to the 1995 Budget. Realizing that deficit reduction would be both long and painful, people reduced their expectations of government dramatically. Not only were they sanguine about many cuts to government spending, they no longer expected government to create jobs directly, but rather just create an environment conducive to private sector hiring. This view, however, never prevailed in Atlantic Canada, which wished for continued high levels of government involvement in people's lives. This region would smoulder silently in the first weeks of the campaign, and later demonstrate their frustration more loudly, before finally rebelling on election day against the Liberals' domination of the region.

The second round of spending cuts to affect Canadians, this time from their provincial governments, was felt harder coast to coast. One level of government cutting public spending they could accept, but when Ralph Klein and Mike Harris started a trend of even greater service rationalization, and other premiers followed their lead, Canadians started to voice a preference for a slower, more cautious approach. As time progressed, they began to yearn for a light at the end of the tunnel, and required a renewal of hope for the future, a reward for their sacrifice.

The response of the pParties: campaign promises

In response to the public desire for a reward, the Reform and PC Parties offered tax cuts. This promise was not effective. Eight in ten Canadians wanted tax cuts, but seven in ten felt they were not affordable. Rather than this, people would prefer the money to be spent on hospitals and education, which they believed would benefit them more. In Ontario, where the Liberals would sweep electorally in 1997, the governing party was inoculated from the PC/Reform tax cut plans by the actions of the provincial PC government — which had cut taxes while simultaneously shutting down hospitals and downgrading the education system. This Ontario experience was a mill-stone around the neck of the federal PCs, and assisted in limiting Reform support in that province. What is more, the Harris advisors who formulated the Charest tax cut plan misread the meaning of the Harris Ontario victory in 1995. Harris's own people continued to underestimate the abilities and "everyman" appeal of their leader, and had given credit for Harris's popularity to a superficial tax cut rather than a skilled politician with strong personal appeal.

One key effect of Canadians' acceptance of the deficit problem and solution in 1995 was to decrease expectations of government's ability to directly increase employment. Since, at least in Central and Western Canada, government was no longer expected to be a direct job creator, the issue did not have the importance in the 1997 election that it did in 1993. Indeed, though the lack of jobs was seen to be no less a problem, and is still considered the most important issue facing Canada by 42 per cent of all Canadians — only 24 per cent thought it to be the most important issue in the election campaign. They did not find any other issues to focus on. Rather, they were left confused by the party leaders' ever-shifting messages, changing sometimes daily from economic management, to tax cuts, or health care, gun control, national unity and accountability. After the election, three in ten Canadians were unable to name the most important issue of the campaign, though all but 6 per cent had an opinion on what it should have been.

Previous elections had been fought on one dominant issue. In 1984 it was jobs. In 1988 it was free trade. In 1993 it was jobs. The lack of single-issue focus of the 1997 campaign was partially a function of the issue menu being used as a foil for leadership, party reputation and regional interests. It was also a result of five parties, each with different and unusually rigid doctrines, being unable to dominate the campaign with its own agenda. Each party would win their place in the spotlight for no more than three days, and usually receive a small lift in public support, only to have it wrestled away by a competitor. The confusion these multiple and competing agendas caused the public was of enormous benefit to the incumbent Liberals, who had only to deal with 2–3 day "raids" from all directions, but no "sustained attack" from a single challenger.

POLLARA's polling for the Liberals showed that they would have to utilize their four major assets in their campaign: 1) The popularity of the Prime Minister, 2) Their success reducing the deficit, 3) The reviving economy, and 4) Their team. As incumbents, the opposition would be expected to attack them primarily. With most media polls continually placing the Liberals in the low 40s in percentage of decided voter support, and not able to anticipate much further growth, they would have to "narrow-cast" their campaign to their own supporters, campaign more intensively among the one in six undecided voters in the country, and be ready to react to sustained attacks from any single opponent who managed to emerge from the pack.

The public, like the media, was on a "death-watch" with respect to the Liberals. They at first paid higher-than-average attention to the campaign, scrutinizing campaign events such as the "leaking" of the Liberal platform document by Preston Manning, and the controversy over calling the election at the outset of the Manitoba Flood, searching for signs of national discontent. Yet, the national level of public support for the Liberals remained solid, and the media polls did not show any significant movement. One week after the debate, with no "horse-race" in sight, the amount of public attention being paid to the Liberal Party decreased, and voters gave up trying to build a consensus as to which party would be the Liberals' national rival.

Parties and leadership

While the Liberals were kept busy defending themselves against attacks, the opposition parties were aggressive, and gained some ground. The Reform Party benefited almost solely from Westerners voting for the party they thought would best represent their region. Reform's "native sons and daughters" image swept much of the West. The Reform Party benefited from regionally popular issues. Our post-election survey shows that leadership was not a key factor in people's support for Reform. Indeed, Reform voters tended to be more impressed with Jean Chrétien than they were with Preston Manning. Manning, however, was the native son, and like Gilles Duceppe and Lucien Bouchard in Quebec, could be counted on to protect his region's interest.

Jean Charest's strength was leadership and strength of personality, which he demonstrated to the public when he, in their opinion, won both leaders' debates. He personally surged in popularity, but these gains did not transfer directly to his party or quickly work to enhance his own credibility. He had momentum, but the momentum had no "traction." He stalled in the polls, limited by a platform that voters perceived as "risky" and "right-wing", and by Ontario's general satisfaction with the existing federal government. His momentum peaked more than a week after the leaders' debates, when his support surged in Atlantic Canada, Quebec, Manitoba, and to a lesser extent, in Ontario and Alberta. These gains, however, came too late in the campaign. In the critical few days which the new pro-Charest attitudes needed to harden, his opponents set out to undermine his credibility. In less than a week, they had destroyed many of his gains. Charest came under strong attack from all four party leaders, the three Liberal Atlantic Premiers, and the Premier of Quebec. The national unity issue, which he had used emotively to enhance his leadership stature, finally provoked a response from the BQ after he began taking votes from Duceppe. Lucien Bouchard's decisive intervention to remind Quebeckers of Charest's role in scuttling the Meech/Charlottetown agreements under Brian Mulroney finished Charest with the soft nationalists he had been wooing. Charest's own references to Mulroney restricted his gains in Ontario, Alberta, Manitoba and the East. In the Atlantic region, where he had been benefiting from weak Reform support, and was splitting the anti-government vote with the NDP, his gains would be reduced significantly, to a 1 per cent plurality over the Liberals.

Alexa McDonough was another of the three leaders to make strong gains as a result of people voting for regional rather than national interests. Newly spotlighted on the national stage, and seen as a fresh face with much potential, she surged strongly in the first two weeks of the campaign. Her early gains were manifested mainly in the Atlantic region but also in Manitoba, where the decision to call the election just before the flood crisis was controversial. She concentrated on jobs, which struck a chord with those Canadians who considered employment the most important issue. The NDP economic platform, however, with its greatly increased spending and taxing policies, was not designed to appeal to more than a niche segment of the electorate. After two years of deficit-related sacrifice, Canadians were not yet ready to "let the good times roll" and after a poor debate performance she faltered everywhere west of Quebec. In Atlantic Canada, which was discontented with the Liberals for withdrawing their "entitlements", and where her economic policies were more in line with public opinion, she was the "native daughter" who would stand up for the region. She would win 8 of her 21 seats in the Atlantic provinces.

Gilles Duceppe was not the man his predecessor was, at least in the opinion of most "soft" Bloc Québécois supporters. His first week of campaigning was an immediate disappointment, with embarrassing photo opportunities, organizational mishaps, and further embarrassment when former Premier Jacques Parizeau's secret intentions to declare independence immediately following the 1995 referendum came to light. Duceppe's support plummeted in the first week, recovered slightly due to voter sympathy in week two, and hardened in the third week as a result of backing from Lucien Bouchard. After the leaders' debate, with national unity once more on the politicians' and media's agenda, he was on more solid ground. Soft sovereigntists, unhappy with Duceppe's leadership, and not as motivated by regional interest as core BQ supporters, galvanized behind the Liberals in the first weeks of the campaign. When national unity arose as an issue, and Charest staked out new ground for himself in addressing it, those soft voters transferred to the PCs, weakening the first-place Liberals, and allowing Duceppe to regain the lead. In the last ten days of the campaign though, Preston Manning would strike with his "anti-Quebec politician", advertising positioning the Reform Party to make national unity both more important and more controversial. Reform's views and evident popularity turned both soft sovereigntists and even some soft federalists back from their experimentation with the PCs and Liberals, and returned some of them to the guardian of their regional interests, Gilles Duceppe.

Regional volatility

The media polling reports did not serve the public well in this election. Most of these polls used sample sizes too small to provide a good picture of any province outside of Quebec and Ontario. While there was some volatility in Quebec, there was none in Ontario. The real movement was in the smaller provinces, and most of it went unnoticed and unreported until the media pollsters boosted their sample sizes in the final week of the election.

The Liberals' first challenge was Manitoba. Calling the election at the outset of the flood improved NDP and PC fortunes in that province immediately, and Reform benefited later in the campaign. The electoral damage to the Liberals in Manitoba could be repaired however, mainly through local Liberal candidates curtailing their campaign activities and using their organizational abilities to combat the flood. The use of the Armed Forces and the attention paid to the region by the government also made an impact. The rest of Western Canada was a different story. The Liberals had started the campaign ahead of Reform and the NDP in British Columbia, behind Reform in Alberta, and with a slight lead over Reform in Saskatchewan. In each province, as the campaign progressed, both Liberal and NDP vote intentions deteriorated proportionally to the exposure of Preston Manning to the public. Manning was not overly popular, and his policies did not at first catch fire, but Westerners considered him more sensitive to their region than any of the alternatives. In the absence of being strongly or traditionally partisan toward the Liberals, they could indulge in voting along lines of regional interest. Reform support became more pronounced when Manning launched his "anti-Quebec politician" ads, which were not seen as offensive in Western Canada. His shift to "accountability" as the closing issue of the campaign, however, did nothing to enhance his fortunes. It was too "soft" a concept to be effective, and followed too closely on the "hard" message about Quebec. In the face of the continuing Liberal and NDP attacks on his credibility, both these parties were able to regain some small amount of ground in Western Canada in the last few days of the campaign.

In Ontario, it was business as usual. There, the Liberals finished the campaign with almost as much support as they started it with. Voters were decidedly happy with the Liberals, and Prime Minister Chrétien was extremely popular. There were some challenges from the NDP in the opening weeks in Southwestern Ontario, post-debate from the PCs in the Metro Belt (905 area code), and in the last week from Reform in Central Ontario, but the opposition parties were blocked from sustaining these challenges by attacks on each other, and by their ever-changing shifts in issue focus. Reform, for example, mounted a serious challenge to the Liberals in Central Ontario using their "anti-Quebec politician" positioning. They initially gained ground, but lost it as soon as two things happened. First, the "bigot" label that was applied to Reform by Charest, while having no effect in Western Canada, was not a label that the more "politically correct" central Ontarians wanted to wear. The resulting Reform decline would not benefit Charest, but would help dash Reform hopes in the province. Second, Reform shifted its message to "recall and accountability", and as a result lost much of their edge just when they needed to reinforce their support.

In Quebec, the vote was polarized along lines of regional interest. Liberal support in Montréal would be largely unchallenged throughout the election. Outside of Montréal, the vote was more volatile, with soft sovereigntists first moving to the Liberals after Duceppe's first week of troubled campaigning, then to the PCs to reflect Charest's new vitality after the leaders' debates, and finally partially back to the Bloc after the prominence of the national unity issue re-galvanized their support. The Bloc ended the campaign weakened, and the Liberals and PCs ended it strengthened. The lasting change was the elevation of Jean Charest to the status of the most popular politician in Quebec, more impressive to Quebeckers than even Lucien Bouchard. While in the polarized Quebec environment he could not translate this into many votes for his PC Party, he now has new importance and prominence in any future discussions on the future of Quebec.

Liberal support in Atlantic Canada was widespread in the opening days of the 1997 campaign, but it was also resentful and reserved. Changes to the employment insurance system rankled, as did federal and provincial government cutbacks, but these were only some of the regional factors that would move support. NDP leader Alexa McDonough, already popular in Nova Scotia, gained exposure and stature when campaigning in Newfoundland, New Brunswick and to a lesser extent, Prince Edward Island. She was viewed as the most regionally sensitive of the leaders, and as their "native daughter" of the Atlantic region. Voters were stirred to anger, and believed that the deficit-related cutbacks which they had never agreed to, would not stop by re-electing Liberals. McDonough, and later Charest, would both incite and benefit from this emotion. There was a new realization on the part of some voters that here were champions for their cause. Charest's gains, having to wait until his momentum achieved "traction", were especially pronounced across all four Atlantic provinces. With a week to go, PC support surpassed both the Liberals and NDP region-wide. The Liberals countered the PCs with aggressive advertising and the active involvement of the three Liberal Premiers of the region. Charest counter-punched, attacking the Premiers as "liars" and "stooges", but this served only to tarnish his image in New Brunswick and Newfoundland where the Liberal Premiers were popular. The Liberals surged in the home-stretch, to within 1 per cent of the PCs and 9 per cent ahead of the NDP, but lost seats to both these parties.

The challenges of victory

Though public opinion polling both before and after the 1997 election has shown that the public expected a Liberal majority government, and preferred a Liberal majority government more than any other option, there is more to this election than Canadians merely electing such a Liberal majority. For the Liberals, the campaign was a success in that, while themselves retaining representation from all regions, they preserved the split between their opponents on the right, protected their flanks on the left, and undermined the BQ/sovereigntist position in Quebec. Many challenges also surfaced from this campaign though, and the new government's popularity and effectiveness in governing will depend on how it meets these challenges. To borrow from Winston Churchill, "The problems of victory are more agreeable than those of defeat, but they are no less difficult."

First, the government must take into account a new economic attitude toward deficit-cutting and government spending in general. The number of Canadians who believe the deficit to be the issue of prime importance has declined by half since before the election. It is not seen to be a major problem any longer. Indeed, more than six out of ten people think that significant gains will be made against the deficit within the next year, and that the government has the issue under control. As a result, Canadians are calling for increased expenditures in 17 of the 19 key areas of government spending. They still deny the need for immediate tax cuts, but are split three ways over what to do when the deficit is eliminated: 1) spend more on health care and social programs, 2) cut taxes, or, 3) contribute toward reducing the national debt.

In general, Canadians believe the government has been moving in the right direction for the country as a whole. A plurality of people in every region still believe that the Liberals are the best party to represent the national interest. They differ however, outside of Ontario, when it comes to determining who would best handle their regional interests, and it currently appears that regional interests are more important to them. As a result, there is a desire for a change in government direction, either major (in the alienated provinces) or minor (in Ontario). In no province in Canada do a majority of residents urge the government to "stay the course."

Regional alienation will be a key challenge for the government both economically and socially. Canada is a confederation in which nine out of ten provinces voted along lines of regional self-interest, rather than national self-interest. "Western alienation", as voiced by Preston Manning and exemplified by the success of his "anti-Quebec politician" message, is as prominent as "Quebec alienation". The newly emerged "Atlantic alienation", which is less historically-based than the others and more oriented toward the government's deficit-related policies, will produce a difficult channel for the government to navigate.

There is some hope however, within this issue of regional alienation. While we must not underestimate the problem, there is no certainty that voting along lines of regional interest will be a permanent fixture in future elections. In the 1997 campaign there was no national alternative party that could be considered a credible replacement for the Liberals. The Liberals had a strong lead in the media public opinion polls, and very few Canadians believed that they would not win a majority. Voting based on regional interests therefore, could be indulged in totally risk-free. The national interest would still be served. The national incumbent government would still be re-elected, and would guard those national interests. The problem that could arise, and almost did, was that of all Canadians voting on regional rather than national interests. This might have triggered either a Liberal minority or defeat, a paradoxical outcome which would have been perceived by the public as being against its own self-interest.

Whether the new trend toward political regionalism endures in the future, or is merely a temporary risk-free indulgence, Canadians and their political parties will need to re-examine their priorities. Either Canada is a unified nation, voting for national interests, or it is a polyglot of provinces, voting along regional lines. If the latter, it is unlikely over time that our national interests will long survive the pressure. We have until the year 2001 to decide this question.

Notes

The contribution of Donald Guy and Angela Marzolini to the analysis and writing of this article is gratefully acknowledged.

Eleven
The Leaders' Debates:
(...And the Winner Is...)
by Lawrence LeDuc

As has become the pattern in recent federal elections, the televised leader debates which took place on May 12th and 13th (with a resumption of the truncated French debate on May 18th) were a central focus, but probably not the critical event of the 1997 campaign. Now generally scheduled about three weeks before election day, televised debates are increasingly thought of as the starting point of the *real* campaign rather than the "defining moment" or critical "turning point" that such events have sometimes been in previous elections. The shorter total length of the 1997 campaign, coupled with the lackluster first two weeks, contributed to the feeling that the debates would serve to finally get the campaign under way. "The phony war ends tonight," observed Edison Stewart of *The Toronto Star* in that newspaper's lead article on the debates. "Swept into the background by the Manitoba flood and the Bre-X mining scandal, Canada's campaigning political leaders have had trouble getting the public's attention."[1]

Televised debates are indeed very good at getting the public's attention. Watched by millions of potential voters, the debates provide one of the best opportunities in a campaign for party leaders to take their message directly to the electorate as a whole and for voters to compare the party leaders. Particularly for new leaders who lack the high visibility of more established political figures, these events present a unique opportunity to shape the agenda and to establish a favourable image in the minds of the voters. They also tend to dominate journalistic commentary for a period of at least several days of the campaign. Thus, many individuals who may not actually watch an entire debate can still form impressions from news clips, post-debate analyses, and other references to these events over the course of the campaign.[2]

Nevertheless, it is important not to overstate the role which televised debates between the party leaders can play in an election campaign. While they are certainly a major focal point, they are only one event of the campaign. Canadian elections are not presidential contests, a fact which is sometimes forgotten in drawing comparisons between leader debates in Canada and the United States. Often discussed in boxing ring imagery such as "landing a blow" or delivering a "knockout punch", it is easy to overstate their effects on the larger campaign. Leaders now generally enter these affairs well prepared and well briefed, and defensive strategies are often as important as the more obvious offensive ones. With as much as three weeks of the campaign remaining after the television lights are turned off, the debates which at one moment appear so critical are rapidly overtaken by other campaign events. In the 1993 election, the debates proved to be an important campaign event, but they did little in themselves to change the overall course of the campaign.[3] A similar argument can be advanced with regard to the effects of the debates on the outcome of the 1997 election.

The evolution of leaders' debates in Canada

Televised debates between the major party leaders are now a semi-institutionalized feature of Canadian federal election campaigns. Although originally associated with the style of American presidential politics, such events have become commonplace in the electoral politics of many other countries besides the United States. Countries as diverse as France, Australia, Japan, Sweden, Turkey and Brazil, to mention only a few examples, have incorporated televised debates into recent election campaigns.[4] In each of these instances, the format and practice has been adapted to fit quite different electoral institutions, party systems, and campaign practices. In those countries where debates have been a regular feature of election campaigns for some time, there has often been considerable variation in format from one election to another, reflecting changes in technology, campaign strategies, and party politics.

Such has certainly been the case in Canada. When the first debate between party leaders in a Canadian federal election took place in 1968, the concept of a televised debate between the leaders was still new and untested in the arena of electoral politics. The famous Kennedy–Nixon debates, which had taken place in the U.S. eight years earlier, provided the only appropriate model for such an event.[5] But, while the 1960 U.S.

debates demonstrated the power of television, then still a relatively young medium, they also made politicians wary of the high risks of a debate. After his defeat in the 1960 U.S. presidential election, Richard Nixon never again debated his opponents in subsequent contests, and televised debates between presidential candidates in the U.S. did not take place again until the Carter–Ford debates of 1976.[6] Until at least the mid-1980's, the question of participating in a televised campaign debate was largely a matter of party strategy. Debates proposed by the media for the 1972 and 1974 Canadian federal elections failed to take place, primarily because it proved impossible to secure the agreement of all of the parties on timing, format and procedure. After extended negotiations between the parties, a debate was held during the 1979 federal election campaign. Unilingual and occurring only a week before election day, the 1979 debate was quite different than those which took place in the most recent election.[7] Again primarily because of the difficulty in obtaining agreement among the parties, there were no debates during the 1980 election campaign.

From 1984 onward however, debates have been a regular feature of Canadian federal elections. The 1984 debates, which featured Brian Mulroney's famous "you had an option" riposte to John Turner's attempted defence of a string of patronage appointments ushered in a new era for these events in Canada and established a new set of norms and expectations.[8] In the earlier years, the question of whether or not to participate in a debate had been largely a matter of party strategy. New leaders generally favoured them, hoping to use the opportunity to establish a favourable personal image with the public. Opposition parties and smaller parties also perceived benefits to be gained through the medium of debates. Incumbent prime ministers were more reluctant to participate, as were incumbent presidents in the U.S. But this tendency changed in Canada with Brian Mulroney's participation in the 1988 debates, as it did in the U.S. with the participation of incumbent presidents Jimmy Carter in 1980 and Ronald Reagan in 1984. By the end of the decade, it could be said that debates were well institutionalized in both presidential elections in the United States and federal elections in Canada. Many other countries had also begun to make such events a routine part of election campaigns.

The 1984 election was the first in which separate French and English debates were conducted, thus placing greater emphasis on the linguistic abilities of the participants. NDP leader Ed Broadbent was significantly disadvantaged by this development, but once the precedent was set, it would never again be possible to propose a single unilingual debate such as that of 1979. This was to be a matter of particular concern regarding Preston Manning's participation in a French debate in 1993 and 1997. 1984 also saw the innovation of a separate debate on women's issues, a practice which has not carried over into subsequent elections. However, the 1988 format did allocate extra time in both the French and English programs for issues of special interest to women, and the question of the content of the debates gradually received greater attention. By the time of the 1988 election, a new set of understandings for such events was firmly in place.

The 1988 debates were memorable for John Turner's dramatic "you've sold us out" indictment of Brian Mulroney on the free trade issue.[9] They also demonstrated that a strong performance by a leader could have a powerful effect on the dynamics of an election campaign. The Liberals surged sharply upward in the polls following the 1988 debates and, although the Conservatives went on to win the election, the lesson regarding the potential effects on a campaign was not forgotten by the media or by the parties.[10] Continuing experience with televised debates in election campaigns was beginning to demonstrate the risks for incumbents, both in Canada and elsewhere. Ronald Reagan's strong performance in the debate with incumbent president Jimmy Carter in 1980 and Reagan's uneven performance as president against Walter Mondale in the first debate of the 1984 U.S. election campaign showed clearly that debates held substantial risks for political leaders defending a record in office. While both Mulroney in 1988 and Reagan in 1984 recovered to win re-election, this lesson was also not lost on future participants. Debates remained the ideal medium for the challenger, and a risky one for incumbents. While they could no longer be avoided as they had been in the earlier years, the risks could be minimized by holding them earlier in the campaign, limiting the number of such encounters, and preparing extensively for the unexpected. Entering the 1990's, debates were firmly established as a necessary and routine part of a modern election campaign. But they were no longer the "wild card" that they had been in the earlier years. While their importance remained, the sense of drama associated with them had begun to decline.

Debates in the two most recent Canadian federal elections have seen changes in format and procedure prompted by the rise of two new federal political parties and by continuing concerns regarding the content of the debates. Prior to 1993, the debates had been largely the preserve of the media, with questions put to the candidates by a panel of prominent journalists, although free exchanges between the participants were increasingly permitted. The leaders debated each other in rotating pairs, adapting the format generally followed in the U.S. presidential debates to the three party world of Canadian federal politics. But by the time of the 1993 federal election, new political realities and concerns had to be accommodated. The adaptation of the 1993 and 1997 format to participation by five party leaders rather than three moved Canadian procedures further away from the U.S. presidential model and closer to those found in some of the European multi-party systems. There has also been a movement toward opening up the process to participation by "ordinary citizens", reducing somewhat the role played by journalists. To some extent, this represents a variation of the "town hall" format used in two of the 1992 U.S. presidential debates, in which questions were asked by members of the studio audience rather than by journalists. In the 1993 Canadian debates, an additional segment in this format was appended to the end of the two programs.[12] In 1997, it was incorporated directly into the main program by concluding each segment with questions to the candidates asked by members of the studio audience. Thus the two 1997 debates, conducted in English and French respectively, with questions asked by both journalists and voters, and involving the leaders of five political parties, would barely have been recognizable to a 1968 or 1979 viewer. While debates have evolved to a considerable degree in all of the countries that have incorporated them into election campaigns, the changes which have taken place over the six federal elections in which they have played a role in Canada have been both dramatic and potentially significant in reducing or limiting somewhat their potential effects on electoral outcomes.

How important are the debates?

At the moment they take place, debates sometimes seem to be the only noteworthy event of an election campaign. "The final result of an exhausting 47 day election campaign could be decided in 4 hours of televised debates" suggested a reporter for *The Globe and Mail* in an article written on the eve of the 1993 debates.[13] But the effects of these encounters on the attitudes of voters are often fleeting. Joe Clark went on to win the 1979 election in spite of evidence that his performance in the debates was inferior to that of both Trudeau and Broadbent.[14] John Turner, in spite of his stunning success in the 1988 debates, went on to lose that election by a decisive margin. The evidence for the effects of campaign debates on the election outcome is at best mixed.[15] Clearly, such events "matter" in terms of their impact on voters' perceptions of the leaders and the issues emphasized during the campaign.[16] Yet it is also seems that the effects of the debates on voters' opinions tend to diminish as the campaign continues on after the event. Thus, the modern defensive strategy of scheduling debates well in advance of election day partially negates their potential effects on the outcome. Still, for new leaders with relatively unformed images, small parties with low visibility, or candidates who find themselves well behind the front runner in a campaign, debates remain one of the best opportunities available to redress the electoral balance. For incumbents, front runners, or veteran political leaders, they are but one more campaign event to be subjected to the "damage control" strategies of modern campaign management.[17]

Table 1

Percentages of National Samples Who Saw All or Part of at Least One Debate, 1968–97

(%)	Total sample	Anglophones	Francophones
1997a	50	49	53
1993b	55	56	55
1988c	63	63	64
1984d	67	67	67
1979e	51	61	26
1968f	61	64	50

a. POLLARA Post-election survey. (N=1688).
b. 1993 Canadian National Election Study. Post-election wave. (N=3340).
c. 1988 CNES. Post-election wave. (N=2922).
d. 1984 CNES. Including the Womens' Debate. (N=3359). There were three debates in the 1984 election campaign, but only two in the three most recent elections and one in 1979 and 1968.
e. 1979 CNES. Random half-sample. (N=1296).
f. 1968 CNES. (N=2767).

Debates are important largely because of the massive audiences that they draw, and the degree of concentrated attention that they place on the party leaders at a critical juncture of the campaign. Generally, somewhat more than half of all eligible voters indicate some exposure to the debates in the course of a federal election campaign in Canada. The television audience for the 1997 debates appears to have been more or less in line with, albeit slightly lower than, expectations based on evidence from past cases (Table 1). About half of a sample of all eligible voters reported watching at least part of one of the debates which took place during the 1997 campaign. As has been found in all of the previous studies, viewers were somewhat more likely to have had higher levels of income and education, to reside in urban areas, and to be older. Residents of Quebec (55 per cent) or Ontario (54 per cent) were somewhat more likely to have tuned in than those in the Atlantic or Prairie provinces (41 per cent). Men (54 per cent) were slightly more likely than women (47 per cent) to report having watched them. As with most indicators of political participation however, the amount of variance which can be explained by these types of sociodemographic variables is rather modest. It is more accurate to say that the debates were seen by a broad cross-section of the public, and that the degree of exposure to them was in turn related to other factors that tend to explain attentiveness to election campaigns, such as general political interest or media exposure.

The possible direct effects of the debates are somewhat diluted by the fact that viewers are also more likely to watch other political programs over the course of the campaign.[18] Viewers of campaign debates tend to have multiple sources of information about the candidates and even the event itself. They are invariably more likely to be exposed to other political programs, political advertising, news programs, news specials, and commentary preceding or following the debates. The secondary use of "bites" from the program in political advertising or in newscasts assures wider exposure, and has the effect of making the debates and their content an even more dominant part of the total campaign coverage. In the process, however, it also confounds attempts to isolate the effects of debates from those of other short term forces associated with campaigns, or from the images which the public may already hold of the party leaders. Viewers of programs such as the debates are substantially more likely to vote, or to otherwise take an interest in the election.[19] The debates are therefore by definition reaching an audience that is more likely to "count" in affecting the election result.

While debates can sometimes act to merely reinforce existing attitudes toward parties and leaders, it is also true that they can cause viewers to form new and distinct impressions of the leaders. Attitudes towards John Turner, for example, became significantly more positive following the 1988 telecast, as the recognition of Turner's strong performance seemed to register almost immediately.[20] Given the very low ratings that many of the same respondents in a panel study gave Turner following the 1984 debates, there can be little doubt that this more positive perception was at least partly driven by his strong performance.[21] But the 1988 case also demonstrates that even strong effects emanating from a single event such as a televised debate are reversible. When a leader has succeeded in gaining an advantage over his/her opponents in a televised campaign debate, it is not an easy matter to sustain that advantage through an additional three or four weeks of a campaign. Both the campaign itself, and the attention of the public, soon move on to other matters.

Debates may have a particularly important influence on public opinion in elections where some of the party leaders are new and relatively unknown faces on the political scene. In the absence of preconceptions about particular leaders, voters may be more easily able to develop "first impressions" on the basis of information gathered from the debates which are not as quickly dispelled by subsequent campaign events. There is some evidence that Mulroney in 1984 may have benefitted from such an effect. As a relatively unknown political figure at the time, his performance in the debates significantly strengthened his image with many voters. The more negative characteristics of Mulroney's image that were later to become dominant were not as evident until well after he had become Prime Minister.[22] In the 1993 contest, Campbell, McLaughlin, Bouchard, and Manning were all new leaders, relatively unknown to the public at large. In 1997, Duceppe, McDonough, and Charest were in a similar position. For them, the debates represented a crucial opportunity to establish a positive image with the public rather than to attempt to dispel or reinforce an existing one. For leaders such as Chrétien or Manning, who had already established an image with much of the electorate through previous campaigns or through holding public office, such encounters take on more of a negative than a positive quality. There is less to gain and more to lose. But, as the example of Turner in 1988 also demonstrates, exceeding public expectations can be a winning strategy for even a well known political figure. A stronger than expected performance can cause voters to at least partially revise perceptions of a party leader which were previously negative. Conversely, a lackluster performance may not inflict serious harm on a well established political leader who has succeeded in lowering expectations during the period prior to the debates.

The 1997 debates

The 1997 format was similar to that of 1993, with the English and French programs scheduled for successive nights (May 12th & 13th, respectively). A total of two hours was allotted for each, with the speaking order for opening and closing statements determined by random draw. The English debate was moderated by Ann Medina of the CBC, who had also presided in 1993.

Ms. Medina indicated in her introductory statement that she intended to intervene as little as possible, thereby signalling to the participants that they would be relatively free to engage in impromptu give and take. With five participants, this announcement all but guaranteed that it would be an unruly and undisciplined affair. ("At times, the debate looked more like a school yard spat", concluded one analyst the following day.[23]) Questions to the participants were put by a panel of journalists consisting of Peter Kent (Global Television), Jason Moscovitz (CBC), and Craig Oliver (CTV). At the end of each 20 minute segment, 10 minutes of questions from members of the studio audience were allowed. The debate thus followed more or less the same format as that of 1993, but with the audience questions integrated into the program rather than reserved until the end.

Opening statements by the leaders covered more or less predictable ground. Alexa McDonough articulated an "old left" message which sought to distance her party from those on the right. Jean Chrétien stressed the fiscal achievements of his government, and the need for a "balanced" approach. Preston Manning contrasted Reform's "fresh start" program with the positions of the "old line parties", and declared himself firmly against any "special status" for Quebec. Gilles Duceppe portrayed the Bloc as "giving Quebec a voice", and interpreted sovereignty for Quebec as the beginning of a "new partnership". Jean Charest stressed his party's platform of tax cuts and a "health care guarantee", and sought to emphasize the need for alternatives to old approaches. During the ensuing give and take on issues such as jobs, health care, and deficit reduction, the discussion sometimes degenerated into a cacophony of all five leaders talking at once. Preston Manning often tried to seize control of the debate and position himself one on one against the prime minister, but the other leaders generally intervened to prevent this. Charest seemed more adept at moving smoothly in and out of the exchanges, and drew the only round of applause from the studio audience with his statement that he had made a commitment to his children to "pass on to them the country I received from my parents. I am determined to make that happen". Indeed, the "national unity" issue invariably generated the most heat, allowing the four federalist politicians to hold the patriotic high ground in simultaneously attacking Duceppe, but also allowing Manning to stress the one issue generally considered to most benefit his party, particularly in the West. Chrétien's approach was for the most part low key and "prime ministerial", but he drew one of the few laughs of the evening from the audience when he motioned toward the other leaders all talking at once and said "you see what I have to put up with in Parliament every day".

All of the leaders and their representatives professed to be satisfied with their performance. Chrétien had held his own, and had not made "the big mistake" that some feared could occur in this high pressure environment. Neither Manning nor McDonough had made any great breakthrough, and Duceppe had little to gain or lose in the English debate. Charest, articulate and often effective, clearly had the most to gain from his performance, but his opponents sometimes succeeded in tying him to his past record of service in the unpopular Mulroney government, thereby limiting the extent to which he could appear as a new and fresh face on the political scene. The media however was generally inclined to pronounce Charest the winner. "Tory leader wins low key debate" read the highline over the next day's analysis by Hugh Winsor of *The Globe and Mail*.[24] *The Toronto Star*'s analyst[25] was even more forthright in declaring Charest the winner, even though the *Star*'s own election panel saw no winner in the debates and seemed on balance to display a slight preference for Chrétien.[26]

The French debate on the following night was similarly structured. The debate was moderated by Claire Lamarche of TVA, who often intervened to prevent the leaders from interrupting too aggressively and to give McDonough and Manning an opportunity. Questions were posed to the candidates by Jean-François Lepine (Radio Canada) and Normand Rheaume (TVA). As in the English debate of the previous night, members of the studio audience were allowed to ask additional questions at the end of each twenty minute segment. Without facility in French, Manning was a presence, but not really a participant, during the evening. McDonough's fluency was sufficient to permit adequate opening and closing statements, but also fell short of real participation. From the beginning, the spotlight was on Duceppe, for whom this was the critical event. It was not only a crucial opportunity to communicate directly with "his" voters, but it had also become a vehicle by which to attempt to reverse the slide in the polls following the disastrous Bloc campaign of the first two weeks. For Charest also, the French debate was critical, both in attempting to position himself to appeal to Quebec voters and in sustaining the momentum flowing from his well regarded performance the previous night.

From the beginning, Duceppe was more forceful than in the previous encounter, seeking to position himself and the Bloc as a "voice" for Quebec and stressing that the result of a future referendum vote must be "respected". Chrétien's performance was for the most part similar to that of the previous night, low-key and prime ministerial. There were a number of one-on-one interchanges between Duceppe and Chrétien, establishing a pattern which served the interests of both candidates well. Charest also gave a strong performance, but was less easily able to intervene smoothly than had been the case the night before, in part because of tighter control by the moderator but also because the other candidates, sensing that Charest had gained by this tactic in the English debate, were less inclined to provide him the opportunity.

Two hours into the debate, just as M. Lepine was opening the section on national unity with a question to Chrétien on possible responses to a narrow YES victory in a future referendum ("Mr. Chrétien, if the YES won by a proportion of 50.6 per cent the next time, would you accept the popular verdict?"), the debate was abruptly suspended when the moderator fell ill. A few minutes later, after she had been taken to hospital, it was announced that the program would not be resumed. This unexpected turn of events quickly overwhelmed any perceptions which viewers may have formed up to that point. "A draw" declared most of the reports in the press the following day.[27] But in one interpretation that developed over the next two days, the suspension had "saved" Chrétien from having to take a position on one of the most difficult questions of the sovereignty debate, namely whether a "50 per cent plus one" referendum result should be allowed to stand without any further challenge.[28] It had also severely disrupted the debate strategies of both Duceppe and Charest, who had been counting on the French debate to improve their standing with Quebec voters. Partly for these reasons, the Liberals initially seemed reluctant to agree to a continuation. By the end of the week however, agreement had been reached for a resumption of the French debate on Sunday, May 18th. This proved anticlimactic. Moderated by Gilles Gougeon with questions again asked by Messrs. Lepine and Rheaume and members of the audience, the discussion covered mainly old constitutional ground (Meech Lake, Charlottetown, "distinct society"), and seemed to lack the intensity of the earlier encounter. Only forty-five minutes long, the sequel added little to the impressions that had been formed from the two earlier sessions.[29] Overall,

Charest had come out of the debates in an improved position, with greater visibility and a more positive public image. Perceptions of Chrétien appeared little changed, perhaps the best outcome that could be expected for an incumbent prime minister.

Table 2

Leader Seen as Having Given the Best Overall Performance in the Debates[a]

(%)

	Charest	Chrétien	Manning	McDonough	Duceppe	DK/None
Total sample[a]	55	13	11	8	1	12
Atlantic provinces	53	10	6	19	*	11
Quebec	70	10	*	5	4	11
Ontario	53	16	10	6	—	14
Prairies	43	14	22	11	*	10
British Columbia	43	13	21	10	—	13
Anglophones	52	14	13	9	*	12
Francophones	67	10	1	4	4	13
Men	54	14	11	8	2	12
Women	57	12	10	8	1	13

a. POLLARA post-election survey. Viewers only. (N=821).
* Less than 1%.

Polls generally confirmed the impression that Charest had gained the most from the debates, as does evidence provided by the POLLARA survey (Table 2).[30] More than half of the respondents who saw at least one of the debates pronounced Charest the "winner". Among francophone viewers, the number who believed that Charest gave the best performance rises to two-thirds. Some predictable regional patterns appear in the data on perceived debate performance (Table 2), as respondents in the Atlantic provinces were somewhat more likely to see McDonough as the winner of the debates than were those from other regions. Likewise, Westerners were more likely to be impressed by Manning's performance. This tendency failed to help Duceppe however, as only 4 per cent of Quebec respondents saw him as the debate winner. And, in spite of this

Table 3

Feelings About Parties and Political Leaders, Pre/Post Debates[a]

(%)	Charest	Chrétien	Manning	McDonough	Duceppe
Would make best prime minister:					
pre-debate wave	22	36	14	6	3
post debate "	27	35	11	4	3
Approve of job X is doing:					
pre-debate wave	49	52	36	27	12
post-debate "	52	51	29	26	11

Vote intention: (decided voters only)	PC	Liberal	Reform	NDP	Bloc
pre-debate wave	21	40	18	11	10
post-debate "	25	39	15	10	10

a. Strategic Counsel poll. (N=1200). *The Toronto Star*, May 17, 1997, pp. A1, A11

modest regionalization of voters' perceptions of the leaders, Charest was clearly seen as having given the best overall performance in the debates by respondents from every region. The percentage of respondents who believed that Chrétien had won the debates was less than half of what it had been in 1993.[31] Yet it was enough. Polls measuring vote intention barely moved following the debates, nor did more general approval ratings of the leaders or opinions about who would make the best prime minister (Table 3). Vote intention however did show some movement toward the Conservatives, particularly in Quebec. The Environics poll conducted immediately following the debates placed the Conservatives at 25 per cent of the popular vote nationally, a gain of about 5 points over polls published about a week earlier.[32] This poll and some others also showed a substantial gain for the Conservatives in Quebec, largely at the expense of the Bloc, placing them in the lead with 36 per cent of the Quebec vote compared to 27 per cent for the Bloc. The *Star*'s Strategic Counsel poll registered a four point gain for the Conservatives between the pre- and post-debate segments of its survey (Table 3).

Did the debates make a difference?

As has been demonstrated in many previous examples, both in Canada and elsewhere, "winning" a debate is not the same thing as winning an election. In part, as we have already noted, this is because the surge in public opinion which may follow a debate is often difficult to sustain through the remaining weeks of the campaign. Once the event is over, other factors soon begin to weigh more heavily in the outcome of the election. In addition, it should be emphasized that Canadian federal elections are not presidential contests. Attitudes toward the leaders are therefore only one variable among the many that may contribute to a particular result.[33] The electoral system itself also becomes a factor. Parties such as Reform or the Bloc that are able to concentrate their votes regionally are often better placed to win seats in a single member district parliamentary system than are those such as the NDP or Conservatives, whose popular vote tends to be spread more widely across the country. For the Conservatives in 1997, this represented a particularly serious risk, since the 25 per cent of the vote predicted by some polls had the potential to deliver relatively few seats.

Table 4

Voting Behaviour in the Election, by Exposure to the Debates[a]

	Watched the debates	Did not watch
Liberal	41%	41%
PC	19	15
Reform	18	21
NDP	12	10
Bloc	8	11
Other	3	2

a. POLLARA post-election survey. Voters only. (N=828).

Although the Liberals continued their slow decline in the public opinion polls over the remaining weeks of the campaign, there was little immediate change following the debates. The "bounce" which the

Conservatives appeared to enjoy in polls taken immediately afterwards gradually dissipated, and final polls published a few days before the election placed them close to where they had been before the debates.[34] The Conservatives' 19 per cent share of the popular vote registered on election day would seem to suggest that few of the gains made by Charest in the debates translated into votes three weeks later. This impression is confirmed by data from the POLLARA survey, which shows little variation between viewers and non-viewers of the debates in voting choice (Table 4). The small patterns which are found however are consistent with expectations based on the debates, with the PCs doing slightly better among viewers than among non-viewers, and the BQ faring more poorly among those who watched the debates.[35] Therefore, as was the case in 1993, one might conclude that the debates had some effect on the images of the leaders, but little on voting behaviour.[36] For the Liberals, the debates had represented one of the most serious potential obstacles to be overcome during the course of the campaign. Chrétien's solid, if low key, performance in the debates can be seen as the successful implementation of a strategy to minimize any possible negative effects. And, Charest's inability to translate his strong performance into votes for his party again demonstrates that success in the debates does not necessarily bring with it comparable success at the polls.

Conclusion

The 1997 case is illustrative of a number of the new realities regarding the role of televised leaders debates in federal elections in Canada. These are now well known and somewhat predictable campaign events. Voters expect them, and use them to form opinions about the leaders, particularly those who are new to the political scene and whose public images are not fully developed. For the parties and leaders, they form a crucial part of the overall campaign strategy. But now occurring closer to the beginning of the campaign than to the end, they are no longer the main event that they may have been in an earlier era. With five parties and leaders participating, and with new innovations in format and execution, they provide fewer opportunities for dramatic one-on-one exchanges between the leaders. As the debates have become an institutionalized feature of federal election campaigns, the risks which may have previously been associated with these high profile events have increasingly been tamed. Parties and leaders plan their strategies for the debates well in advance of the campaign and prepare for them intensively. As a result, there are fewer surprises to be expected in such encounters. While it is now difficult to imagine a Canadian federal election without televised debates in both French and English between the leaders, it is equally difficult to envision these affairs as the high stakes, high risk events that they may have once been. The days of the "knockout punch", if indeed they ever really existed, are clearly over.

Notes

[1] Edison Stewart, "Millions Expected to Watch Leaders' Debates", *The Toronto Star*, May 12, 1997, p. A1

[2] Richard Johnston, et al. *Letting the People Decide* (Montréal, McGill-Queen's Press, 1992),
pp. 168-96.

[3] See Lawrence LeDuc, "The Leaders' Debates: Critical Event or Non-Event?", in Allan Frizzell et al., *The Canadian General Election of 1993* (Carleton University Press, 1994), pp. 127-141.

[4] See Holli Semetko, "The Media" in Lawrence LeDuc, et al. *Comparing Democracies: Elections and Voting in Global Perspective* (Beverly Hills CA, Sage, 1996), pp. 276-78. See also Robert Bernier and Denis Monière, "The Organization of Televised Leaders Debates in the United States, Europe, Canada and Australia", in Frederick J. Fletcher, *Media and Voters in Canadian Election Campaigns*, Research Studies of the Royal Commission on Electoral Reform and Party Financing, vol.18 (Toronto, Dundurn Press, 1991), pp. 157-211.

[5] On the 1960 Kennedy-Nixon debates, see Sidney Kraus, *The Great Debates* (Bloomington IN, University of Indiana Press, 1962). On U.S. presidential campaign debates more generally, see Austin Ranney (ed.), *The Past and Future of Presidential Campaign Debates* (Washington DC, American Enterprise Institute, 1980), and Kathleen Jamieson & David Birdsell, *Presidential Debates* (NY, Oxford University Press, 1988).

[6] On the 1976 debates, see Sidney Kraus, *The Great Debates: Carter vs. Ford, 1976* (Bloomington IN, University of Indiana Press, 1979). See also Ranney, *passim.*

[7] On the 1979 debate, see Lawrence LeDuc and Richard Price, "Great Debates: the Televised Leadership Debates of 1979", *Canadian Journal of Political Science*, 18 (1985), pp 135-53. On the evolution of debates more generally in Canada, see Cathy Widdis Barr, "The Importance and Potential of Televised Leaders' Debates", in Frederick J. Fletcher, *Media, Elections and Democracy*, Research Studies of the Royal Commission on Electoral Reform and Party Financing, vol.18 (Toronto, Dundurn Press, 1991), pp. 107-56.

[8] On the 1984 debates, see David J. Lanoue, "Debates that Mattered:

Voters' Reactions to the 1984 Canadian Leadership Debates", *Canadian Journal of Political Science*, 24 (1991), pp. 51– 65. See also Lawrence LeDuc, "Party Strategies and the Use of Televised Campaign Debates", *European Journal of Political Research*, 18 (1990), pp. 121–41.

[9] See Harold Clarke, et al. *Absent Mandate: Interpreting Change in Canadian Elections*, 2nd edition (Toronto, Gage, 1991), pp. 101–104. See also Johnston, et al, *Letting the People Decide*, pp. 185-91.

[10] The Gallup poll showed a surge of 11 points for the Liberals, and polls by other organizations found similar, albeit smaller, shifts in opinion following the 1988 debates. *The Gallup Report*, November 7, 1988. See also Harold Clarke, et al, *Absent Mandate: Canadian Electoral Politics in an Era of Restructuring* (3rd edition), pp. 80-83, and Johnston, et al, *Letting the People Decide*, pp. 169-74.

[11] See, for example, the discussion by Bernier & Monière of debates in Germany, the Netherlands, and the Scandinavian countries. "The Organization of Televised Leaders Debates...", pp. 171–78.

[12] One half hour at the end of the French debate, and 45 minutes in the English debate.

[13] Ron Howard, "Leaders Hoping Effort Won't Go Down the Tube". *The Globe and Mail*, October 2, 1993, p. A1

[14] LeDuc & Price, "Great Debates...", pp. 144-46.

[15] See LeDuc, "Party Strategies...".

[16] Johnston et al, *Letting the People Decide*, pp. 194-96.

[17] For an analysis of debates from the perspective of a practitioner, see Myles Martel, *Political Campaign Debates: Images, Strategies, Tactics* (Ny, Longmans, 1983). For some examples of strategies followed by the party leaders in preparation for the 1988 debates, see Graham Fraser, *Playing for Keeps* (Toronto, McClelland & Stewart, 1989), pp. 264-66.

[18] LeDuc, "Party Strategies...", pp. 130-31. See also Johnston et al, *Letting the People Decide*, pp. 184-90.

[19] LeDuc, "Party Strategies...", p. 131.

[20] Johnston et al, *Letting the People Decide*, pp. 180-82. See also Fraser, *Playing for Keeps*, p. 295.

[21] Clarke et al, *Absent Mandate* (2nd edition), pp. 102-04.

[22] *Absent Mandate* (2nd edition), pp. 97-99. See also *Letting the People Decide*, pp. 168-80.

[23] James Travers and David Vienneau, "National Unity Sets Off Sparks in Leaders' Debate", *The Toronto Star*, May 13, 1997, pp. A1, A11

[24] Hugh Winsor, "Charest Scores Best Line", *The Globe and Mail*, May 13, 1997, p. A1

[25] Antonia Zerbisias, "Charest's Strong Form Makes Him TV Debate Winner," *The Toronto Star*, May 13, 1997, p. A11

[26] Particia Orwen, "Debate Fails to Sway *Star* Election Panel", *The Toronto Star*, May 13, 1997, p. A1

[27] See, for example, Rosemary Speirs, "Debate Ends in Disappointing Draw", *The Toronto Star*, May 14, 1997, p. A1

[28] Tim Harper & David Vienneau, "Separation Vote Query Sidestepped," *The Toronto Star*, May 15, 1997, p. A1. See also Murray Campbell, "Chrétien Seems Reluctant to Resume Debate", *The Globe and Mail*, May 15, 1997, p. A4

[29] Rosemary Speirs, "Leaders Perform Well With Little New to Say", *The Toronto Star*, May 19, 1997, p. A1

[30] See Scott Feschuk, "Charest Perceived as Debate Winner", *The Globe and Mail*, May 17, 1997, p. A10; and James Travers, "Liberals Hold Massive Lead, New Poll Says", *The Toronto Star*, May 17, 1987, p. A1, A11, The poll for *The Globe and Mail* was conducted by Environics between May 13th and May 15th., and the *Star* poll by Strategic Counsel between May 10th and May 14th. The latter included a split sample, with half of the respondents interviewed before the debates and the other half afterward. The POLLARA survey is more fully described in Chapter 12 of this volume.

[31] In a similar survey in 1993, 36 per cent of the respondents stated that Chrétien had given the best performance. See LeDuc, "The Leaders Debates...", p. 136

[32] Hugh Winsor & Edward Greenspon, "Tories Gaining Strength in Quebec", *The Globe and Mail*, May 17, 1997, pp. A1, A10

[33] See *Absent Mandate* (3rd edition), pp. 101–05.

[34] A poll by Ekos Research published in *The Globe and Mail* on May 27th had the Conservatives at 21 per cent, while one by Strategic Counsel sponsored by *The Toronto Star* placed them at 19 per cent. Edward Greenspon, "Poll Predicts Slim Majority for Chrétien", *The Globe and Mail*, May 27, 1997, pp. A1, A9; and James Travers, "Liberals Still Hold Big Lead, Poll Shows," *The Toronto Star*, May 29, 1997, pp. A1, A16

[35] Cramer's V=.09. The overall relationship however between watching the debates and voting behaviour in the election shown in Table 4 is not statistically significant.

[36] LeDuc, "The Leaders Debates...", pp. 136-38.

Twelve
The Voters Decide
by Jon H. Pammett

It was supposed to be a sure thing, a reelection of the only party with a defensible claim to be able to form a national government. It ended as a cliffhanger, with the Liberals finally managing to secure a bare majority. However, only the splintered nature of support for parties other than the Liberals, coupled with an electoral system which allowed a majority of seats in Parliament to be won with less than 40 per cent of the vote, permitted this result. The Canadian General Election of 1997 was an election in which every major party could claim a victory of sorts, but was also an election in which every party had reason to be disappointed in the results.

The 1997 election victory for the Liberal Party was fashioned predominantly by their ability to hold on to a substantial enough number of their 1993 voters to hold off the challengers. While the party benefitted from converting some voters who had previously supported other parties, those switching to the Liberals were more than offset by the larger group of former Liberals who moved away from the party in 1997. Similarly, although there were groups of new voters, and transient "sometimes" voters who chose the Liberals in 1997, these groups were not unusually high relative to other parties. So the 1997 Liberal victory was a "holding operation", one that barely succeeded.

The consolidation of regional support bases in this election was the result, if not necessarily the intention, of the campaigns of all the parties. Even the victorious Liberals are in that situation largely because "their region", Ontario or, to be charitable, Central Canada, has so many seats in Parliament. The four opposition parties have carved up the rest of the country into regional strongholds, and owe their positions to the success of their appeals to regional interests (see Chapter Ten of this volume.) Issues championed by the parties in the 1997 election were often designed to appeal to specific parts of the country. Even advertising was different in different places.

In some ways the Canadian public went along with the emphasis on regionalization. Many voters made their choices in support of parties which made such appeals, either overt (as in Quebec) or covert (as in the West.) But there are disturbing signs in this election that all is not well with Canadian democracy. Most obviously, a lower percentage of eligible voters turned out to the polls at this federal election than at any time since the Second World War, continuing a downward trend begun in 1993. Almost a third of the public did not feel there was an important issue in the campaign, despite all the party publications, advertising and strategizing that have been detailed in the chapters of this book, and despite the hundreds of hours of campaign coverage in the media of print, radio, television, and the internet. Only half of Canadians turned on the leader's debates, and those who did may not have been very excited at what they saw. Indeed, many people felt the election should not have been called in the first place, as a majority government had not even served four years since they were previously elected. Public disaffection with electoral politics was palpable during the 1997 election campaign.

The flow of the vote

This chapter examines the reasons for the 1997 election outcome. It does so with data from a national survey of Canadians conducted in the days immediately following the election by POLLARA Research.[1] Tables 1, 2 and 3 provide the basic information for an examination of the support given to the parties in the 1997 election. Table 1 provides an outline, drawn from questions in the survey, of the patterns of behaviour of Canadian voters (and non-voters) in this election and the preceding one of 1993. The small numbers in the cells of that table are a result of the fact that the entire table is percentaged to add to 100 per cent, rather than columns or rows as we are more accustomed to seeing. The partitioning of the entire 1997 electorate according to their behaviour at two time points gives us an overall indication of the extent of stability and change over the three and a half year period between the two federal elections.

Table 1

Canadian Electoral Behaviour, 1993–1997

1997

1993	LIB	PC	NDP	REF	BQ	OTH	Did Not Vote
LIB	20.9	3.7	2.2	2.5	.4	.4	2.9
PC	1.5	4.9	.4	1.9	.1	—	.8
NDP	.9	.3	4.0	.6	—	.1	.9
REF	.7	.2	.2	7.0	—	.2	.5
BQ	.1	.4	.1	.1	4.5	—	.6
OTH	.5	.3	.2	.2	.1	.4	1.1
Did Not Vote	5.9	2.5	1.3	2.3	1.6	.5	8.8
Not Eligible	2.4	1.6	.6	1.0	1.1	.3	3.1
							100%

Note: The entire table adds to 100%
Source: POLLARA Perspectives Canada survey. N=997

Summary and Comparison to 1993

	1993	1997
Voted for same party as previous election (1993–1988; 1997–1993)	27%	42%
Switched vote from previous election	35	18
Voted, but did not vote or behaviour not known in previous election*	13	14
Did not vote, but voted in previous election	8	7
Did not vote either time	9	9
Newly eligible (not all voting)	8	10

*Includes those not voting in previous election, as well as those who did not know whether they voted or who they had voted for.

The largest concentration of people in Table 1 appears in the top left-hand corner, and represents the proportion of the electorate who reported voting Liberal in both 1993 and 1997. While this number may not appear particularly large on first glance, it dwarfs the other figures on the diagonal of Table 1, which represent the groups of people who voted consistently for the other Canadian political parties at these two times. The closest contender to that 20.9 per cent of the total electorate which voted Liberal in 1993 and 1997 was the 7 per cent which voted for the Reform Party in these two elections. The other three parties trail behind in terms of the share of the electorate choosing to continue to support them a second time. Of course, we must remember that these are figures for Canada as a whole; if we were to partition the vote within any one province or region, these figures would look different because of the different strengths of the parties in the regions. In Quebec, for example, the share of the vote retained by the Bloc Québécois would appear much higher.[2]

Table 2
Where the Vote Went in 1997

1993 Behaviour

1997	LIB	PC	NDP	REF	BQ	OTH	Did Not Vote	Not Yet Eligible
LIB	63%	15%	13%	8%	2%	19%	26%	24%
PC	11	51	4	2	7	10	11	16
NDP	7	5	59	9	2	7	6	6
REF	8	20	9	80	2	8	10	10
BQ	1	1	—	—	78	3	7	11
OTH	1	—	2	2	—	15	2	3
Did Not Vote	9	8	13	6	10	38	38	31

Source: POLLARA Perspectives Canada Survey

Retention of its support from the previous election was extremely important to the Liberal victory in 1997. Another perspective on this finding may be obtained from Table 2, which shows what the 1993 voters did in 1997. From this table, we can see that almost two-thirds (63 per cent) of those who voted Liberal in 1993 did so again in 1997. This retention rate is higher than either of the other two "old line parties", as the NDP retained 59 per cent of its 1993 voters and the Conservatives only 51 per cent. However, all three of these parties pale beside the ability of Reform and the Bloc Québécois to keep their vote intact. In the case of both of these parties which have more specific regional, ideological or nationalistic appeals, four-fifths of their previous voters chose to support the party a second time.

Consolidation of past support may provide the core of every party's cadre of voters, but conversion of those who had previously supported others is the goal of all parties during the campaign. The flows of *vote switching* between the 1993 and 1997 elections are all visible in Table 1. Any cell of that table not on the diagonal represents a group of voters who did something different in the two elections. Thus, looking once again at the top left-hand corner of the table, we note that 1.5 per cent of the total electorate cast a 1993 vote for the Progressive Conservatives, but a 1997 Liberal vote. This once again appears to be a small number, but it represents over a quarter of a million people! Thus, we can say that even if the Liberal campaign did not appear to be a great success to most observers, it obviously convinced an appreciable number of voters to switch to them.

The off-setting flows of vote-switching between the Liberals and other parties were not favourable to the Liberals, however. We noted above that 1.5 per cent of the total electorate changed to that party after voting for the PCs in 1993. If we look for the opposite pattern, it is easy to see that there were over twice as many people (3.7 per cent) who switched to the PCs after a 1993 Liberal vote. This same pattern of differential vote-loss is apparent when we compare those who switched to the Liberals from any of the other parties with those who went the other way. Over three times as many people switched to Reform from the Liberals as did the reverse. Similarly, the switching between previous supporters of the Liberals and the Bloc Québécois, though it involved relatively small numbers of people when seen in the overall national picture, was heavily in favour of the latter party.

Table 3
Sources of 1997 Party Support

1997 1993	LIBERAL	PC	NDP	REFORM	BQ
LIBERAL	64%	27%	24%	16%	5%
PC	4	35	5	12	1
NDP	3	2	44	4	0
REFORM	2	2	2	45	0
BQ	0	3	1	0	58
OTHER	2	2	2	1	1
DID NOT VOTE	18	18	15	15	20
NOT ELIGIBLE	7	11	7	7	14

Source: POLLARA Perspectives Canada survey.

Table 3 gives us a way of determining how important attracting converts was to the support base of each of the major parties in 1997. For the Liberals and the Bloc Québécois, conversion was of secondary importance, though in the case of the former party what little there was served to offset some of the heavy losses the party suffered. For the Progressive Conservatives and the New Democratic Party, on the other hand, switchers from the Liberals alone made up around one quarter of the total number of votes the parties received! For Reform, the picture looks slightly different. The Reform Party also gained substantially from switches away from a previous Liberal vote (16 per cent of their vote total fell into this category.) To this group of people, however, was added a further 12 per cent of their 1997 voters who had supported the Progressive Conservatives in 1993. Clearly, the Reform Party campaign had an effect on previous supporters of both the "old line parties." We have already seen (Table 2) that relatively few previous supporters of the Reform Party deserted them in this second general election held since their formation.

The Reform Party only operates in federal politics, and therefore cannot depend on the symbolic and organizational support of provincial party equivalents as can the other parties under normal circumstances. It is interesting, however, to look at the voting behaviour of supporters of those provincial parties in several of the provinces where Reform did well federally. In British Columbia, for example, over one-third of provincial Liberals voted Reform in the 1997 election, virtually the same percentage as those voting Liberal. In contrast, only 8 per cent of provincial NDPers in BC voted Reform in the federal election. In the three Prairie provinces, it was the provincial Conservatives who provided Reform votes; 45 per cent of those intending to vote P.C. in the next provincial election chose to cast their ballots for Reform federally.

Finally, the situation in Ontario merits examination of the pattern of provincial and federal party choice. In a controversial decision, the provincial Conservative government in Ontario chose not to endorse the federal Conservative Party in the election campaign. (see chapter Four of this volume). The Harris government was apparently wary of the retaliation by Reformers that might follow a decision to advise its supporters not to support Reform in the federal election, and Harris himself was opposed to Jean Charest's support for "distinct society" status for Quebec. In any case, the survey data show that those intending to vote PC in the next provincial election (fewer people, incidentally, than said they were going to vote Liberal) split their federal votes almost evenly between three parties. Provincial Conservatives in Ontario voted: 30 per cent for the Liberals; 29 per cent for the Conservatives; 1 per cent for the NDP; 25 per cent for Reform; with the rest not voting. In contrast, of provincial Liberals in Ontario, only 1 per cent voted Reform. Whether a Harris endorsement of the federal Tories would have meant more votes and seats for them is of course speculation. As in 1993, some seats in the province were won by the Liberals in situations where Reform and the PCs split the vote in opposition to them. Since only a quarter of provincial Conservatives voted for the Reform Party, and since some of these people undoubtedly would have done so in any case, a Harris endorsement might not have been very effective in this direction.

The Reform Party, on the admittedly limited evidence of two elections, has a credible claim to be building on an established base of support. While this feat may seem unremarkable, it has not been the norm for other major Canadian parties, despite occasional rhetoric to the contrary. The Liberals, Conservatives, and to an even greater extent, the NDP, have not been able to count on a consistent committed base of voters from one election to the next. Rather, they have had to assemble electoral coalitions during each campaign on the basis of short-term party images, issues, and leader identifications. The partisan ties of a majority of Canadian voters have been remarkably *flexible*, changing readily from one occasion to the next on the basis of changing political times and fortunes.[3] If Reform can "break the mould" in this regard by engendering widespread partisan loyalties which can deliver votes consistently election after election, their chances of survival are greatly enhanced. There are indications from Table 2 that Reform supporters are unusually loyal. However, we must enter a cautionary note about these conclusions since the Reform vote overall did not increase in 1997, and the party's strength is now even more regionally concentrated in the West than it was four years previously.

Table 1 also shows that the Liberal Party was hurt by the decisions of a group of their 1993 supporters not to vote at all in 1997. The number in the top right-hand corner of the table documents that 2.9 per cent of the electorate falls into this category. Of course, all parties suffer from the decisions of "transient voters" not to go to the polls a second time in a row, as Table 2 shows. However, the group of these "sometime voters" abandoning the Liberals was substantially larger in terms of sheer numbers than that for any other party.

One of the secrets of the Liberal Party's success in winning Canadian federal elections has been its ability to attract the votes of young people coming into the electorate and casting a ballot for the first time.[4] Table 1 shows that, in absolute numbers, the Liberals were again the beneficiaries of an influx of new voters to a greater extent than any of the other parties. However, relative to other sources of support, Table 3 shows that the cadre of new supporters who decided to vote Conservative was more important to that party's total vote than was the Liberal group of newcomers. The Bloc Québécois also benefitted substantially from the first-time ballots of young Quebeckers. Because the Bloc Québécois loses relatively few voters to other parties through conversion (Table 2), this replacement effect is important. However, it must be noted that overall the Bloc Québécois vote totals in 1997 were lower than they were in 1993, suggesting that sympathizers with that party are not so dedicated as to necessarily turn out to vote every time, particularly in federal elections.

Factors in the vote decision

The 1997 election is the seventh in which we have data from a specific sequence of questions asked of national samples of Canadians to determine the relative importance of factors in the vote decision. The first question asks whether the respondent found the party leaders, the local candidates or the parties taken as a whole to be the most important factor in their own vote decision. The second question is a follow-up, asking whether this choice was motivated by issues, or by the leader or candidate's "personal qualities" or, in the case of parties, by their "general approach to government." The purpose of this way of questioning people about their motives is to avoid giving an initial choice involving issues, which might be a more socially-approved response, but to see if there was an issue basis behind other factors important to the vote decision.

Table 4
Most Important Factors in Voting, 1974-1997
(Percent citing issue basis in parentheses)

ELECTION	PARTY LEADERS	LOCAL CANDIDATES	PARTY AS A WHOLE
1997	20% (71)	22 (58)	58 (57)
1993	22% (62)	21 (52)	57 (54)
1988	20% (71)	27 (57)	53 (57)
1984	30% (56)	21 (46)	49 (37)
1980	36% (53)	20 (40)	44 (43)
1979	37% (54)	23 (43)	40 (45)
1974	33% (58)	27 (48)	40 (43)

Sources: 1974–84 Canadian National Election Studies. 1988 reinterview of 1984 CNES. 1993 Insight Canada Research post-election survey. 1997 POLLARA Perspectives Canada survey.

Table 4 shows the factors which have been cited as most important to the vote decisions in all Canadian elections since 1974. The 1997 results are very similar to those of the previous two elections. Party, taken as a whole, is by far the most important factor cited in the survey, with 58 per cent of voters picking this choice. Well behind are those primarily motivated by local candidates (22 per cent) and party leaders (20 per cent). This dominance of "party" as a reason for vote choice has slowly established itself over the past twenty years. Looking back to our first survey in 1974, 40 per cent of Canadian voters said they decided on this basis. Once the Conservative resurgence under Brian Mulroney's leadership of that party got underway in the early 1980s, party substantially increased in importance, to 49 per cent in 1984 and to 53 per cent in 1988.

It is instructive that Mulroney himself was not a more important factor in motivating vote choice. Indeed, the heyday of "party leader" in guiding the vote came with the final elections involving Pierre Trudeau, those of

1979 and 1980. It was the appeal of Trudeau himself which limited the extent of the Liberal defeat in 1979 and which propelled the party back to victory in 1980.[5] From that point on, leaders have declined in importance in actually motivating voters' choices, even while they have structured the electoral debate and dominated the media coverage. In 1997, only a fifth of the voting public made their decision primarily on the basis of the party leaders. Furthermore, as Table 4 shows, less than one-third of the "leader motivated vote" was decided on the basis of the personal characteristics of the leaders. When asked whether issue or personal qualities lay behind their choice of leader as the most important factor for them, 71 per cent of respondents said that issues were the key. Despite the fact that popular commentary is fond of debating the effects of the leaders' appearance, dress, hairstyles or speaking styles on the public, the bulk of the population does not rate these things highly when it comes to making up their minds.

A similar, if somewhat less dominant, role is played by issues in structuring the public's choices motivated by local candidates or parties taken as a whole. Table 4 shows that 57 per cent of those citing party as the reason for their vote decision said there was an issue basis for this, rather than the party's general approach to government. In fact, the level of issue-voting in the 1997 election, by this measure, resembles the election of 1988 more closely than that of 1993. The 1988 election, it will be remembered, was dominated by the issue of the Free Trade Agreement between Canada and the United States; the amount of attention paid to this issue was so great that the event has been considered a major contender for the title of most issue-dominated election of the century. Does 1997 really measure up to this?

In 1988, only 5 per cent of the electorate said there were no important election issues, and there was a virtual consensus among the rest that the election was about free trade. Table 5 shows that only a scattering of 1988 respondents picked issues other than free trade. The political parties were either committed to the FTA (the Progressive Conservatives) or pledged to not enact it if elected (the Liberals and NDP.) The atmosphere during the 1988 election was highly charged, political interest was at a peak, and 75 per cent of eligible Canadians turned out to vote. The 1993 election also appears to have focused the attention of the Canadian public to a relatively high degree. Even though turnout declined to 70 per cent, only 10 per cent of the electorate found no important election issues, and attention centred on two of them, unemployment/job creation and reducing the deficit (Table 5).

The picture for 1997 appears rather different. Although the high levels of unemployment and the need for job creation was still the

Table 5
Most Important Election Issues, 1988–1997

ISSUE	1988	1993	1997
Unemployment, jobs	1%	44%	24%
Economy	1	8	4
Deficit, debt	2	18	10
Taxes	1	–	3
Free Trade	82	1	–
National unity, Québec, separation	1	4	13
Resources, environment	2	–	1
Social issues	2	4	10
Government, trust, accountability, etc.	2	7	3
Other	3	4	3
None, don't know	5	10	29

Sources: (1988) Carleton University reinterview of 1984 Canadian National Election Study respondents (1993) Insight Canada Research Post election survey. 1997 POLLARA Perspectives Canada survey. N=1200 in all three studies

number-one issue concern of the voters, it was not in the dominant position it had been four years before. Only about a quarter of the electorate chose it as most important issue, as opposed to the 44 per cent who did so in 1993. Similarly, concern with deficit and debt reduction was drastically reduced during the 1997 campaign, mirroring the actual reduction in the deficit produced by a succession of actions by the Liberal Finance Minister during the party's tenure in office. Concern for social issues increased in 1997, largely as a result of the cutbacks in funding of these programs in the pursuit of deficit reduction. As this illustrates, discussion of social issues in Canadian elections has become essentially reactive, embodying protests against reductions in spending on social services, rather than proactive, involving proposals for new social programs. Even the NDP, which has not entirely abandoned its championship of a national daycare program, has not been able to structure a national debate about this proposal in recent years.

Issues involving Quebec were more prominent in the 1997 election campaign than in any recent Canadian election. We would need to think back to the campaigns of 1979 and 1980, occurring as they did immediately before the first referendum on sovereignty-association, to find a precedent for as much discussion of Quebec during a federal election. The occasion this time was the decision of the Reform Party to "play the Quebec card" by overtly raising the scenario of Quebec independence and proposing various "hard line" arguments designed mainly to attract support for itself in the West, where such positions play well by invoking resentment of "special treatment" for Quebec. They hoped this issue would also work for them in Ontario.

Issue discussion in the 1997 election campaign was somewhat reminiscent, therefore, of the elections of 1979 and 1980 in that there was no one single issue of dominant concern but rather a set of issues which either occupied the entire stage for short periods of time or else allowed several parties to take the stage at the same time to promote their own issues while ignoring the others who happened to be talking about something else. Thus, the Liberals could insist that deficit reduction and the health of the economy were paramount, at the same time as Reform was proposing to play hardball with Quebec, the NDP was arguing for the maintenance of social programs and the stimulation of regional economic growth, and the Conservatives were promoting the benefits of a tax cut and national unity. At times, the parties engaged each other in a dialogue on these issues, as when they reacted to the Reform statements on Quebec by denunciations of that party. Mainly, however, the parties were content to promote their own issues.

The lack of public interest in the 1997 election campaign is not only illustrated by the drop in the voting turnout rate, which declined to 67 per cent of eligible voters. It can be seen in Table 5 in the category of people who, when asked about the most important issue to them in the election said they did not know or that there was none. It is not unprecedented for one-third of the electorate to declare that there was no important issue, as happened in 1997. This was also the case in elections during the 1970s. As late as the 1984 federal election, one quarter of the respondents to the National Election Study said there was no important issue.[6] And it may be that political interest will "bounce back" in future. But the combination of the increase in nonvoting with the lack of issue identification make the situation appear potentially different, and more worrisome for the health of Canadian democracy.

But perhaps there is a hopeful sign. We concluded our discussion of Table

4 with the observation that there was an unusually high number of people who claimed to have an issue basis for their choice of leader, candidate or party as the most important factor in their voting decision. Our subsequent examination of the issues in the campaign does not sustain the impression this table gives, that 1997 was a campaign where issues overwhelmed the other factors. However, the Table 4 results can perhaps be interpreted as "wishful thinking" on the part of many voters. The issues in the 1997 campaign may not have been as central as in some previous campaigns, but voters were still looking for them. They were not willing to judge the leaders and candidates solely on the basis of their personalities, and the parties on generalities. Canadian voters had become used to substance on which to base their judgements, conditioned by two campaigns (1988 and 1993) in which issues were paramount. They were not now easily deterred from their habit of evaluating the parties and politicians on the basis of issues. If the public continues to look for issues of substance in future, perhaps ambitious political parties will do better on the policy front.

Table 6
Party Closest on Most Important Issue, 1993, 1997

	LIB	PC	NDP	REF	BLOC	OTH	NONE
Unemployment/jobs							
1997	33%	14	22	11	1	1	18
1993	61%	7	4	7	5	–	16
Taxes							
1997	22%	27	6	30	–	1	14
1993	46%	18	18	9	–	–	9
The deficit/debt							
1997	62%	8	2	19	3	1	6
1993	24%	21	4	29	4	1	17
Quebec issues							
1997	27%	19	7	29	8	–	11
1993	41%	6	2	16	16	4	14
Social issues							
1997	31%	10	25	17	–	1	17
1993	40%	8	21	9	4	4	15
All issues							
1997	35%	14	14	20	2	2	14
1993	48%	9	4	13	6	2	18

Source: (1993) Insight Canada Research post-election survey. (1997) POLLARA Perspectives Canada survey

When we turn to the question of which parties may have benefitted from the issues identified as important in the election, Table 6 shows several significant differences in 1997 from the pattern in 1993. The contents of Table 6 are the results of the follow-up question "Which party is closest to you on this issue?" which was asked once the respondent had cited an election issue which was important. Almost all categories of issues were less favourable to the Liberal Party in 1997 than they had been in 1993. The summary line "all issues" at the bottom of the table shows that little more than one-third of the respondents in 1997 picked the Liberals as closest to them on the most important issue, down from close to half in 1993. The decline in Liberal support is most noticeable on the unemployment issue, since this was the leading issue in the election, and had been particularly important to the Liberals in fashioning their 1993 victory. In that election, the party had proposed a short-term job creation plan, which caught the public's attention and helped to associate the issue with the Liberals. No such plan was forthcoming in the 1997 campaign— the Liberals relied on general statements about the health of the economy, and the growth and investment benefits of the reduced deficit, to try to maintain their lead on this issue. (see Chapter Three of this volume). Table 6 shows that much of their dominance from 1993 was lost, but that it was the NDP, not the Conservatives and the Reform Party, which picked up the slack. The NDP was able to use the unemployment issue against the Liberals mainly in the Atlantic region, however, and was limited in its ability to gain from it elsewhere.

The fact that the PCs and Reform were not very credible on the unemployment issue meant that the Liberals were less threatened by it in Ontario and the West than they might have been. The Conservatives were haunted by the Mulroney legacy of promising "jobs, jobs, jobs" in 1984 and then not doing very much to create them. Reform's main agenda had been to cut down on the activities of government, and they had ridiculed the Liberals' short term job creation plan in 1993. They were therefore not in a position to pose as the champions of job creation either, except by cheering on the private sector. However, the Liberals were limited in their ability to forge a link in the public's mind between themselves and job creation, even if they had proposed more specific plans. The fact was that they had been in government for almost four years, and the unemployment rate, while it had decreased during their time in office, was still close to 10 per cent nationally and higher in the Eastern half of the country.[7]

Faced with this situation, the Liberals shifted their issue emphasis. In a fascinating turnabout from 1993, the Liberals seized the issue of deficit reduction, on which they had been particularly weak in 1993, and made it theirs in 1997. Cutting the deficit in order to reduce the national debt had been an electoral battleground in 1993 between the Conservatives, who were campaigning as a government that had taken a gradualist approach to budget cutting, and the Reform Party, who advocated much more drastic methods of getting spending down. In 1997, both the Conservatives and Reform lost considerable credibility on the deficit reduction issue, since both parties were proposing tax cuts, a move which the Liberals argued would negate savings which accrued from budgetary belt-tightening. The proposed tax cuts were cited as most important issue by 3 per cent of Canadians (Table 5), and those to whom this was important were indeed more likely to choose Reform and the PCs (Table 6), but this issue was not salient enough to swing the large numbers of votes that these two parties had hoped for. The electorate by-and-large accepted its budget reduction "medicine", and even gave the Liberals credit for making them take it; this was true even though the Liberals had maintained during the 1993 campaign that a large helping of the medicine was not necessary and might even kill the patient!

Finally, Table 6 shows us the pattern on the most controversial of the 1997 issues, those dealing with Quebec. In reality, there were a number of forms in which this subject was discussed during the campaign. First, and most generally, there was the desire for "national unity", a traditional rallying-cry of federalists, who, in its service, advocated bilingualism and biculturalism for the country, as well as a tolerance for diversity represented in the various provinces, so long as people, in the end, believed in the country. Second, there were plans for restructuring the constitution in order to give "special status" to Quebec, and to recognize that province as a "distinct society" where the provincial government would have enhanced powers. Third, there was the matter of potential independence for Quebec, and the proper response for the Federal Government and the Rest of Canada if a future referendum in that province were to approve such a plan, with or without a proviso for negotiation of an agreement for economic cooperation.

In previous decades, first the Trudeau Liberals and then the Mulroney Conservatives were identified by the public as the political party best able to "deal with Quebec." In the 1990s, however, the advent of the Bloc Québécois and the Reform Party meant that some of this support was siphoned off. This effect was noticeable in the 1993 election (Table 6), even though these Quebec-related issues were mentioned by relatively few people as the most important issue in that campaign (Table 5). In 1997, the

Liberals would have been quite content had the Quebec question continued to simmer on the back burner outside of that province itself. However, sensing opportunity, the Reform Party campaigned on the untrustworthiness of federal and provincial party leaders from Quebec, and their unwillingness to take a hard line on the consequences of separation (see Chapter Six of this volume.) In response, as we have already seen, the Quebec issue was more prominent in the campaign than in many previous elections.

It is debateable, however, whether this decision to raise the profile of the Quebec question should be considered a campaign success for Reform. On the one hand, as Table 6 shows, 29 per cent of the electorate who regarded Quebec as the most important election issue felt that Reform was the party closest to them on the issue. Given the raised salience of the issue, this amounted to a considerable number of people, most of whom ended up voting for Reform. On the other hand, only in the West did the Reform Party have a clear lead in the ultimate voting decisions of those finding the Quebec issue the most important; it might

Table 7
Effects of Selected Issues, 1997
(percentages of all voters)

Most Important Issue	1997 Vote					
	Lib	PC	NDP	Ref	BQ	Oth
Unemployment						
Switch to:	3.0	3.1	2.2	1.7	.5	.4
Remain:	6.8	1.9	2.1	1.0	1.7	–
Total	9.8	5.0	4.3	2.7	2.2	.4
Deficit						
Switch to:	1.7	.9	.3	1.0	.5	.1
Remain:	5.3	.4	.1	1.2	.3	.1
Total	7.0	1.3	.4	2.2	.8	.2
Quebec						
Switch to:	1.6	1.5	.4	2.1	.9	.5
Remain:	3.2	1.2	.5	2.3	.7	.1
Total	4.8	2.7	.9	4.4	1.6	.6
Social						
Switch to:	2.2	1.0	1.1	1.2	.4	.1
Remain:	1.8	.3	.8	–	.8	–
Total	4.0	1.3	1.9	1.2	1.2	.1

Source: POLLARA Perspectives Canada survey

well be argued that many of these people would have ended up voting Reform anyway. In Ontario, where the party hoped to pick up converts by raising the Quebec issue, over half the electorate preferred the moderate positions of the Liberals or Conservatives on this issue, as opposed to the 28 per cent who favoured Reform. In fact, fear of the consequences of the Reform position on Quebec may have solidified the Liberal vote in the key province of Ontario.

Some indication of the electoral effects of the four most important issues in the 1997 election may be obtained from Table 7. This table shows the proportion of the whole group of voters who switched to, or remained with, each party, while choosing these issues as most important. Continuing our examination of the Quebec issue, the electoral effects of this subject may be seen here. A total of 4.4 per cent of 1997 voters picked the Quebec issue as most important, and voted Reform. Of these, slightly less than half (2.1 per cent of the voters) switched to Reform in 1997 from some other form of behaviour in 1993. The rest (2.3 per cent) represent people who had voted Reform previously. Still considering those people who identified the Quebec issue as most important, a glance at the figures for the other parties shows that Reform was not the only party collecting significant numbers of votes. In total, more people found this issue a reason to vote Liberal than Reform, though the numbers indicate that it was particularly important to people staying with the Liberals rather than switching to them. Considering only vote-switchers, however, the proportion of the 1997 voters switching to parties other than Reform totals over twice as many people (4.9 per cent) as that 2.1 per cent who were converted to the Reform Party over their position on Quebec.

Another way of considering the modest nature of the impact of the Quebec issue on voting in 1997 is to compare this issue with some of the other important issues in the election. For example, the 2.1 per cent of voters who switched to Reform over Quebec is actually a slightly smaller group of people than those who switched to the NDP over the question of unemployment and job creation (2.2 per cent), and substantially smaller than those switching to the Conservatives or the Liberals on that same issue. Indeed, more people in total switched to Reform itself over economic issues like unemployment and the deficit (shown in Table 7), as well as taxes and the economy generally (not shown in the table) than were convinced to turn to them in order to stand up to Quebec. All in all, it seems reasonable to conclude that the Reform Party's decision to campaign so strongly on the Quebec issue in the 1997 election served mainly to consolidate its appeal in the West at the expense of the more moderate parties. In many places, however, this decision reinforced the party's image as a group of "hardliners", an image Preston Manning had taken steps to alleviate in the social and economic areas. The party seemed to be gambling that if, in the future, the mood in the country hardened against Quebec, people would remember that Reform had "told them so."

The importance of economic issues to the Liberal victory can be clearly seen from Table 7. In particular, the issues of unemployment and the deficit gave a substantial proportion of the party's 1993 voters a reason to stay with the party again in 1997. Retention of past support, as we noted from Table 1, was the key to the Liberal victory. Not all voters, of course, needed an issue basis to motivate or justify their actions in 1997. We have already noted (Table 5) that a high number (29 per cent) of the 1997 electorate could identify no issue at all as important in the election. Significantly, of those people citing no issues as important, 40 per cent voted Liberal, over twice as many as favoured any one of the other parties (data not shown).

Table 8
1997 Vote, By Time of Vote Decision

| | Time of Vote Decision | | | |
	Before Election Called (54%)	When Called (10%)	During Campaign (13%)	Final Days (23%)
1997 Vote				
Liberal	44%	45%	28%	41%
Progressive Conservative	12	18	20	25
New Democratic Party	11	12	15	11
Reform	21	18	27	15
Bloc Québécois	12	8	11	7

Source: POLLARA Perspectives Canada survey

Our findings about the importance of the retention of past supporters to the Liberal Party are consistent with the findings presented in Table 8, which looks at the voting behaviour of those making their voting decisions at various times. Those people who had made up their minds before the election was called, or who decided at the moment the "writ was dropped", were quite likely to have decided in favour of the Liberals;

this group involved almost two-thirds of all voters. Those deciding during the campaign, on the other hand, spread themselves relatively evenly among all the parties. In particular, the Reform Party did relatively well among the 13 per cent of voters who made their decisions during the mid-campaign period. Among that group of 23 per cent of Canadian voters who left their decision until the campaign's final days (in some cases until election day itself) support for the Reform Party dropped off, and the Liberals and Conservatives did well.

Table 8 appears to tell the following story about each of the parties during the campaign of 1997. The Liberals started the campaign with a strong lead, but their support weakened considerably during the campaign once the attacks of the other parties revealed the shortcomings of their program and leadership. At the end of the campaign, a number of late-deciding voters realized that the party might have been weakened to the extent that an undesirable minority government might result. The Progressive Conservatives started slowly but picked up strength consistently as the campaign rolled along, buoyed no doubt by leader Jean Charest's performance in the television debates. While winning only 12 per cent of those voters who had already decided before the election was called, the PCs won 20 per cent of mid-campaign deciders and 25 per cent of those who made up their minds at the last minute. The NDP ran a targeted and effective campaign which produced a small improvement of their fortunes among those who paid attention to the campaign and decided midway along. The Reform Party started with a group of decided supporters second only to the Liberal Party, and added to them during the campaign. However, the momentum of their campaign did not sustain itself, and by the end the attacks mounted on the party from all other quarters had begun to take their toll; among those deciding at the last minute, fewer opted for Reform than among those making up their minds earlier in the campaign. Finally, the Bloc Québécois displayed a pattern not unlike that of Reform, a strongly committed group of initial supporters at the inception of the campaign, a burst of enhanced appeal along the way, and diminished chances among those hesitant late-deciders perhaps frightened by the hardline stances of the parties.

Who Voted for Whom?

Traditionally, the Canadian political parties have been relatively centrist in ideology. This is not to say the parties believe or say exactly the same thing, but that their differences are of degree, and not of kind.[8] In keeping with this picture, the parties have not been supported by substantially different kinds of people. Another way of saying this is that the social characteristics of Canadians have not explained much of the variance in voting choice in Canada. Models of voting behaviour in Canadian Political Science have rested on psychological factors rather than the social cleavages in the electorate. However, there are some differences between the support-bases of Canada's political parties, and we are able to illustrate these by considering the data in Table 9.

Table 9
Characteristics of Supporters of the Canadian Federal Parties, 1997

	LIBERAL	PC	NDP	REFORM	BLOC
AGE % of party voters under 35 years old	31	37	32	30	40
GENDER % of party voters female	51	52	59	41	46
EDUCATION % of party voters with high school or less	36	35	36	47	49
INCOME % of party voters with household income of $45,000 or less	53	53	62	48	65
COST OF LIVING % of party voters feeling their income is falling behind the cost of living	43	45	59	50	42
FEAR OF JOB LOSS % of party voters feeling they or family member may lose job in next year	30	25	49	21	27

Source: POLLARA Perspectives Canada survey.

Some of the parties reveal themselves to appeal differentially to certain groups in the population. The Bloc Québécois, for example, is the "youngest party", with 40 per cent of its 1997 voters under 35 years old. Along with its youth, it appeals to that portion of the Quebec population which has lower educational levels, and also lower household income. The Bloc Québécois has the highest proportion of any Canadian party of supporters with only a high school or lower education, and it also has a lower average income level than even the NDP. Interestingly, however, additional questions in the POLLARA survey reveal that, despite their low income, the Bloc voters are not particularly dissatisfied with their standard of living (fewer feel that their income is falling behind the cost of living than voters for any other party). The lower income and education of the BQ voters reflects that party's greater strength in areas of Quebec outside the metropolitan hub of Montréal. It appeals particularly to young, male, lower income, lower educated people, who are committed to enhanced power or independence for Quebec. The correspondence between support for independence among Quebec voters and Bloc Québécois vote in the election is very strong: 83 per cent of those "very favourable" to independence voted BQ, whereas only 4 per cent who were "very unfavourable" voted for them.

Despite the antipathy between the two, the supporters of the Bloc Québécois and the Reform Party have a number of characteristics in common. We have already noted that these two Canadian parties retain a relatively stable support base from one election to the next. The Reform voters in 1997 resembled the Bloc in that they were much more likely to be male than female, and also were low in education, with almost half of them having only reached high school or primary school. Unlike the Bloc, however, Reform's supporters are older than average, and more (rather than less) likely to feel that their income is falling behind the cost of living. So, rather than idealistic young men, Reformers are more likely to be disgruntled older men. Despite the fact that more of them have an income over $45,000 than voters for any other Canadian party, and fewer fear job loss in the next year, half of them are dissatisfied with their standard of living. They made it on their own, and they don't have much patience with other people (especially in "pampered" regions like Quebec) who want special treatment.

The New Democratic Party appeals much more strongly to women than any other Canadian party (Table 9) for several reasons, among them its commitment to social programs, concern for the unemployed and its choice of two female leaders in a row. This profile is not the traditional one for the party, long supported disproportionately by unionized male workers. The education level of NDP voters is similar to the Liberals and the Conservatives, considerably higher than Reformers. Economically, however, their household income level is much lower, with 62 per cent having families which earn $45,000 or less. In addition, a whopping 59 per cent feel that their income is not keeping up with the cost of living, and half of them (49 per cent) think that they or a family member will lose their job in the coming year. The NDP has therefore captured a lot of support from the economically disadvantaged (many of whom are from the Atlantic region) and from those, particularly women, concerned with the maintenance of social services and support programs.

In contrast to the other three parties, the two which have traditionally competed to form the government, the Liberals and Progressive Conservatives, take the middle ground on most of the categories of supporters' characteristics. Furthermore, the supporters of these two parties resemble each other to a considerable degree. Aside from the somewhat younger age profile, the Conservative Party voters look almost identical to the Liberals, with a proportion of men and women which resembles the distribution of sexes in the population, a relatively high number of university-educated people, a moderately high income level and lower levels of feeling that this income is becoming unsatisfactory over the years. These are middle-of-the-road parties in terms of policy (even though the road itself has veered to the right in recent years) and they have middle-of-the-road voters.

Conclusion

As we started this book by remarking, the Canadian General Election of 1997 was simultaneously the best of times and the worst of times for the parties which contested it. All parties claimed victories of sorts, and all had some bright spots in their performance. But in many ways, 1997 was a static election. Despite a normal amount of vote shifting from the previous election, the parties found it difficult to significantly improve their positions, and all are vulnerable to sudden diminutions of their fortunes at the next opportunity.

The Liberals, whose victory was obtained primarily through hanging on to enough of their previous voters to eke out a parliamentary majority, can take very little comfort from this feat. Not only are they vulnerable to a few by-election defeats or defections over the next several years, but they appear to have been backed into defensive positions on many of the issues in Canadian politics, including Quebec, social services, and even the economy, should there be a general slump in economic growth. The one issue clearly associated with them in the 1997 election was reduction in the deficit, but there is little "growth potential" in this area once the reductions are completed. New leadership, and new policy initiatives would appear to be imperative when the Liberals position themselves for the next election.

The other parties, however, have little to gloat about either. Reform's move to Official Opposition status was largely fashioned through a consolidation and expansion of its existing Western base. The party's championship of a hardline position on Quebec likely limited its appeal to Central Canada in 1997, and may provide a barrier to future hopes of forming a national government. In a sense, the result of the 1997 election was to replace one regional party (the BQ) as Official Opposition by another regional party (Reform). Reform may try to *act* more like a national party than the Bloc, but they have yet to prove themselves to be one. Their overall vote percentage did not increase, and their seats are even more concentrated in the West than they were in 1993. The Bloc Québécois, with the limited opportunities for national exposure which were provided by its previous status as Official Opposition removed, now no longer needs to make even a pretense of taking positions on national issues, and can concentrate even more singlemindedly on promotion of Quebec independence.

And what of the other two "old line parties?" The Conservatives can take some satisfaction from the increases in their vote share and seat numbers from the disastrous result of the previous election. However, the limited and geographically concentrated nature of these improvements tempers the party's credibility when it attempts to act like "the real national opposition party." The appeal of the party's leader, Jean Charest, played some role in the party's comeback in 1997, but in four more years he may not look so new and refreshing as he did during this recent campaign. Much the same story can be told about the NDP; its gains were modest and regionally concentrated as well. And of course the NDP brings to its present situation its history of ups and downs while never threatening seriously to break through into major party status in Canadian federal politics.

Perhaps the most serious aspect to the 1997 Canadian election was the revelation of the decline in the political interest and participation of the Canadian people which has occurred in the last decade. Rather than the anomaly it might have appeared at the time, the 1993 election now looks like the beginning of a downward trend in voting turnout in federal elections. This decline in voting (from a norm of 75 per cent in the past to 70 per cent in 1993 and 67 per cent in 1997) has ironically taken place as some of the recommendations of the Royal Commission on Electoral Reform and Party Financing designed to improve voting turnout were being implemented (see Chapter Nine of this volume). Persistent nonvoting, that is decisions on the part of individuals to continue to abstain from casting ballots, may be on the rise, raising fears that alienation from politics, rather than just discontent, may become more characteristic of the Canadian public.

The current situation just described presents a serious challenge to the men and women elected to Canada's new Parliament, and to those unelected members of the party executives and research staffs. The country appears to have been less than pleased with the election campaign of 1997 and the conduct of Canadian politics generally. The future of the country may depend on whether some improvement is forthcoming.

Notes

[1] The sample size was 1688, which reduces with corrective weighting for oversampled areas of the country (primarily the Atlantic region and Quebec) to 1200 analytic cases. Although POLLARA does survey work for the Liberal Party (see Chapter Ten of this volume) this survey has no partisan connection.

[2] If Table 1 is constructed for Quebec only, the proportions in the two groups of people voting Liberal in both elections and Bloc Québécois in both elections are almost identical.

[3] Harold D. Clarke, Jane Jenson, Lawrence LeDuc and Jon H. Pammett, *Absent Mandate: Canadian Electoral Politics in an Era of Restructuring*, third Edition, (Toronto, Gage, 1996).

[4] *Ibid*, chapter 6. See also, by the same authors, *Political Choice in Canada*, (Toronto: McGraw-Hill Ryerson, 1980) Chapter 12.

[5] Harold D. Clarke, Jane Jenson, Lawrence LeDuc and Jon H. Pammett, *Absent Mandate: Canadian Electoral Politics in an Era of Restructuring* Third edition (Toronto: Gage, 1996) pp129-34.

[6] *Absent Mandate*, op cit, p 29.

[7] As reported by Statistics Canada, the national unemployment rate was 11.2 per cent in 1993, 10.4 per cent in 1994, 9.5 per cent in 1995, and 9.7 per cent in 1996. In the immediate pre-election period, the rate was 9.5 per cent in May, 1997.

[8] See the various articles in George Perlin, ed., *Party Democracy in Canada: The Politics of National Party Conventions* (Scarborough: Prentice Hall, 1988). Other sources are Robert Alford, *Party and Society: The Anglo-American Democracies* (Chicago: Rand McNally, 1963); F. G. Engelman and M.A. Schwartz, *Canadian Political Parties: Origin, Character, Impact* (Scarborough: Prentice-Hall, 1975); Janine Brodie and Jane Jenson, *Crisis, Challenge and Change* (Ottawa: Carleton University press, 1988); Colin Campbell and William Christian, *Parties, Leaders and Ideologies in Canada* (Toronto: McGraw-Hill Ryerson, 1995).

The Results

Standing of Parties

Unofficial Results

Source: Library of Parliament (Internet address: http://www.parl.gc.ca)

Prepared by Elections Canada: July 2, 1997

Provinces	Lib. Caucus	R.P. Caucus	B.Q. Caucus	N.D.P Caucus	P.C. Caucus	Ind.	Vacancy	Total
Alberta	2	24						26
British Columbia	6	25		3				34
Manitoba	6	3		4	1			14
New Brunswick	3			2	5			10
Nfld.	4				3			7
Nova Scotia				6	5			11
Ontario	101				1	1		103
P.E.I.	4							4
Quebec	26		44		5			75
Sask.	1	8		5				14
N.W.T.	2							2
Yukon Territory				1				1
National Total	155	60	44	21	20	1	0	301

The Results   251

By Constituency

KEY

ACTION	Canadian Action Party
BQ	Bloc Québécois
CHP	Christian Heritage Party of Canada
GP	The Green Party of Canada
IND	Independent
LIB	Liberal Party of Canada
M-L	Marxist-Leninist Party of Canada
NDP	New Democratic Party
NLP	Natural Law Party of Canada
NIL	No Affiliation
PC	Progressive Conservative Party of Canada
REF	Reform Party of Canada

Percentage of Votes Received By Province

	LIB.	REF.	B.Q.	N.D.P.	P.C.	OTHERS
NFLD	37.86%	2.52%	0%	21.97%	36.77%	0.87%
P.E.I.	44.79%	1.50%	0%	15.13%	38.28%	0.31%
NS	28.35%	9.67%	0%	30.41%	0.77%	0.79%
NB	32.92%	13.11%	0%	18.37%	34.97%	0.63%
QC	36.68%	0.29%	37.86%	1.96%	22.17%	1.03%
ON	49.51%	19.14%	0%	10.69%	18.81%	1.85%
MB	34.30%	23.70%	0%	23.16%	17.75%	1.09%
SK	24.69%	36.02%	0%	30.89%	7.79%	0.62%
AB	23.05%	54.66%	0%	5.74%	15.38%	1.17%
BC	28.81%	43.04%	0%	18.19%	6.23%	3.73%
NWT	43.13%	11.74%	0%	20.86%	16.66%	7.62%
YT	21.95%	25.26%	0%	28.94%	13.94%	9.91%
Totals	38.37%	19.35%	10.67%	11.05%	18.92%	1.63%

NEWFOUNDLAND
1997
%

BONAVISTA-TRINITY-CONCEPTION
LIB	35.3
PC	28.2
NDP	33.7
NIL	2.9

BURIN-ST.GEORGE'S
LIB	38.6
PC	45.7
NDP	15.7

GANDER-GRAND FALLS
LIB	52.2
PC	33.7
NDP	14.1

HUMBER-ST. BARBE-BAIE VERTE
LIB	39.8
PC	39.1
NDP	14.6
REF	6.5

LABRADOR
LIB	50.6
PC	6.9
NDP	37.8
REF	4.7

ST. JOHN'S EAST
LIB	27.2
PC	39.0
NDP	28.1
REF	4.5
GP	0.9
NLP	0.4

ST. JOHN'S WEST
LIB	37.1
PC	44.1
NDP	15.6
REF	2.5
NLP	0.7

PRINCE EDWARD ISLAND
1997
%

CARDIGAN
LIB	45.0
PC	44.5
NDP	10.5

EGMONT
LIB	48.4
PC	44.2
NDP	7.4

HILLSBOROUGH
LIB	40.9
PC	24.6
NDP	30.8
REF	2.5
CHP	0.8
NLP	0.4

MALPEQUE
LIB	45.1
PC	41.0
NDP	10.6
REF	3.3

NOVA SCOTIA

1997
%

BRAS D'OR

LIB	38.4
PC	20.3
NDP	41.3

CUMBERLAND-COLCHESTER

LIB	25.8
PC	43.6
NDP	14.2
REF	14.0
NLP	0.5
IND	1.9

DARTMOUTH

LIB	27.2
PC	26.9
NDP	32.6
REF	11.7
NLP	0.4
IND	1.2

HALIFAX

LIB	21.6
PC	23.3
NDP	49.0
REF	5.4
M-L	0.2
NLP	0.4

HALIFAX WEST

LIB	30.9
PC	23.5
NDP	34.6
REF	10.5
M-L	0.2
NLP	0.4

KINGS-HANTS

LIB	30.3
PC	36.3
NDP	19.0
REF	13.4
NLP	0.6
NIL	0.5

PICTOU-ANTIGONISH-GUYSBOROUGH

LIB	29.9
PC	42.3
NDP	19.3
REF	7.9
NLP	0.5

SACKVILLE-EASTERN SHORE

LIB	26.3
PC	30.3
NDP	30.4
REF	12.6
NLP	0.5

SOUTH SHORE

LIB	29.0
PC	36.0
NDP	20.7
REF	13.5
NLP	0.8

SYDNEY-VICTORIA

LIB	26.3
PC	22.6
NDP	51.1

WEST NOVA

LIB	25.7
PC	34.3
NDP	20.5
REF	18.8
NLP	0.7

NEW BRUNSWICK

<u>1997</u>
%

ACADIE-BATHURST

LIB	35.4
PC	24.1
NDP	40.5

BEAUSÉJOUR-PETITCODIAC

LIB	34.8
PC	16.0
NDP	39.0
REF	10.2

CHARLOTTE

LIB	25.7
PC	44.9
NDP	7.4
REF	21.1
NLP	0.9

FREDERICTON

LIB	34.1
PC	30.2
NDP	13.1
REF	21.8
NLP	0.9

FUNDY-ROYAL

LIB	25.3
PC	41.5
NDP	9.4
REF	22.9
NLP	0.8

MADAWASKA-RESTIGOUCHE

LIB	37.0
PC	50.3
NDP	10.4
NLP	2.3

MIRAMICHI

LIB	40.4
PC	30.7
NDP	15.3
REF	13.6

MONCTON

LIB	44.6
PC	25.5
NDP	16.0
REF	13.0
NLP	0.9

SAINT JOHN

LIB	15.9
PC	63.1
NDP	10.4
REF	9.8
NLP	0.7

TOBIQUE-MACTAQUAC

LIB	30.2
PC	35.9
NDP	6.2
REF	27.7

QUEBEC

1997
%

ABITIBI

LIB	43.7
PC	17.0
NDP	2.4
BQ	36.9

AHUNTSIC

LIB	49.3
PC	16.2
NDP	1.8
BQ	31.8
NLP	1.0

ANJOU-RIVIÈRE-DES-PRAIRIES

LIB	47.3
PC	18.4
NDP	1.5
BQ	32.4
M-L	0.4

ARGENTEUIL-PAPINEAU

LIB	34.0
PC	21.5
NDP	1.6
BQ	40.9
CHP	1.0
NLP	1.0

BEAUCE

LIB	49.1
PC	20.8
NDP	1.6
BQ	26.6
IND	1.9

BEAUHARNOIS-SALABERRY

LIB	33.5
PC	25.6
NDP	1.3
BQ	39.7

BEAUPORT-MONTMORENCY-ORLÉANS

LIB	27.1
PC	24.9
NDP	1.7
REF	2.5
BQ	43.0
M-L	0.8

BELLECHASSE-ETCHEMINS-MONTMAGNY-L'ISLET

LIB	33.5
PC	30.5
NDP	1.2
REF	1.5
BQ	33.4

BERTHIER-MONTCALM

LIB	24.3
PC	21.5
NDP	1.6
BQ	52.6

BONAVENTURE-GASPÉ-ILES-DE-LA-MADELEINE-PABOK

LIB	40.8
PC	16.3
NDP	1.7
BQ	41.3

BOURASSA

LIB	52.2
PC	13.0
NDP	2.2
BQ	32.5

BROME-MISSISQUOI

LIB	42.4
PC	28.1
NDP	1.7
BQ	27.8

BROSSARD-LA PRAIRIE

LIB	46.6
PC	18.9
NDP	1.7
BQ	32.8

CHÂTEAUGUAY

LIB	33.6
PC	19.5
NDP	1.4
BQ	45.5

CHAMBLY

LIB	26.5
PC	22.3
NDP	1.9
BQ	49.3

CHAMPLAIN

LIB	27.5
PC	27.2
NDP	1.3
BQ	44.0

CHARLESBOURG

LIB	31.4
PC	24.6
NDP	1.7
REF	2.0
BQ	38.4
M-L	0.5
NLP	1.3

CHARLEVOIX

LIB	26.9
PC	17.6
NDP	1.2
BQ	54.2

CHICOUTIMI

LIB	11.4
PC	43.7
NDP	2.0
BQ	42.9

COMPTON-STANSTEAD

LIB	20.0
PC	44.6
NDP	1.4
BQ	32.9
NLP	1.1

DRUMMOND

LIB	23.1
PC	33.6
NDP	1.0
BQ	42.3

FRONTENAC-MÉGANTIC

LIB	35.9
PC	25.4
NDP	0.6
BQ	37.1
NLP	0.9

GATINEAU

LIB	46.4
PC	29.0
NDP	1.8
BQ	20.9
CHP	0.8
M-L	0.3
NLP	0.8

HOCHELAGA-MAISONNEUVE

LIB	34.2
PC	15.9
NDP	1.7
BQ	46.0
M-L	0.9
NLP	1.2

HULL-AYLMER

LIB	54.1
PC	17.7
NDP	2.8
REF	2.0
BQ	20.8
GP	1.2
CHP	0.6
M-L	0.3
NLP	0.6

JOLIETTE

LIB	15.3
PC	35.9
NDP	1.0
BQ	46.5
NLP	1.2

JONQUIÈRE

LIB	14.4
PC	34.9
NDP	1.0
BQ	48.6
NLP	1.0

KAMOURASKA-RIVIÈRE-DU-LOUP-T...MISCOUATA-LES BASQUES

LIB	32.7
PC	26.9
NDP	1.0
BQ	38.3
NLP	1.1

LÉVIS

LIB	28.0
PC	23.7
NDP	3.1
BQ	45.2

LAC-SAINT-JEAN

LIB	21.0
PC	14.3
NDP	1.2
BQ	63.5

LAC-SAINT-LOUIS

LIB	69.0
PC	18.3
NDP	2.5
REF	2.5
BQ	7.0
NLP	0.6

LASALLE-ÉMARD

LIB	60.9
PC	12.1
NDP	1.7
BQ	24.4
NLP	0.9

LAURENTIDES

LIB	30.4
PC	22.5
NDP	1.3
BQ	45.7

LAURIER-SAINTE-MARIE

LIB	23.0
PC	12.0
NDP	4.5
BQ	54.7
GP	2.4
M-L	0.7
IND	2.6
NIL	0.3

LAVAL CENTRE

LIB	35.3
PC	23.0
NDP	2.1
BQ	39.6

LAVAL EAST

LIB	32.1
PC	28.2
NDP	1.3
BQ	38.5

LAVAL WEST

LIB	48.9
PC	19.2
NDP	1.7
BQ	30.3

LONGUEIL

LIB	29.3
PC	18.6
NDP	2.0
BQ	50.1

LOTBINIÈRE

LIB	28.5
PC	27.5
NDP	1.3
BQ	37.1
IND	5.6

LOUIS-HÉBERT

LIB	33.6
PC	21.9
NDP	2.0
REF	1.7
BQ	39.9
NLP	0.9

MANICOUAGAN

LIB	41.2
PC	7.7
NDP	4.0
BQ	47.1

MATAPÉDIA-MATANE

LIB	30.1
PC	22.8
NDP	1.2
BQ	44.8
NLP	1.1

MERCIER

LIB	29.1
PC	17.6
NDP	1.6
BQ	51.1
M-L	0.6

MOUNT ROYAL

LIB	62.3
PC	10.3
NDP	2.0
BQ	4.1
NLP	0.4
IND	20.9

NOTRE-DAME-DE-GRÂCE-LACHINE

LIB	56.6
PC	19.8
NDP	4.4
BQ	16.8
NLP	1.1
IND	0.7
IND	0.6

OUTREMONT

LIB	50.1
PC	12.2
NDP	6.4
BQ	28.4
M-L	0.9
NLP	2.0

PAPINEAU-SAINT-DENIS

LIB	53.9
PC	12.8
NDP	2.5
BQ	28.9
M-L	1.0
NIL	1.0

PIERREFONDS-DOLLARD

LIB	66.4
PC	18.2
NDP	1.8
REF	2.0
BQ	10.8
NLP	0.8

PONTIAC-GATINEAU-LABELLE

LIB	45.8
PC	18.5
NDP	2.2
BQ	32.0
CHP	0.5
NLP	1.0

PORTNEUF

LIB	29.5
PC	24.6
NDP	2.6
BQ	43.3

QUEBEC

LIB	32.4
PC	18.5
NDP	4.6
BQ	44.5

QUEBEC EAST

LIB	31.4
PC	24.6
NDP	2.1
REF	2.5
BQ	39.4

REPENTIGNY

LIB	21.1
PC	21.0
NDP	1.5
BQ	56.3

RICHELIEU

LIB	28.9
PC	14.2
NDP	2.1
BQ	54.8

RICHMOND-ARTHABASKA
LIB	20.3
PC	41.5
NDP	1.2
BQ	37.0

RIMOUSKI-MITIS
LIB	30.2
PC	21.5
NDP	1.3
BQ	47.0

ROBERVAL
LIB	26.3
PC	20.3
NDP	1.3
BQ	52.1

ROSEMONT
LIB	32.2
PC	15.6
NDP	3.3
BQ	47.0
M-L	0.9
NIL	1.0

SAINT-BRUNO-SAINT-HUBERT
LIB	32.8
PC	20.1
NDP	2.0
BQ	45.1

SAINT-EUSTACHE-SAINTE THÉRÈSE
LIB	29.3
PC	22.5
NDP	1.7
BQ	46.5

SAINT-HYACINTHE-BAGOT
LIB	22.3
PC	33.2
NDP	1.6
BQ	42.9

SAINT-JEAN
LIB	27.2
PC	24.5
NDP	1.5
BQ	46.1
M-L	0.7

SAINT-LÉONARD-SAINT MICHEL
LIB	69.8
PC	11.6
NDP	2.3
BQ	16.3

SAINT-LAMBERT
LIB	41.2
PC	17.1
NDP	2.0
BQ	39.1
ACTION	0.6

SAINT-LAURENT-CARTIERVILLE
LIB	70.1
PC	13.9
NDP	1.8
REF	1.4
BQ	12.7

SAINT-MAURICE
LIB	47.3
PC	7.8
NDP	1.0
BQ	43.9

SHEFFORD

LIB	26.2
PC	36.9
NDP	1.1
BQ	35.8

SHERBROOKE

LIB	8.7
PC	59.5
NDP	1.2
BQ	29.7
NLP	0.9

TÉMISCAMINGUE

LIB	31.9
PC	19.8
NDP	1.6
BQ	46.6

TERREBONNE-BLAINVILLE

LIB	26.4
PC	21.3
NDP	2.0
BQ	50.4

TROIS-RIVIÈRES

LIB	31.3
PC	24.2
NDP	1.1
BQ	42.5
NLP	1.0

VAUDREUIL-SOULANGES

LIB	45.0
PC	18.6
NDP	1.0
REF	1.1
BQ	33.4
NLP	0.9

VERCHÈRES

LIB	22.7
PC	22.2
NDP	1.3
BQ	53.7

VERDUN-SAINT-HENRI

LIB	46.9
PC	15.0
NDP	2.5
REF	0.8
BQ	33.2
M-L	0.4
NLP	1.1

WESTMOUNT-VILLE-MARIE

LIB	60.1
PC	17.4
NDP	5.7
BQ	11.3
GP	1.7
M-L	0.4
NLP	0.5
IND	3.0

ONTARIO

1997

%

ALGOMA-MANITOULIN

LIB	41.3
PC	10.1
NDP	23.6
REF	25.0

BARRIE-SIMCOE-BRADFORD

LIB	43.5
PC	19.8
NDP	4.8
REF	29.6
GP	0.9
CHP	0.8
ACTION	0.6

BEACHES-EAST YORK

LIB	47.9
PC	12.3
NDP	23.5
REF	14.3
GP	1.3
NLP	0.6

BRAMALEA-GORE-MALTON

LIB	46.4
PC	26.1
NDP	5.6
REF	21.3
M-L	0.7

BRAMPTON CENTRE

LIB	48.9
PC	14.8
NDP	7.7
REF	28.4
M-L	0.3

BRAMPTON WEST-MISSISSAUGA

LIB	60.0
PC	18.6
NDP	4.8
REF	16.6

BRANT

LIB	53.0
PC	12.7
NDP	11.4
REF	22.9

BROADVIEW-GREENWOOD

LIB	49.8
PC	7.6
NDP	32.8
REF	7.7
GP	1.0
M-L	0.2
NLP	0.5
IND	0.5

BRUCE-GREY

LIB	36.8
PC	22.9
NDP	7.1
REF	33.2

BURLINGTON

LIB	44.1
PC	32.7
NDP	5.1
REF	17.3
ACTION	0.7

CAMBRIDGE

LIB	36.7
PC	19.3
NDP	20.4
REF	22.4
IND	0.6
IND	0.5

CARLETON-GLOUCESTER

LIB	59.0
PC	19.7
NDP	5.6
REF	14.6
ACTION	0.5
NLP	0.7

DAVENPORT

LIB	65.9
PC	10.1
NDP	18.4
GP	2.1
M-L	1.0
ACTION	1.1
NIL	0.7
NIL	0.7

DON VALLEY EAST

LIB	59.2
PC	20.1
NDP	6.9
REF	12.0
ACTION	0.9
NLP	0.4
NIL	0.4

DON VALLEY WEST

LIB	52.9
PC	30.4
NDP	5.9
REF	9.4
GP	0.8
M-L	0.2
NLP	0.3

DUFFERIN-PEEL-WELLINGTON-GREY

LIB	42.6
PC	22.6
NDP	4.8
REF	30.0

DURHAM

LIB	43.3
PC	19.6
NDP	7.1
REF	28.5
CHP	1.5

EGLINTON-LAWRENCE

LIB	59.2
PC	22.7
NDP	9.0
REF	8.1
NLP	0.9

ELGIN-MIDDLESEX-LONDON

LIB	40.0
PC	25.7
NDP	7.3
REF	23.0
GP	1.1
CHP	2.8

ERIE-LINCOLN

LIB	42.8
PC	15.4
NDP	6.1
REF	31.2
CHP	3.2
ACTION	0.7
NLP	0.6

ESSEX

LIB	46.1
PC	6.4
NDP	29.6
REF	17.9

ETOBICOKE CENTRE

LIB	54.6
PC	22.0
NDP	5.3
REF	17.2
M-L	0.4
NLP	0.5

ETOBICOKE NORTH

LIB	61.8
PC	11.9
NDP	9.3
REF	15.6
M-L	0.5
ACTION	0.4
NLP	0.5

ETOBICOKE-LAKESHORE

LIB	46.2
PC	22.9
NDP	8.9
REF	19.0
GP	0.7
M-L	0.3
ACTION	1.7
NLP	0.3

GLENGARRY-PRESCOTT-RUSSELL

LIB	72.0
PC	12.6
NDP	4.7
REF	9.5
GP	0.9
NLP	0.4

GUELPH-WELLINGTON

LIB	47.7
PC	21.3
NDP	10.4
REF	17.3
GP	1.1
CHP	1.9
M-L	0.3

HALDIMAND-NORFOLK-BRANT

LIB	45.5
PC	21.0
NDP	5.4
REF	27.1
GP	0.9

HALTON

LIB	47.2
PC	25.0
NDP	4.5
REF	22.2
GP	1.1

HAMILTON EAST

LIB	49.5
PC	11.4
NDP	20.0
REF	16.6
CHP	1.1
M-L	0.5
NIL	0.9

HAMILTON MOUNTAIN

LIB	45.8
PC	19.2
NDP	16.1
REF	17.7
M-L	0.3
ACTION	0.8

HAMILTON WEST

LIB	50.0
PC	15.5
NDP	18.3
REF	15.0
M-L	0.4
NLP	0.8

HASTINGS-FRONTENAC-LENNOX AND ADDINGTON

LIB	39.5
PC	26.2
NDP	7.0
REF	25.8
CHP	1.1
NLP	0.4

HURON-BRUCE

LIB	51.3
PC	19.5
NDP	6.4
REF	21.0
CHP	1.7

KENORA-RAINY RIVER

LIB	41.9
PC	8.3
NDP	20.6
REF	29.1

KENT-ESSEX

LIB	50.2
PC	15.5
NDP	10.1
REF	20.9
GP	0.7
CHP	1.5
ACTION	1.1

KINGSTON AND THE ISLANDS

LIB	49.5
PC	21.8
NDP	12.4
REF	13.1
GP	1.7
CHP	1.5

KITCHENER CENTRE

LIB	48.0
PC	22.8
NDP	9.4
REF	19.9

KITCHENER-WATERLOO

LIB	47.7
PC	22.1
NDP	9.0
REF	20.0
M-L	0.3
ACTION	0.5
IND	0.5

LAMBTON-KENT-MIDDLESEX

LIB	46.2
PC	15.9
NDP	5.3
REF	27.5
GP	0.6
CHP	3.9
IND	0.6

LANARK-CARLETON

LIB	45.3
PC	21.3
NDP	4.9
REF	27.0
GP	0.7
ACTION	0.5
NLP	0.3

LEEDS-GRENVILLE

LIB	39.5
PC	32.3
NDP	3.6
REF	21.6
GP	2.3
CHP	0.5
NLP	0.2

LONDON NORTH CENTRE

LIB	51.7
PC	17.5
NDP	12.3
REF	15.2
GP	1.5
CHP	0.8
M-L	0.3
NIL	0.7

LONDON WEST

LIB	48.6
PC	21.5
NDP	10.4
REF	17.4
GP	1.0
CHP	1.0
M-L	0.2

LONDON-FANSHAWE

LIB	51.2
PC	13.7
NDP	16.9
REF	17.1
GP	1.1

MARKHAM

LIB	36.7
PC	44.7
NDP	3.2
REF	10.8
ACTION	0.5
NLP	0.6
NIL	3.5

MISSISSAUGA CENTRE

LIB	65.0
PC	15.2
NDP	4.8
REF	14.5
M-L	0.5

MISSISSAUGA EAST

LIB	59.9
PC	19.8
NDP	5.4
REF	14.2
ACTION	0.7

MISSISSAUGA SOUTH

LIB	49.9
PC	23.7
NDP	5.4
REF	19.6
M-L	0.2
ACTION	0.4
NLP	0.5
IND	0.3

MISSISSAUGA WEST

LIB	61.2
PC	16.2
NDP	4.3
REF	18.3

NEPEAN-CARLETON

LIB	48.8
PC	19.0
NDP	4.8
REF	26.4
ACTION	0.6
NLP	0.4

NIAGARA CENTRE

LIB	49.7
PC	12.0
NDP	11.4
REF	24.8
CHP	1.1
M-L	0.3
NLP	0.7

NIAGARA FALLS

LIB	38.4
PC	24.0
NDP	9.8
REF	26.6
GP	0.9
NLP	0.4

NICKEL BELT

LIB	48.9
PC	4.4
NDP	33.5
REF	12.0
ACTION	0.9
NLP	0.4

NIPISSING

LIB	56.3
PC	16.1
NDP	6.5
REF	21.0

NORTHUMBERLAND

LIB	45.8
PC	24.8
NDP	5.8
REF	22.9
CHP	0.8

OAK RIDGES

LIB	54.7
PC	24.4
NDP	4.8
REF	15.1
ACTION	0.3
NLP	0.6

OAKVILLE

LIB	47.7
PC	30.1
NDP	4.6
REF	17.6

OSHAWA

LIB	37.7
PC	16.5
NDP	17.4
REF	28.4

OTTAWA CENTRE

LIB	45.2
PC	16.3
NDP	23.7
REF	11.6
GP	1.5
M-L	0.3
ACTION	0.4
NLP	0.4
IND	0.3
IND	0.2
IND	0.2

OTTAWA SOUTH

LIB	59.0
PC	15.1
NDP	8.1
REF	15.9
GP	0.8
M-L	0.3
ACTION	0.5
NLP	0.3

OTTAWA WEST-NEPEAN

LIB	54.0
PC	15.5
NDP	7.6
REF	21.2
GP	0.8
M-L	0.2
NLP	0.3
IND	0.4

OTTAWA-VANIER

LIB	61.9
PC	13.6
NDP	12.0
REF	9.8
GP	1.3
M-L	0.3
NLP	0.7
NIL	0.5

OXFORD

LIB	36.0
PC	32.5
NDP	7.5
REF	21.1
CHP	2.1
ACTION	0.4
NLP	0.4

PARKDALE-HIGH PARK

LIB	48.3
PC	13.8
NDP	20.4
REF	13.7
GP	1.6
M-L	0.7
ACTION	0.8
NLP	0.6

PARRY SOUND-MUSKOKA

LIB	41.6
PC	26.8
NDP	4.0
REF	25.6
GP	1.2
ACTION	0.6
NLP	0.3

PERTH-MIDDLESEX

LIB	44.0
PC	24.9
NDP	8.6
REF	20.6
CHP	1.9

PETERBOROUGH

LIB	46.5
PC	15.9
NDP	8.9
REF	28.7

PICKERING-AJAX-UXBRIDGE

LIB	52.1
PC	21.6
NDP	5.2
REF	21.1

PRINCE EDWARD-HASTINGS

LIB	51.6
PC	21.4
NDP	5.8
REF	21.2

RENFREW-NIPISSING-PEMBROKE

LIB	40.3
PC	25.4
NDP	6.7
REF	26.8
ACTION	0.5
NLP	0.4

SARNIA-LAMBTON

LIB	47.4
PC	14.6
NDP	8.1
REF	24.7
CHP	3.6
ACTION	0.4
NLP	0.3
IND	1.0

SAULT STE. MARIE

LIB	44.5
PC	7.9
NDP	27.1
REF	19.9
NLP	0.6

SCARBOROUGH CENTRE

LIB	57.4
PC	15.9
NDP	8.2
REF	18.5

SCARBOROUGH EAST

LIB	54.3
PC	19.5
NDP	7.8
REF	16.5
GP	0.7
CHP	0.4
ACTION	0.4
NLP	0.3

SCARBOROUGH SOUTHWEST

LIB	53.4
PC	13.7
NDP	11.2
REF	20.5
GP	1.2

SCARBOROUGH-AGINCOURT

LIB	65.1
PC	17.8
NDP	6.3
REF	10.8

SCARBOROUGH-ROUGE RIVER

LIB	74.8
PC	11.4
NDP	4.9
REF	8.1
ACTION	0.4
NLP	0.4

SIMCOE NORTH

LIB	44.4
PC	21.1
NDP	4.8
REF	28.0
GP	0.8
ACTION	0.4
NLP	0.4

SIMCOE-GREY

LIB	35.2
PC	23.1
NDP	6.1
REF	34.3
CHP	1.3

ST. CATHARINES

LIB	43.5
PC	13.4
NDP	9.6
REF	31.0
CHP	1.4
ACTION	0.6
NLP	0.5

ST. PAUL'S

LIB	54.3
PC	23.7
NDP	12.4
REF	7.3
GP	1.2
M-L	0.3
ACTION	0.4
NLP	0.5

STONEY CREEK

LIB	50.0
PC	19.9
NDP	7.1
REF	21.5
CHP	1.0
NLP	0.5

STORMONT-DUNDAS

LIB	52.5
PC	20.1
NDP	6.1
REF	20.6
NLP	0.7

SUDBURY

LIB	55.4
PC	8.6
NDP	21.1
REF	13.0
ACTION	1.3
NLP	0.6

THORNHILL

LIB	59.0
PC	26.4
NDP	4.6
REF	7.9
NLP	0.6
IND	0.5
IND	0.3

THUNDER BAY-ATIKOKAN

LIB	42.7
PC	16.3
NDP	24.2
REF	16.8

THUNDER BAY-NIPIGON

LIB	51.8
PC	11.0
NDP	20.8
REF	16.4

TIMISKAMING-COCHRANE

LIB	59.4
PC	14.1
NDP	13.3
REF	13.1

TIMMINS-JAMES BAY

LIB	50.3
PC	6.7
NDP	35.7
REF	7.4

TORONTO CENTRE-ROSEDALE

LIB	49.2
PC	19.3
NDP	20.6
REF	7.8
GP	1.2
M-L	0.4
ACTION	0.6
NLP	0.6
NIL	0.3

TRINITY-SPADINA

LIB	45.3
PC	6.9
NDP	40.8
REF	4.1
GP	1.0
M-L	0.3
ACTION	0.3
NLP	0.5
IND	0.3
NIL	0.4

VAUGHAN-KING-AURORA

LIB	64.3
PC	16.5
NDP	4.3
REF	13.9
NIL	1.0

VICTORIA-HALIBURTON

LIB	34.0
PC	26.7
NDP	6.5
REF	31.8
ACTION	0.9

WATERLOO-WELLINGTON

LIB	44.0
PC	18.0
NDP	7.0
REF	31.1

WENTWORTH-BURLINGTON

LIB	41.6
PC	28.7
NDP	7.9
REF	21.8

WHITBY-AJAX

LIB	47.7
PC	20.5
NDP	6.8
REF	24.3
ACTION	0.8

WILLOWDALE

LIB	58.4
PC	21.5
NDP	6.1
REF	12.9
ACTION	0.6
NLP	0.6

WINDSOR WEST

LIB	55.2
PC	6.2
NDP	23.7
REF	13.4
GP	1.0
M-L	0.5

WINDSOR-ST. CLAIR

LIB	39.9
PC	10.3
NDP	34.4
REF	14.3
GP	0.9
M-L	0.3

YORK CENTRE

LIB	72.1
PC	8.6
NDP	9.4
REF	7.4
GP	1.0
M-L	0.4
ACTION	0.5
NLP	0.6

YORK NORTH

LIB	45.3
PC	22.3
NDP	3.9
REF	26.1
CHP	1.6
ACTION	0.4
NLP	0.4

YORK SOUTH-WESTON

LIB	33.4
PC	5.1
NDP	9.3
REF	6.2
GP	0.4
M-L	0.3
NIL	45.0
NIL	0.3

YORK WEST

LIB	73.6
PC	7.5
NDP	9.9
REF	9.0

MANITOBA

<u>1997</u>
%

BRANDON-SOURIS

LIB	17.7
PC	35.6
NDP	13.4
REF	32.0
CHP	0.6
NIL	0.7

CHARLESWOOD-ASSINIBOINE

LIB	43.0
PC	23.4
NDP	10.6
REF	22.7
M-L	0.4

CHURCHILL

LIB	29.3
PC	10.5
NDP	41.2
REF	19.0

DAUPHIN-SWAN RIVER

LIB	20.8
PC	21.6
NDP	21.2
REF	35.5
IND	0.9

PORTAGE-LISGAR

LIB	14.6
PC	35.9
NDP	7.2
REF	40.2
CHP	1.5
ACTION	0.5

PROVENCHER

LIB	40.0
PC	16.3
NDP	8.6
REF	35.1

SAINT BONIFACE

LIB	51.2
PC	12.3
NDP	18.0
REF	18.0
M-L	0.5

SELKIRK-INTERLAKE

LIB	28.1
PC	14.8
NDP	27.8
REF	28.3
CHP	0.9

WINNIPEG CENTRE

LIB	36.9
PC	9.1
NDP	40.9
REF	11.5
M-L	0.5
IND	0.6
IND	0.4
IND	0.2

WINNIPEG NORTH CENTRE

LIB	28.7
PC	6.4
NDP	50.3
REF	13.5
M-L	0.5
NLP	0.6

WINNIPEG NORTH-ST. PAUL

LIB	37.5
PC	15.0
NDP	26.3
REF	19.7
CHP	1.2
M-L	0.3

WINNIPEG SOUTH

LIB	49.6
PC	17.3
NDP	12.2
REF	19.8
M-L	0.2
NLP	0.4
IND	0.5

WINNIPEG SOUTH CENTRE

LIB	55.9
PC	14.0
NDP	16.0
REF	12.5
M-L	0.5
NLP	0.6
IND	0.6

WINNIPEG-TRANSCONA

LIB	21.5
PC	9.0
NDP	50.3
REF	17.2
CHP	1.3
M-L	0.3
IND	0.5

SASKATCHEWAN

<u>1997</u>

%

BATTLEFORDS-LLOYDMINSTER

LIB	20.0
PC	9.4
NDP	27.8
REF	42.7

BLACKSTRAP

LIB	28.3
PC	6.6
NDP	27.6
REF	36.9
NLP	0.6

CHURCHILL RIVER

LIB	28.4
PC	5.1
NDP	34.5
REF	32.0

CYPRESS HILLS-GRASSLANDS

LIB	21.3
PC	10.2
NDP	19.4
REF	49.1

PALLISER

LIB	23.1
PC	8.5
NDP	38.2
REF	29.2
NLP	1.1

PRINCE ALBERT

LIB	21.2
PC	8.2
NDP	31.7
REF	38.1
ACTION	0.8

QU'APPELLE

LIB	23.7
PC	5.6
NDP	42.4
REF	26.9
ACTION	1.3

REGINA-LUMSDEN-LAKE CENTRE

LIB	23.6
PC	5.4
NDP	42.3
REF	27.8
ACTION	0.9

SASKATOON-HUMBOLDT

LIB	26.4
PC	7.4
NDP	32.4
REF	33.1
NLP	0.7

SASKATOON-ROSETOWN-BIGGAR

LIB	16.0
PC	7.0
NDP	43.7
REF	32.6
ACTION	0.7

SOURIS-MOOSE MOUNTAIN

LIB	27.2
PC	13.0
NDP	18.6
REF	41.2

WANUSKEWIN

LIB	24.4
PC	7.9
NDP	26.8
REF	39.2
NLP	0.4
IND	1.3

WASCANA

LIB	41.9
PC	7.4
NDP	28.4
REF	21.6
ACTION	0.8

YORKTON-MELVILLE

LIB	18.9
PC	6.1
NDP	25.0
REF	50.1

ALBERTA

1997
%

ATHABASCA

LIB	30.0
PC	9.2
NDP	4.7
REF	54.6
GP	1.5

CALGARY CENTRE

LIB	32.6
PC	18.6
NDP	6.1
REF	40.1
GP	1.8
M-L	0.3
NLP	0.5

CALGARY EAST

LIB	22.8
PC	24.6
NDP	6.5
REF	45.0
NLP	1.1

CALGARY NORTHEAST

LIB	24.1
PC	16.2
NDP	3.4
REF	52.1
NLP	0.6
IND	3.6

CALGARY SOUTHEAST

LIB	18.2
PC	23.6
NDP	2.6
REF	55.0
NLP	0.5

CALGARY SOUTHWEST

LIB	20.2
PC	17.9
NDP	2.7
REF	58.0
GP	0.6
CHP	0.2
NLP	0.4

CALGARY WEST

LIB	29.0
PC	18.2
NDP	4.0
REF	47.2
GP	1.1
NLP	0.6

CALGARY-NOSE HILL

LIB	25.2
PC	17.4
NDP	3.8
REF	51.8
GP	1.3
NLP	0.5

CROWFOOT

LIB	9.7
PC	15.5
NDP	3.8
REF	71.0

EDMONTON EAST

LIB	34.6
PC	7.3
NDP	11.8
REF	44.6
GP	0.6
CHP	0.8
NLP	0.3

EDMONTON NORTH

LIB	32.5
PC	7.7
NDP	14.9
REF	44.3
NLP	0.6

EDMONTON SOUTHEAST

LIB	46.0
PC	6.2
NDP	5.9
REF	41.5
NLP	0.5

EDMONTON SOUTHWEST

LIB	33.6
PC	10.0
NDP	4.7
REF	51.3
NLP	0.5

EDMONTON WEST

LIB	43.4
PC	7.1
NDP	8.3
REF	40.0
GP	0.5
M-L	0.3
NLP	0.3

EDMONTON-STRATHCONA

LIB	35.4
PC	7.2
NDP	14.5
REF	41.3
GP	0.8
ACTION	0.2
NLP	0.3
NIL	0.2

ELK ISLAND

LIB	19.7
PC	12.5
NDP	5.9
REF	60.6
IND	1.3

LAKELAND

LIB	17.6
PC	17.8
NDP	4.4
REF	59.3
NIL	0.8

LETHBRIDGE

LIB	19.2
PC	18.1
NDP	5.4
REF	55.5
CHP	1.0
ACTION	0.8

MACLEOD

LIB	11.6
PC	15.6
NDP	4.1
REF	68.0
NLP	0.7

MEDICINE HAT

LIB	17.5
PC	12.1
NDP	4.9
REF	65.4

PEACE RIVER

LIB	19.1
PC	16.1
NDP	5.9
REF	58.9

RED DEER

LIB	11.4
PC	15.7
NDP	4.0
REF	68.4
NLP	0.5

ST. ALBERT

LIB	28.5
PC	10.6
NDP	4.9
REF	55.2
IND	0.8

WETASKIWIN

LIB	14.2
PC	13.2
NDP	4.8
REF	66.0
CHP	1.8

WILD ROSE
LIB	12.1
PC	19.0
NDP	3.6
REF	63.8
GP	1.5

YELLOWHEAD
LIB	17.8
PC	12.4
NDP	5.0
REF	64.8

BRITISH COLUMBIA
<u>1997</u>
%

BURNABY-DOUGLAS
LIB	26.1
PC	3.4
NDP	43.1
REF	26.5
M-L	0.2
NLP	0.7

CARIBOO-CHILCOTIN
LIB	20.7
PC	11.8
NDP	14.1
REF	51.1
GP	2.3

DELTA-SOUTH RICHMOND
LIB	37.1
PC	5.5
NDP	9.2
REF	46.5
CHP	0.6
NLP	0.5
IND	0.6

DEWDNEY-ALOUETTE
LIB	25.1
PC	6.1
NDP	19.2
REF	47.3
GP	1.5
CHP	0.5
NLP	0.5

ESQUIMALT-JUAN DE FUCA
LIB	26.2
PC	4.5
NDP	22.2
REF	43.4
GP	2.5
ACTION	0.6
NLP	0.7

FRASER VALLEY
LIB	22.0
PC	3.3
NDP	8.9
REF	62.9
GP	0.6
CHP	2.0
NLP	0.2
NIL	0.2

KAMLOOPS
LIB	31.8
PC	2.2
NDP	36.1
REF	28.9
GP	1.0

KELOWNA
LIB	22.4
PC	16.8
NDP	7.6
REF	50.0
GP	3.2

KOOTENAY-COLUMBIA

LIB	17.6
PC	4.1
NDP	14.2
REF	61.9
GP	2.2

LANGLEY-ABBOTSFORD

LIB	24.9
PC	3.5
NDP	6.7
REF	62.0
GP	1.5
CHP	1.0
NLP	0.3

NANAIMO-ALBERNI

LIB	20.9
PC	5.2
NDP	22.2
REF	49.9
GP	1.3
NLP	0.6

NANAIMO-COWICHAN

LIB	21.1
PC	4.2
NDP	26.0
REF	45.0
GP	1.8
ACTION	1.4
NLP	0.4

NEW WESTMINSTER-COQUITLAM-BURNABY

LIB	29.1
PC	3.9
NDP	30.5
REF	34.5
GP	1.5
M-L	0.2
NLP	0.3

NORTH VANCOUVER

LIB	33.9
PC	4.9
NDP	9.2
REF	48.9
GP	1.8
ACTION	0.4
NLP	0.3
IND	0.7

OKANAGAN-COQUIHALLA

LIB	26.4
PC	5.4
NDP	11.8
REF	53.1
GP	2.2
CHP	0.7
NIL	0.4

OKANAGAN-SHUSWAP

LIB	24.7
PC	6.7
NDP	12.4
REF	53.1
ACTION	1.7
NIL	0.8
NIL	0.5

PORT MOODY-COQUITLAM

LIB	29.5
PC	5.5
NDP	19.7
REF	43.6
GP	1.3
NLP	0.4

PRINCE GEORGE-BULKLEY VALLEY

LIB	21.9
PC	8.1
NDP	12.2
REF	54.3
GP	1.6
CHP	0.9
NIL	1.0

PRINCE GEORGE-PEACE RIVER

LIB	17.1
PC	5.7
NDP	9.0
REF	66.9
GP	1.3

RICHMOND

LIB	43.8
PC	8.3
NDP	9.6
REF	36.0
GP	1.4
CHP	0.4
M-L	0.2
NLP	0.4

SAANICH-GULF ISLANDS

LIB	31.5
PC	7.5
NDP	14.3
REF	43.1
GP	2.7
ACTION	0.4
NLP	0.4

SKEENA

LIB	20.3
PC	3.5
NDP	31.2
REF	42.4
CHP	2.7

SOUTH SURREY-WHITE ROCK-LANGLEY

LIB	30.1
PC	4.5
NDP	7.9
REF	54.9
GP	1.6
CHP	0.4
ACTION	0.3
NLP	0.3

SURREY CENTRAL

LIB	29.0
PC	8.6
NDP	14.0
REF	34.7
GP	0.8
CHP	1.9
ACTION	1.3
NLP	0.3
IND	0.3
IND	9.1

SURREY NORTH

LIB	28.2
PC	3.2
NDP	19.1
REF	46.8
GP	0.8
CHP	0.8
M-L	0.1
ACTION	0.3
NLP	0.2
IND	0.6

VANCOUVER CENTRE

LIB	40.8
PC	9.2
NDP	20.9
REF	22.6
GP	3.0
M-L	0.2
ACTION	1.0
NLP	0.4
IND	1.4
NIL	0.2
NIL	0.2

VANCOUVER EAST

LIB	37.1
PC	2.7
NDP	42.3
REF	12.1
GP	3.4
CHP	0.6
M-L	0.4
NLP	0.5
NIL	0.5
NIL	0.3

VANCOUVER ISLAND NORTH

LIB	20.9
PC	3.4
NDP	23.3
REF	47.5
GP	3.3
CHP	1.1
NLP	0.5

VANCOUVER KINGSWAY

LIB	40.6
PC	4.0
NDP	30.5
REF	18.4
GP	2.3
M-L	0.5
NLP	0.6
IND	2.6
NIL	0.3
NIL	0.2

VANCOUVER QUADRA

LIB	42.1
PC	16.9
NDP	10.0
REF	27.6
GP	2.6
M-L	0.3
NLP	0.5

VANCOUVER SOUTH-BURNABY

LIB	42.7
PC	5.9
NDP	19.1
REF	29.7
GP	1.6
M-L	0.4
NLP	0.6

VICTORIA

LIB	34.8
PC	6.9
NDP	21.9
REF	29.5
GP	5.4
ACTION	0.7
NLP	0.7
NIL	0.3

WEST KOOTENAY-OKANAGAN

LIB	17.5
PC	5.6
NDP	21.9
REF	46.8
GP	6.1
CHP	0.8
ACTION	0.9
NLP	0.5

WEST VANCOUVER-SUNSHINE COAST

LIB	34.5
PC	8.4
NDP	11.9
REF	40.1
GP	4.6
NLP	0.5

WESTERN ARCTIC

LIB	41.6
PC	12.6
NDP	19.3
REF	14.7
IND	11.7

YUKON TERRITORY

	1997 %
YUKON	
LIB	22.0
PC	13.9
NDP	28.9
REF	25.3
CHP	1.0
IND	8.9

NORTHWEST TERRITORIES

	1997 %
NUNAVUT	
LIB	45.9
PC	24.1
NDP	23.8
REF	6.2

Notes on Contributors

Keith Archer is Professor of Political Science and Dean of Graduate Studies at the University of Calgary. He is author of *Parameters of Power: Canada's Political Institutions*, and co-author of *Political Activists: The NDP in Convention*.

Andre Bernard is a longtime member of the Department of Political Science at the University of Quebec in Montreal. He is author of several books on Quebec politics, including *La vie politique au Quebec et au Canada*, *What Does Quebec Want?*, and *Les institutions politiques au Quebec et au Canada*.

Stephen Clarkson is Professor of Political Science at the University of Toronto. He is author of *Canada and the Reagan Challenge* and co-author of the two-volume biography *Trudeau and Our Times*.

Christopher Dornan is head of the School of Journalism and Communications at Carleton University. He is an active writer and commentator on Canadian politics and the activities of the media.

Faron Ellis teaches political science and history at Lethbridge Community College. He has published articles on the Reform Party in several books, and in the *Canadian Journal of Political Science*.

Edward Greenspon is Ottawa Bureau Chief of *The Globe and Mail*. He is co-author of *Double Vision: The Inside Story of the Liberals in Power* and appears frequently as a television commentator on political events.

Lawrence LeDuc is Professor of Political Science at the University of Toronto. He is co-author of *Political Choice in Canada, Absent Mandate: Canadian Electoral Politics in an Era of Restructuring*, and *Comparing Democracies*. He has published several articles about debates between political leaders.

Michael Marzolini is founder and president of POLLARA, one of Canada's most respected public opinion polling and consulting firms.

Louis Massicotte teaches in the Department of Political Science at the University of Montreal. His published work specializes in the fields of constitutional law and electoral reform.

Jon H. Pammett is Professor of Political Science at Carleton University. He is co-author of *Political Choice in Canada* and *Absent Mandate: Canadian Electoral Politics in an Era of Restructuring*. His articles on voting behaviour have appeared in previous volumes in this series.

Anthony Westell was a political reporter and columnist in Ottawa before joining the Carleton University School of Journalism. With **Alan Frizzell** he founded the series of election studies of which this volume is the fourth. In retirement, he is an associate editor of *The Literary Review of Canada*.

Alan Whitehorn is Professor of Political Science at the Royal Military College of Canada. He is author of *Canadian Socialism: Essays on the CCF–NDP* and co-author of *Political Activists: The NDP in Convention*. He was the first holder of the J.S. Chair in Humanities at Simon Fraser University.

Peter Woolstencroft is Associate Professor of Political Science and Associate Dean of Arts at the University of Waterloo. His published work deals with the federal and Ontario Progressive Conservative parties, the selection of party leaders, electoral geography, urban politics, and education policy.